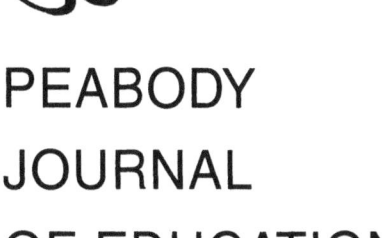

# PEABODY JOURNAL OF EDUCATION

James W. Pellegrino, Editor
Susan A. McDowell, Managing Editor

EDITORIAL BOARD—Peabody College of Vanderbilt University

Alfred Baumeister
Camilla Benbow
Leonard Bickman
David Bloome
John Bransford
Penelope Brooks
Vera Chatman
Paul Cobb
David Cordray
Anne Corn
Robert Crowson
Paul Dokecki
Carolyn Evertson
Douglas Fuchs
Lynn Fuchs
Judy Garber
Susan Goldman

Ellen Goldring
James Guthrie
Philip Hallinger
James Hogge
Ann Kaiser
Mark Lipsey
Joseph Murphy
Charles Myers
J. R. Newbrough
Daniel Reschly
Victoria Risko
Howard Sandler
Sharon Shields
Patrick Thompson
Travis Thompson
Tedra Walden
Neils Waller

# PEABODY JOURNAL OF EDUCATION

*Volume 75, Number 3, 2000*

Collaboration—Across Campus, Across Town, and With K–12 Schools

| | |
|---|---|
| Setting the Stage for Collaboration<br>*Jill F. Russell*<br>*Richard B. Flynn* | 1 |
| The Boston College–Allston/Brighton Partnership: Description and Challenges<br>*Mary E. Walsh*<br>*Mary M. Brabeck*<br>*Kimberly A. Howard*<br>*Francine T. Sherman*<br>*Catalina Montes*<br>*Timothy J. Garvin* | 6 |
| Winburn Community Academy: A University-Assisted Community School and Professional Development School<br>*Sara Delano Moore*<br>*Sharon Brennan*<br>*Ann R. Garrity*<br>*Sandra W. Godecker* | 33 |
| Manufacturing and Production Technician Youth Apprenticeship Program: A Partnership<br>*Lawrence M. Kenney*<br>*Lana Collet-Klingenberg* | 51 |

*(Continued)*

Creating the 21st-Century School of Education:
Collaboration, Community, and Partnership in
St. Louis     64
*Charles D. Schmitz*
*Susan J. Baber*
*Delores M. John*
*Kathleen Sullivan Brown*

Florida Early Literacy and Learning Model: A
Systematic Approach to Improve Learning at
All Levels     85
*Cheryl Fountain*
*Janice Wood*

Springfield College Collaboration With the Springfield
Public Schools and Neighboring Community     99
*Dale Lucy-Allen*
*Dennis Brunton*
*Jenny McDade*
*Jennifer Seydel*
*Dennis Vogel*

Twenty-Five Years of Collaboration for Interprofessional
Education and Practice at The Ohio State University     115
*Steven A. Harsh*
*Jilaine W. Fewell*
*R. Michael Casto*

Collaborating to Promote Effective Elementary
Practices Across Seven School Districts     133
*Sheri Rogers*
*Kathy Danielson*
*Jill F. Russell*

Beyond Collaboration: Accounts of Partnership From
the Institute for Educational Renewal Based at Miami
University     145
*Bernard Badiali*
*Randy Flora*
*Iris DeLoach Johnson*
*James Shiveley*

Growing Teacher Inquiry: Collaboration in a Partner
School     161
*Thomas S. Poetter*
*Bernard Badiali*
*DJ Hammond*

*(Continued)*

The Changing Role of Schools and Higher Education
Institutions With Respect to Community-Based
Interagency Collaboration and Interprofessional
Partnerships                                                                 176
*Dean Corrigan*

Commonalities Across Effective Collaboratives                                196
*Jill F. Russell*
*Richard B. Flynn*

# Setting the Stage for Collaboration

Jill F. Russell
Richard B. Flynn

Recommendations for the reform of education, both P–12 and postsecondary, almost always include calls for increased collaboration. Educators are urged to collaborate among themselves, with business and community leaders, and with parents and human service agencies, to name a few. However, collaboration is not an easy entity to capture. Calling a meeting does not a partnership make.

Collaboration can, in fact, be a continuum. At the minimum level, collaboration would involve two individuals or two units or organizations communicating together for a specific undertaking. Further along the continuum, two or more units or organizations may agree to establish a process or structure to enable joint decision making, and even further into the collaborative mode would be an ongoing working partnership with two or more parties having a formal, legal contractual arrangement with responsibilities specified and, in essence, with the partnership taking on a life and purpose of its own.

---

JILL F. RUSSELL *is Assistant Dean of the College of Education, and Executive Director of the Metropolitan Omaha Educational Consortium, University of Nebraska at Omaha.*

RICHARD B. FLYNN *is the President of Springfield College, Springfield, Massachusetts.*

Requests for reprints should be sent to Jill F. Russell, Assistant Dean, College of Education, Kayser Hall 208, University of Nebraska at Omaha, Omaha, NE 68182. E-mail: jill_russell@unomaha.edu

*J. F. Russell and R. B. Flynn*

In many respects, educational entities and educators have acted as closed systems, rather than as open, widely interacting systems. For example, a history of education, both P–12 and postsecondary, is one that depicts an individual teacher working with his or her students and the lone scholar following his or her research interests. As educators, we typically have not been taught how to team teach, much less how to create and sustain working collaboratives. Yet, true collaboration can, as the saying goes, achieve the almost magical outcome of the whole being greater than the sum of the parts. Where else can you add two and two together and come up with five or six or even seven? In that sense, collaboration is a paradox, and there are many more paradoxes implicit within the process of collaboration. Somehow, taking the time to get to know one another builds trust, relinquishing power and control results in cohesiveness, and talking achieves goals.

The title of this theme issue is "Collaboration—Across Campus, Across Town, and With K–12 Schools." The issue provides descriptions of a range of ways in which universities and schools and colleges of education can provide leadership for collaborative ventures involving the wider community. The collaborative undertakings include working with community agencies, other schools or colleges within or external to the institution, P–12 schools, and business groups.

The rationale for the theme is that in today's world the problems we are facing are so complex that solutions can no longer be generated and successfully implemented in a vacuum. Cross-disciplinary and cross-sector collaboration is required to have the desired impact. This necessitates collaboration. For example, the educator working singly can have little impact on the health of a student. Yet, the student's health may be a critical factor in the child's readiness or capacity to learn or achieve—for which the educator may be held accountable. The teacher educator may also need to venture into the information technology business world in order to have access to the resources to prepare teachers to help P–12 students succeed in the 21st century. Unfortunately, collaboration does not always come naturally or easily. There is a skill to successful collaboration. We can learn from those who have been successful in this arena and avoid making mistakes and jeopardizing relationships.

The theme issue provides case descriptions of 10 collaboratives in which a postsecondary unit, typically a school or college of education, has played a key role in working with other academic units on campus, with schools, or with various community entities to problem solve or reach new goals together. Cases for inclusion were identified and selected by a three-step process:

1. Nominations of successful collaborative projects or entities were solicited of deans and directors or schools and colleges of education who

were members of (a) the Association of Colleges and Schools of Education in State Universities and Land Grant Colleges and Affiliated Private Universities, (b) the Teacher Education Council for State Colleges and Universities, and (c) the Council of Great Cities College of Education. This comprised a list of 305 possible institutions.

2. One hundred ten nominations of projects were received from 68 institutions. The nominations were reviewed and narrowed to those that depicted a range of collaborative partners, purposes, and processes, and which seemed highly successful.

3. The narrowed list was contacted by telephone, and on the basis of a telephone interview selected project contacts were asked to prepare a description of their collaborative undertaking.

The authors of the case descriptions outline their goals, partners, structure, history, process, and outcomes. Public and private institutions of varying sizes from across the country are featured. A wide range of reasons for collaborating are included, from neighborhood development to technology connections. Partners include child care center staff, artists and musicians, cooperating teachers for student teaching, professors from the Law School, CEOs from major corporations, and government officials. Following the case descriptions are two analyses and commentary articles that critique and present conclusions across the cases.

The first case description is provided by Walsh, Brabeck, Howard, Sherman, Montes, and Garvin. They describe the Boston College–Allston/Brighton Partnership. This partnership includes a number of school reform projects involving faculty and staff from multiple departments that grew out of Boston College's commitment to social justice.

The Winburn Academy associated with the University of Kentucky College of Education is described by Moore, Brennan, Garrity, and Godecker. The Winburn Academy partnership includes the Winburn Middle School, the Lexington Parks and Recreation Department, and the university. Although it is a professional development school, it is much more than that, with a number of community services and networking relationships expanding the activity and outcomes.

Kenney and Collet-Klingenberg of the University of Wisconsin–Whitewater describe the Manufacturing and Production Technician Youth Apprenticeship Program for at-risk youth from the Watertown, Wisconsin area. This project includes the P–12 schools, private industry, and the University. It is a joint venture that incorporates a high school education with apprenticeship training for youth, a nontraditional setting for teacher preparation, and workforce development for business and industry.

*J. F. Russell and R. B. Flynn*

Creating the 21st Century School of Education is what the dean of the school at the University of Missouri–St. Louis set out to do. In this article, Schmitz, Baber, John, and Brown describe their vision and implementation. The intent was to change the way of doing business through involvement with new partners. This model is heavy on technology, economic development, and partnerships. It assumes educators of the future will need to "have firsthand knowledge of employer expectations, community resources, and needs."

Fountain and Wood of the University of North Florida share their story of working with state departments, child care agencies, civic organizations, and private companies to provide early literacy experiences for young children. The program, entitled Early Literacy and Learning Model, supports the formation of family and community partnerships as well.

Springfield College (in Springfield, MA) is featured for its efforts to fulfill its Humanics Mission: to prepare students in spirit, mind, and body for service to humanity. This mission has been the impetus for multiple projects involving volunteerism, service learning, and partnering with local entities to address community needs. Coauthors Lucy-Allen, Brunton, McDade, Seydel, and Vogel, representing both the college and the Springfield Public Schools, share their thoughts on factors contributing to the success of their joint endeavors.

The Ohio State University's Interprofessional Commission of Ohio has a 25-year history of cross-disciplinary professional preparation. The organizational structure, funding, and emphasis changes over that time period are chronicled by Harsh, Fewell, and Casto and provide useful information for those who plan on long-term collaboration.

Sharing information across seven districts about effective elementary practices was accomplished in Omaha, Nebraska through a collaborative process described by Rogers, Danielson, and Russell. Under the umbrella structure of the Metropolitan Omaha Educational Consortium, which is part of the University of Nebraska at Omaha's College of Education, P–12 teachers, administrators, and university faculty came together with a common purpose of improving practice through the sharing of research.

Badiali, Flora, Johnson, and Shively describe Miami University's Institute for Educational Renewal (IER) and provide examples of initiatives in different schools. This is followed up by an in-depth description by Poetter, Badiali, and Hammond of a single IER school in which student teaching incorporates inquiry.

Following the 10 case descriptions are two commentary articles. Corrigan (of Texas A & M University) provides commentary on family-based and interprofessional collaborations, drawing on both the case descriptions and his long experience with interprofessional collaborations. He offers comments on barriers, lessons learned, helpful resources, and practices for effective collaboration.

The theme coeditors, Russell and Flynn, took advantage of this assembling of collaborative projects to further their research on effective practices within successful partnerships. The authors from each of the projects represented in this issue were asked to complete a survey regarding the extent to which various factors and practices influenced the success of their collaborative results. The findings are presented in the article, "Commonalities Across Effective Collaboratives."

Knowing that collaboration is a messy, time-consuming activity up front is helpful in that it can give hope to collaborators who are feeling frustrated when all does not go as planned or as quickly as desired. Seeing how colleagues in other institutions have approached collaborative initiatives offers ideas for one's own department, school, or college. Knowing what should be included, as well as what should be avoided, can make the path a little smoother.

As coeditors, our intent has been to share information about the process of collaboration, provide models, and encourage further successful involvement with collaboration. The articles should prove especially useful to educator-preparation faculty and administrators, and to P–12 educators who wish to work in partnership with higher education. We are hopeful this theme issue is a step in that direction.

# The Boston College–Allston/Brighton Partnership: Description and Challenges

Mary E. Walsh, Mary M. Brabeck, Kimberly A. Howard, and Francine T. Sherman
Catalina Montes
Timothy J. Garvin

MARY E. WALSH *is Professor in the Department of Counseling, Developmental, and Educational Psychology, Lynch School of Education, Boston College, and Codirector of the Boston College Center for Child, Family, and Community Partnerships, Chestnut Hill, Massachusetts.*

MARY M. BRABECK *is Dean of the Lynch School of Education, Boston College, Chestnut Hill, Massachusetts.*

KIMBERLY A. HOWARD *is a doctoral candidate in the Department of Counseling, Developmental, and Educational Psychology, Lynch School of Education, Boston College, Chestnut Hill, Massachusetts.*

FRANCINE T. SHERMAN *is Adjunct Associate Professor at the Boston College Law School, Director of the Juvenile Rights Advocacy Project, and Codirector of the Boston College Center for Child, Family, and Community Partnerships, Chestnut Hill, Massachusetts.*

CATALINA MONTES *is Principal of the Gardner Extended Services School, Allston, Massachusetts.*

TIMOTHY J. GARVIN *is Executive Director of the Allston–Brighton Family YMCA, Brighton, Massachusetts.*

Requests for reprints should be sent to Mary E. Walsh, Lynch School of Education, Boston College, Campion Hall 305C, Chestnut Hill, MA 02467. E-mail: mary.walsh.1@bc.edu

Over the last decade, universities have increasingly begun to recognize their responsibility to address the issues and problems confronting society. Many universities are responding to this challenge by developing formal partnerships with communities. This article describes a specific partnership between Boston College and its local contiguous community. It outlines the development of the partnership from a simple school–university engagement between a school principal and a school of education faculty member to a complex set of relationships involving (a) multiple disciplines and professions; (b) a set of complicated projects; (c) multiple funders; (d) a large number of faculty, students, practitioners, and community members; (e) multiple institutions interacting at multiple levels; and (f) many kinds and levels of outcomes. The centrality of the processes of colearning and interprofessional collaboration is highlighted. The factors contributing to the success of the partnership, as well as the ongoing challenges it faces, are examined. The partnership has led to a deepened understanding on the part of both the university and community regarding the research–practice relation.

In its recent report on the "engaged university," the Kellogg Commission (1999) concluded that in addition to offering "first rate undergraduate and graduate programs that prepare students to respond effectively to the complex issues of the society they will enter, [universities] must directly respond to the social and economic concerns of the communities [they serve]" (p. 9). Over the last decade, universities have increasingly begun to recognize their responsibility to address the issues and problems confronting society. Many universities are responding to this challenge by developing formal partnerships with communities.

The effort to address significant societal problems has transformed many of the traditional forms of relation between universities and communities (Kellogg Commission, 1999). It has resulted in a movement in research away from university-based laboratory research to new ways of joining science with practice, inquiry with action. Underlying these new approaches is the assumption that social inquiry will not be effective unless it is combined with social action, and likewise, that social action must be guided by social inquiry. Action gives inquiry a validity that can only come from useful knowledge, and it adds complexity to problems that are otherwise understood to be simplistic (Walsh, Thompson, Howard, Montes, & Garvin, 2000). In parallel fashion, inquiry adds reflection, evaluation, and direction to action. In action inquiry and reflective practice, researchers and community members become collaborators in the search for useful coconstructed knowledge (Gergen, 1991).

Recent efforts to develop stronger ties between inquiry and action have resulted in the university's traditional posture (of remaining distant from and passing knowledge on to the community) shifting toward more direct involvement of the university in the life of the community. University–community collaborations have begun to move toward more symmetrical partnerships in which the partners are colearners and share the power of the knowledge they each hold. Although their domains of expertise are different, they are nonetheless complementary (McKenzie & Richmond, 1998). This approach to scholarship transforms the university as well as the community. Both the university and the community change one another and are themselves changed in the process (Bibace, Dillon, & Dowds, 1999).

Partnerships between the community and the university are increasingly being discussed in the literature of education and other professions including psychology, medicine, law, and social work (Bibace, 1999; Harkavy, 1999; Knapp et al., 1998; Sherman, 1998). Schools of education are natural leaders in this work not only because they have long valued the contribution of the community to the preparation of educators, but also because of their prominence in the scholarship of action inquiry and reflective practice (Holmes Group, 1990).

Although many advocate the implementation of university–community partnerships, there is little guidance available for the difficult act of partnering. The literature is replete with data on the outcomes of partnerships (e.g., Chibucos & Lerner, 1999). However, there is less significant information about the process of partnering (i.e., how partnerships come about and are sustained).

The purpose of this article is to describe a specific partnership between a private university and its local contiguous community. We discuss the centrality of the processes of colearning and interprofessional collaboration to the work of this partnership. We describe how the partnership has developed from a simple school–university engagement between a school principal and a school of education faculty member to a complex set of relationships involving (a) multiple disciplines and professions; (b) a set of complicated projects; (c) multiple funders; (d) a large number of faculty, students, practitioners, and community members; (e) multiple institutions interacting at multiple levels; and (f) many kinds and levels of outcomes. We present some of the challenges of having education schools assume a leadership role on the campus and the challenge this work presents to faculty within schools of education.

## Boston College–Allston/Brighton Partnership

Boston College, a private university that literally sits on the boundary between the City of Boston and a neighboring suburb, is currently engaged in a long-term partnership with a section of the City of Boston known as "Allston–Brighton." The partnership consists of a number of interconnected projects—some older, some new, some small, some large—that engage Boston College staff, faculty, and students in a wide range of activities, most involving local schools.

At its most general level, the goal of the partnership is to link inquiry and action (i.e., to join the knowledge bases and conceptual expertise of the university with the practical expertise and problems in the community). At a more concrete level, the partnership provides the university with opportunities to engage in research that directly addresses the questions of the community and, in so doing, to better prepare students for real world settings. Simultaneously, the partnership provides the community with access to knowledge bases that can contribute to improving the quality of life for its residents. The goal of the partnership joins the goals and resources of the university with the goals and resources of the community in a way that strengthens each partner and privileges neither. To meet both sets of goals simultaneously, the university and community must engage in colearning and share power in a complementary rather than a competitive manner.

However, in linking the university with the community there is an obvious mismatch. The problems and issues confronting the community do not neatly align themselves with the academic disciplines of the university. "Although society has problems, our institutions have 'disciplines.' ... Despite the resources and expertise available on our campuses, our institutions are not well organized to bring them to bear on local problems in a coherent way" (Kellogg Commission, 1999, p. viii). Many advocates of interdisciplinary approaches to the study of human problems have pointed out that the real problems of society do not come in discipline-shaped boxes (Hammer & Champy, 1993; Petrie, 1992; Roy, 1979; Senge, 1991). Interprofessional collaboration becomes essential to bridge this divide (Walsh, Brabeck, & Howard, 1999). The university's ability to work with the community is directly related to the capacity of university faculty to collaborate across disciplines and professions.

*Contexts for the Partnership*

*University.* Each institution of higher education has a unique history and mission that shapes its particular approaches to collaboration, outreach, and scholarship. Boston College, a Jesuit liberal arts university, is committed to the application of knowledge to solve human problems and the preparation of students "to serve others" in the tradition of Catholic social justice teaching. The University's stated commitment to social justice provides the shared value system and language that facilitates collaboration among the diverse schools and departments on campus to address the needs of children and families in today's society, particularly in its local community (Brabeck et al., 1998).

The university houses a graduate school of arts and sciences and five professional schools whose solid reputations in national rankings have been built through faculty and student scholarship as well as sponsored projects. However, scholarship at the graduate level is also balanced by the mission to engage in work that serves others. Although basic research is pursued, scholarship in the real world is encouraged, particularly among faculty and students in the professional schools. These dual commitments to reflection and action are realized through what Boyer (1990) called the "scholarship of application" (p. 16). Such scholarship results in learning that is useful to the community and requires a two-way relationship with the community to make certain that the research questions are relevant and that the knowledge is valid, useful, and used. Thus, the partnership between Boston College and the community emerges from a culture that values service-oriented scholarship. In this regard, Boston College has a climate conducive to creating what Boyer (1994) called the "new American college" (p. A48) and what the Kellogg Commission (1999) called the "engaged university" (p. 11). This climate helped support a formal effort to develop collaboration across the professional schools and academic departments (Brabeck et al., 1998).

Although Boston College faculty have always engaged in some interdisciplinary collaborative work, particularly around curriculum development, there is and has always been a tension among academic departments that must compete for resources and retain independence and autonomy in accounting for productivity. History and departmental organizational structures have made interdisciplinary collaboration and cross-unit efforts a challenge (Brabeck et al., 1998). However, as a result of a lengthy campus-wide planning effort to develop consensus regarding its mission and goals, the University describes its distinct contribution as including "producing nationally and internationally significant research that advances insight and understanding, thereby both enriching culture and addressing important societal needs" (Brabeck et al., 1998, p. 339).

Within the Boston College School of Education, psychology and education faculty had engaged in a year-long discussion of the school's mission that resulted in an explicit commitment to collaboration, partnership, and outreach to achieve social justice. This, however, has not resolved all tensions. Some of the education faculty are not ready to trust any initiatives led by psychologists or to develop initiatives that include psychologists. The power to influence the way teachers are prepared is closely guarded by some, and perceived status hierarchies heighten the mistrust and impede collaboration with our own colleagues. Nevertheless, some faculty have been able to overcome stereotypes and mistrust to focus on the needs of children. One by one they are joining in the work.

*Community.* The Allston–Brighton community, which is adjacent to one side of the university campus, contains 70,000 people and is the most ethnically and culturally diverse section of the City of Boston. Long a working class community comprised mainly of European immigrants, an influx of new immigrants over the last 15 years has resulted in a very heterogeneous community. Immigrants come from a wide range of places: Asia, Africa, South America, and Central America. A significant number of residents are undocumented, and one third of the community residents speak no English. This section of the City of Boston has a poverty rate that is somewhat higher than the city average. The geographical boundaries of the community constitute 1 of 11 major geographical areas of the Boston Public School System. The Allston–Brighton area is referred to as Cluster 5 of the Boston Public Schools. The geographic area of Cluster 5 includes over 70 community agencies and coalitions (health, mental health, etc.). The cluster includes 13 schools and educates 5,500 students who come from the Allston–Brighton area as well as from more distant sections of the city. Court-ordered school desegregation in the 1970s resulted in large-scale busing across the school system's 11 clusters. Among the needs identified by the community is an integration of these services to better support the healthy development of the community's children, youth, and families.

*Beginnings of the Partnership: The Goals*

The Boston College–Allston/Brighton Partnership began at roughly the same time in two different settings—the university and the local community (Allston–Brighton). Neither university faculty nor community members were aware that parallel lines of thoughts and efforts were occurring in the other setting. At the university, a group of faculty, recognizing that many of them were working on common issues impacting children, families, and communities, came together to discuss how they might collaborate to (a) engage in research of significance to the community, (b) prepare students in a range of disciplines (e.g., psychology, law, social work, etc.) to collaborate across professions, and (c) partner to produce better integrated services (Waddock & Walsh, 1999). The Lynch School of Education played a leading role.

Independently, the community was working on a variety of strategies to integrate services to children and families. This effort had been underway for several years. The schools and community agencies were reaching out to one another to address efforts to coordinate fragmented services. They recognized that their community reflected the national situation in which uncoordinated services resulted in families falling through the cracks (Crowson & Boyd, 1993). The neighborhood coalition, known as "Allston–Brighton Healthy Boston Coalition," began to develop linkages with the schools, conducted a large study of the needs of the community, and identified a large number of agencies to be involved in this project. Although the coalition wanted the University to be involved, they were uncertain what this involvement may be.

These two parallel tracks—of university and community—were joined when a local principal asked the first author for help in how to figure out ways to simultaneously meet the academic and nonacademic needs of children. The principal recognized what national leaders in education (Stallings, 1995; Wang & Kovach, 1996) have been addressing: Children's and families' problems could not be divided into the "neat boxes" of distinct professions and the university could and should play a significant role in working with the community to enhance the life chances of children and families. She asked for no less than new models of professional practice and university involvement. Her wishes were echoed by the leader of the School Linked Services Project of the Neighborhood Coalition. She expressed a desire to work directly with faculty, whom she referred to as "the guts of the university." As discussions expanded and deepened, it became clear that the university's desire to work with a community and the local community's desire to work with a university were beginning to converge.

*Implementing the Partnership: Structure and Funding*

The first grant to be written—joint preparation of preservice teachers and social workers in school settings—was a response to an innovative call by the DeWitt Wallace–Readers' Digest Foundation for universities to develop better ways to prepare professionals, specifically teachers and social workers, to address the nonacademic needs of children and families in school settings. The Request for Proposals (RFPs) called for projects that included joint practicum placements in schools, development of a joint social work–education course, joint supervision, and a commitment by the university to make this activity a permanent part of the curriculum. The grant implementation was coordinated by faculty in teacher education and social work (Mooney,

Kline, & Davoren, 1999). This was the first concrete proposal for a Boston College faculty group to engage in an effort that would actively involve more than a single profession. The second grant proposal (Walsh & Savage, 1995) was a response to an RFP from the U.S. Department of Education's Fund for the Improvement of Postsecondary Education. The University faculty saw RFPs as an opportunity to widen the interprofessional effort by engaging a wide range of professions (law, social work, nursing, management, psychology, and education) in a collaborative effort to bring the knowledge bases of those professions to bear on the preservice preparation of student teachers and counselors. This grant was coordinated by two School of Education faculty members—one from counseling psychology and one from teacher education. The proposal delineated a series of steps in which faculty would learn "at the elbows of community practitioners" how to better prepare students to collaborate with other professionals. In addition to joint practica, collaborative seminars, and other activities, the proposal suggested that the knowledge bases of various professions relevant to school-based work would be enhanced by consulting with practicing professionals in the local schools and community.

Funding led to a significant amount of engagement with the local schools and to the establishment of the Boston College Center for Child, Family, and Community Partnerships. The Center focused on addressing the needs of children and families through interprofessional collaboration and colearning projects with the local community, the Greater Boston area, and the State of Massachusetts. The Center became central to Boston College's efforts to be an engaged university. The faculty and students involved in the Center were committed to linking inquiry and action across the professions in what they referred to as "outreach scholarship" (Lerner, 1995, p. 103). For the community, the Center served as a point of access for technical assistance, policy analysis, demonstration projects, youth and family program evaluation, consultation, needs assessment, training and continuing education, and community-collaborative action research. For the University, the Center coalesced and furthered the faculty's efforts to join inquiry with action. It provided opportunities for student training and for the application of knowledge to issues of youth, family, and community life. Collaboration with local public schools became a major focus of the Center and its most active aspect. The director was a faculty member in the Lynch School of Education. To reflect its interprofessional nature, the Director of the Center reports to all deans, to the Academic Vice President for Research, to a Faculty Advisory Committee, and to an External Advisory Committee. The Center provides the University the structure that supports the Boston College–Allston/Brighton Partnership and houses the major projects in the partnership.

## Projects in the Boston College–Allston/Brighton Partnership: The Outcomes

The Boston College–Allston/Brighton Partnership is currently comprised of 10 projects of various sizes, ranging from the school-specific projects, such as facilitating the school-to-work transition for high school students, to the community-wide organization of support services for children, youth, and families. Within this partnership, a *project* is generally defined as any long-term set of activities that has a broad but clear goal of enhancing the life chances of individuals (child or adult) and families, involves both faculty and students from across professions and disciplines, and includes collaborating and colearning with community members (practitioners and consumers) to plan or implement a response to a particular community issue. The project activities include research-based inquiry on questions of importance to the community and opportunities for community-based practice for both students and faculty. In this article, we describe in some detail one of the most substantial projects in the partnership.

### The Thomas A. Gardner School—An Extended Services School

The project described here was directed toward the transformation of a local elementary school—the Thomas A. Gardner School—into a school that would address the wide spectrum of student and familial issues that often impede academic achievement. The mechanism for catalyzing the partnership with the Gardner School was another RFP from the DeWitt Wallace–Reader's Digest Foundation. The goal of the RFP was to promote educational reform by directly addressing the nonacademic barriers to learning that are experienced by a significant number of children and their families. This specific project is an attempt to transform a traditional urban elementary school into what is known as an Extended Services School that would extend school hours as well as the range of services and opportunities offered to children and families. The Extended Services School is more broadly known as a community school (Denham & Etzioni, 1997; Dryfoos, 1994, 1995; Walsh, Howard, & Buckley, 1999). The Gardner Extended Services School is modeled loosely after the Children's Aid Society Community School in New York City (Coltoff, 1998). By one definition, a community school seeks to integrate education and human services by drawing on both school and community resources to create a "seamless, one-stop" environment with extended hours and days (Dryfoos, 1998).

The goal of providing a "seamless" set of programs that address a wide range of needs (e.g., physical, psychological, social, economic, legal) is consistent with the Gardner School principal's belief that the students in her school experience a wide array of needs that constitute barriers to learning (Brabeck, Walsh, Kenney, & Comilang, 1997; Corrigan, 1996; Lawson & Briar-Lawson, 1997; Sailor & Skrtic, 1996). The Extended Services School project matched the school's desire to address the many nonacademic needs of children as well as the university's desire to bring professionals together to collaborate around issues confronted by children and families. The school, which educates 500 children from K–5, is located in the most culturally and linguistically diverse section of Boston. Over 36 languages are spoken among the faculty and children. Eighty percent of the children participate in the Free or Reduced Lunch Programs, and 80% of families have limited English proficiency. Lack of adequate housing and employment plague the families.

A core planning team, which included representatives from the school (parents and staff), the university (faculty), and the community (Allston–Brighton Healthy Boston Neighborhood Coalition—an organization that included community members and many school parents), was established to prepare a proposal. A community agency (the Allston–Brighton Family YMCA) was later invited to join as the official partner or "lead agency" of the Extended Services School. This core team met weekly, and in the give-and-take of these meetings, the dance behind the partnership was enacted. The initial movements of the partners, some of whom were new to the partnership, were often awkward and always tentative. As the various partners began to discuss potential programs for the Extended Services School, they gradually became more aware and respectful of the strengths and struggles of each other. Their negotiations increasingly required them to accommodate to differences as they assimilated new ways of thinking and acting. For example, parents, community members, the community agency, and the university faculty began to develop an appreciation for the complexities involved in the day-to-day operations of an elementary school. Similarly, all the partners gained insight into the fiscal and staffing constraints of community agencies, and the barriers to work outside the campus that present challenges for university faculty.

A similar process of give-and-take also characterized the larger community-wide meetings that included agency and business representatives, parents, and local citizens. The meetings involved an exchange of information, proposals, opinions, and decisions. Bilingual and trilingual group leaders made certain that non-English speakers were included in the conversation. Volunteer subcommittees of relative strangers—parents, teachers, university faculty, and community agency staff—were established to hammer out a design for the various aspects of the Extended Services School. In numerous meetings of the core group of partner representatives, as well as of the larger community, a partnership developed that would transform each of the partners in significant ways. A successful proposal for the Planning Grant led to a successful proposal for the Implementation Grant.

The Extended Services School (ESS)—now in the middle of its second year of implementation funding—(a) developed programs for children (before school, after school, and summer), (b) arranged for new or expanded school-based or school-linked services (dental and medical care, mental health, and social services), (c) developed evening programs for parents and other adults (ESL, GED, immigration counseling, housing access, and health education), and (d) raised matching funds. The Steering Committee, still comprised of representatives from the four institutional partners (school, university, community agencies, and the community coalition) continues to meet on a regular basis and is being evaluated by both internal (university-based) and external evaluators. The university has also provided a cadre of "coaches" (Boston College faculty and staff) to the school to assist with implementation of new curriculum standards, frameworks, and teaching methods and has provided faculty to work with school staff in developing new models of student support to address the nonacademic barriers to learning.

The school and the YMCA have provided opportunities for graduate and undergraduate student internships in a range of professions: social work, nursing, education, psychology, and law (see, e.g., Brabeck et al., 1997). Working with undergraduate students, the university has collaboratively developed and coordinated mentoring and tutoring programs for the Gardner ESS After-School Program. They have welcomed students doing special projects (e.g., an MBA student examining the management issues in linking schools and community agencies). Faculty and students are engaged in a variety of research projects that address questions framed initially by the school staff and parents (e.g., "How can we know if the after-school program is helping our children?"). Undergraduate students regularly do credit-earning independent studies on various aspects of the project. Evaluations of the outcomes of various aspects of the Gardner ESS have involved doctoral students from the Lynch School of Education. For example, Howard, Thompson, Warter, and Walsh (1999) examined the impact of a tutoring program on college student tutors. An on-going national evaluation of extended services schools (Public/Private Ventures, 1999), in which the Gardner School is a participant, has increased opportunities for graduate students to engage in research with significant community implications. Thus, the university's participation at the Gardner ESS has expanded its capacity to meet its traditional tasks of research, teaching, and service using a model of colearning in which all partners contribute various types of expertise. The colearning model was recently described by the principal at a national conference:

> When we sit down to work on a task—write a grant, develop a new program, evaluate what we have—we are really, at that moment, unaware of who is Boston College and who is Gardner staff. We think of ourselves as one—all working for the children. (C. Montes, personal communication, March 27, 1999)

As a single school project, the Gardner ESS has provided significant, rich learning opportunities to each of the partners and, at the same time, benefitted substantially from the varied and strong resources that each partner contributed.

## Factors Contributing to Success

A number of factors have contributed to positive outcomes in the development of Boston College's partnership with the Allston–Brighton community. These include a shared theory of change, engagement in reflective practice, a long-term commitment, and agreed-on funding arrangements.

### Shared Theory of Change

One of the most critical dimensions in the development of these projects was a shared set of assumptions among the partners regarding how to enhance the life chances of children and families. Across all of the projects, protracted discussions between the community and the university faculty revealed that, at their core, the partners had a common understanding about how individuals develop. Although expressed in varying ways, these assumptions led the partners to espouse a similar theory of change. In general, the community and university partners agreed on four fundamental principles of human development. First, they were clear that individuals develop not just in a single context, but rather in a wide array of contexts including family, school, neighborhood, and the wider community (Bronfenbrenner, 1979; Lerner, 1986). Second, the partners agreed that individuals develop simultaneously across multiple domains—biological, psychological, and social (Lerner, 1978, 1986). Third, the partners also agreed that development occurred across the life span, in adults as well as children (Lerner & Lerner, 1987). They explicitly recognized that the traditional assumption that development stops at age 18 was incorrect. Although their respective institutions focused primarily on either adults or children, they eventually agreed that child-oriented programs that did not include parents and other adults would not be effective. The final assumption about human development on which the various partners in the projects agreed was the importance of recognizing and building on strengths as well as addressing the deficits exhibited by children and families (Lerner, 1995; Lerner, Walsh, & Howard, 1998; Pittman & Cahill, 1992). They concluded that positive development could be enhanced by the protective factors present in the lives of children and families (e.g., community centers, caring neighbors, and churches). They had an interest in fostering competencies that could lead to the resilience in children, youth, and families (Howard, Barton, Walsh, & Lerner, 1999; Werner, 1989, 1990).

*Engagement in Reflective Practice*

Developing the link between inquiry and action required constant and deliberate attention. As they began to concretize the theory–action link, the partners gradually became aware of the need to step back periodically from the world of action to reflect on the processes and outcomes. Much of this reflection was guided by the on-going process evaluation. In this reflection, the participants grappled with the theoretical issues involved in both partnering with the community and collaborating across professions. Reflection on these issues in a variety of venues led to the adoption of explicit theoretical frameworks to guide further work in the community and across professions.

A clear example of the value of reflective practice occurred with respect to the partners' arriving at the shared theory of change described above. In the process of reflecting on the practices in which they were engaged, it became clear to the university and the community that their individual theories about human development were surprisingly consistent with one another. The university's view of change, which emerged from theory and research, converged with the community's view, which emerged from the world of action or practice. Coming to understand the similarity in their assumptions was a transforming experience for both the university and the community.

Reflecting with the community participants on the issues and problems involved in the development and implementation of the projects has led to a number of products. These products document the changes that have occurred. At the university, these outcomes have included a number of changes in courses and curriculum, research questions, and grant proposals. At the schools, the colearning is evident in the changes in the school's curriculum and extended services. The recorded notes from the countless meetings and conversations demonstrate the numerous ways each of the partners has changed over the months and years of partnering. The most obvious examples of the colearning that has occurred are evident in the joint conference presentations and joint evaluation projects (Walsh & Madaus, 1997). In this way, the community became critical participants in knowledge generation and theory building.

*Long-Term Commitment*

Another ingredient necessary to the partnership's success is an explicit long-term commitment from each of the partners to stay engaged over the long term. Extended involvement is essential to accommodate the changes in practice that resulted within each institution. At the University, for example, the lessons from these projects are being integrated gradually into curriculum and teaching. Using the methodologies of action inquiry, some of the faculty are redirecting and shaping their research to address the questions generated by the community. Students are becoming heavily engaged in interprofessional practice and action inquiry models of research. The University curricula utilized to train new professionals have changed in significant ways to incorporate the learnings acquired in the community as well as from other professions. These changes in university practices have substantial impact on the research and teaching of the faculty and on the preparation of students. They reflect a substantial commitment of intellectual resources and cannot be temporary in nature.

Similarly, the community agency and school have begun to change their practices in ways that cannot easily be reversed. For example, the local branch of the community agency put the development of ESS on the agenda of the larger agency. It has promoted this type of collaboration at local and national levels of the organization. To some extent, it has staked its reputation in statewide political and community circles on the successful implementation of this project. Other agencies are budgeting considerable time to engage in planning effective school–community linkages. Some have changed their funding practices to incorporate a partnership with a school. The community agencies are willing to invest in and develop new models of collaboration with schools on the assumption that the University would not abandon the project "when the money ran out."

The schools also have changed practices in significant and nonreversible ways. For example, the Gardner School, the principal, and the staff integrated many aspects of the ESS into the school day (e.g., coordinating in-school and after-school literacy instruction for individual students by hiring an ESS coordinator who works with day-school as well as after-school teachers). As a model of ESS, the progress at the Gardner ESS is closely watched by other local and statewide systems.

The changes in practice within each of the partner institutions do not lend themselves to brief, time-limited implementation, but rather require a long-term commitment to become standard practice. In light of the realization that a sustained commitment was necessary for the successful implementation of the projects and for transformation of practices in each institution, the partners made an explicit and repeated commitment to stay with it over time. To solidify this commitment, they sought the backing of the leadership of each of their institutions. Boston College's president, the city wide directors of several community agencies, and the superintendent of the Boston Public Schools have spoken positively and publicly about the work. Their public pledges led to some concrete acts of support.

However, despite significant support for long-term involvement, there is not complete agreement within the membership of each institution about the value of this type of long-term commitment. In the university, many faculty members feel that it is not appropriate for faculty to remain in the community over a long period of time. They believe that faculty should be in the community only long enough to share their expertise and empower the community to act on its own behalf—not to colearn with the community. Within the community agency, some individuals wonder if this type of engagement is appropriate for an institution whose primary identity is delivering a focused service. Some school staff members are concerned that the school's mission of teaching and learning may become diverted or diluted by the ongoing partnership with "outsiders." Parents sometimes wonder if the time required by this partnership is worth the effort. To varying degrees and in varying ways, the partners recognize the demands as well as the uncertainties of their collaborative enterprise.

Yet, as they reflect on the various concerns of their respective institutional colleagues, their fears are somewhat tempered. The university faculty who are involved in the projects believe that empowering others presumes that someone has power to give to the other. The involved faculty do not believe they have that kind of power. Rather, they view sustained collaboration and colearning as more likely to eventually empower everyone—themselves as scholars, the community professionals as practitioners, and the community members as parents and caring adults. The contribution of each was viewed as different but vital to the development of the human community. The leadership of the community agencies believe that a more holistic orientation is an important expansion of their narrower missions (e.g., to provide recreational opportunities or health or social services). The schools' staffs generally believe that schools can not do it alone, but must work with varied professions and with groups external to the schools to enhance the academic success of students. The parents and community members believe that a different model of schooling and collaboration across agencies and schools may provide increased positive opportunities for their children. These ongoing and frequent reassessments repeatedly led the partners to conclude that the opportunity to enhance the life chances of children, youth, and families by engaging in focused inquiry and by changing some key aspects of their own practices was worth the significant cost involved in building the long-term partnership.

Over time, even though the respective roles of the partners have changed dramatically, the relationship among the partners evolved to a point of near-permanence. In the midst of difficult negotiations on key aspects of the project, they sometimes remarked to one another, "We are in this so deeply now, there's no turning back. The only place to go is forward—together" (T. J. Garvin, personal communication, March 27, 1999). The pledge to a long-term and sustained relationship among the partners constituted a significant transformation and cultural sea change for both university and community.

*Funding Arrangements*

The potential success of the project was also significantly enhanced by a shift in the usual arrangements for funding. Although the planning grants for the various projects were typically awarded to Boston College, several funders stipulated that the implementation grants should reside in the community. Coming to terms with this requirement involved significant trust and sharing of power. It required a fundamental change in the orientation of the University, which typically received the "overhead" from faculty-authored grants. As a Jesuit university whose mission statement explicitly calls for the generation of knowledge that can make a difference in human lives, Boston College administrators recognized the central importance, for faculty and students, of engaging in scholarship that was linked at its core to action. For this reason, the University was willing to relinquish both the control and the funds related to the implementation of the various projects in the partnership. Further stipulations by some funders required that grants for community-school collaborations reside in the community agency. This required a shift in the policy of the schools, which ordinarily house any grants involving community collaboration. This represented a fundamental shift for the public schools, which recognized that locating the grant in the community agency meant sharing control of the program with the community agency. Shared control between schools and agencies is not always a simple task, particularly in institutions that compete for scarce resources.

Although the initial implementation grants supported the early stages of the projects, their long-term survival depends on raising new funds. The process of securing these funds required continued sharing of responsibility among the partners. Potential sources of funds are available to one or another of the institutions represented by the partners, but typically not to all. For example, certain grants, such as the Federal 21st Century Schools grants, could only be awarded to local educational agencies. Other grants were available only to community agencies or universities. Thus, each partner has to agree to support the fund-raising efforts of one or another partner, even though with respect to any particular grant or source of funds, there may be "nothing in it for them." This approach was a significant shift for institutions that were accustomed to operating in an isolated manner.

To manage the operational aspects of some of the projects, partners also had to agree to develop a joint accounting system. Over time, they had to agree to a common reporting arrangement in which data about all of the funds available, the income, and the expenses would be kept in a common accounting system to which all members could have access at any time. This arrangement required a significant transformation of the ordinary practice of each institution. Opening "the books" was a new way of doing business for school, community, and university. It requires deep and abiding trust, a complex understanding of the nature of partnerships (Walsh et al., 2000), and a governance structure that allows positive resolution of problems. Designing the governance structure, defining the community, and changing the understanding of professionalism constituted three of the major challenges in developing and implementing the partnership.

Ongoing Issues and Challenges

*Governance*

As details were worked out for implementing the projects, the members gradually developed and agreed on a model for governing the projects through steering committees. Determining the functioning and structure of these committees constituted one of the most difficult aspects of the project. The myriad and sometimes unspoken concerns about trust and coequal participation in each of the projects became concretized in the design of the steering committees. For example, in the final implementation plan for the Gardner ESS, the partners agreed to two representatives from the community agencies, two representatives from the university, two representatives from the parent group in the school, and three representatives from the school staff. The preponderance of school staff on the steering committee reflected the fact that the school would be the single institution most impacted by its transformation into an ESS. In agreeing to move toward an ESS model, the greatest number of risks would be assumed by the school. For this reason, it was agreed that the school needed additional representation.

The issue of governance through a Steering Committee raises critical issues. As long as the tasks involve the development and implementation of services, the Steering Committee appears to function effectively. However, when the issues begin to border on empowering one or another segment of the committee (e.g., parents), the model of governance is substantially challenged. Crowson (1998) noted the differences, sometimes incompatibilities, between service models and empowerment models. An empowerment approach will not only challenge collaboration among the schools and community agencies, but also among most institutions and the university.

*Defining "Community"*

The process of defining the community is an early and critical task in most university–community partnerships (Einbinder & Sloane, 1998; Kellogg Commission, 1999; Knapp et al., 1998; Tippins, Bell, & Lerner, 1998). The definition of community typically emerges from the goal of the particular project around which the partnership is organized. In the case of the partnership projects, the overriding goal was to establish functional linkages between the schools and the community that would give children and their families access to a wide range of services and resources. The definition of the community to which the schools would be linked was vital.

Although the partners initially thought that the definition of who and what comprised the community could be arrived at in one or two meetings, analysis of the process notes reveals that this issue was a recurring theme that was revisited over months and years, at increasingly deeper levels. In community–school linkage projects across the country, the definition of community has been fairly straightforward. Typically, the geographical area immediately surrounding the school or schools is defined as the school's community. However, this geography-bound definition of community was not applicable in the context of the Allston–Brighton community. Court ordered desegregation in the City of Boston had resulted in over half of the schools' students living far outside the geographic community. Partnership members were confronted with the task of building linkages that would not be limited to the community boundaries.

After extensive and difficult discussions, the Steering Committees decided to establish close working relationships with a large number of agencies in the Allston–Brighton community because these agencies had the greatest potential to deliver services within the school buildings. However, although they could not set up interinstitutional contracts with more distant agencies, they committed to developing strategies for working with these agencies around the needs of individual students who lived outside of the school's immediate geographic zone. Some of the local agencies that had branches in other areas of the city (e.g., the YMCA) also saw the possibilities of working with those branch agencies to accommodate individual students. Finally, the partners agreed that, to the extent financially possible, all members of the local geographic community should have access to the projects' resources and services, whether or not they had children attending the school.

The partnership's commitment to include within the community every student in the school and his or her family, from all sections of the city, was a decision in which each partner felt invested. It also was a decision that presented many complications. For example, at the Gardner ESS, the Steering Committee recognized the massive transportation issues that would result in implementing this definition of community at the level of practice. The committee foresaw the difficulty of running after-school programs for children who had no transportation to return to their distant neighborhoods in the late afternoon. Recognizing this and similar barriers, the partnership members united as a team to advocate with the school district for a solution to the transportation problem. This team lobbied and continues to lobby city officials, local politicians, and grant funders for increased transportation for school children and their families.

This new sense of cohesiveness led to an important transformation in each partner's understanding of who constituted the community. Partners who had previously thought of themselves as other than the community came to realize that they, too, were part of the community. For example, the schools, which had traditionally considered themselves as distinct from the community, now came to refer to themselves as "the community" in their requests to city officials. In contrast to their earlier "we–they" posture vis-à-vis the community, they now spoke of "us." Over the course of these discussions, it became clear to the school personnel that they—teachers, school staffs, and administrators—were part of the very community they served. A similar transformation of identity occurred in the university faculty. The traditional stance among university faculty, as they spoke about going out to the community, had been to see themselves as apart from, rather than a part of, the community. As they joined the other partners in seeking transportation and other resources for all of the children, the university also came to realize that it could not exclude itself from membership in the community. Similarly, these shifts in the understanding of community impacted the community agencies and coalitions. Up until this point, it had been useful in certain ways for agencies and coalitions to consider both the schools and the university as separate from themselves. Taking on the big institutions such as the universities or the school department had the potential to become a cause for the community agencies who perceived themselves as Davids challenging the Goliaths. Negotiating the design and implementation of the community–school linkage facilitated the community agencies' coming to view these institutions as part of the community and to see themselves as partners with the university and the school.

As the partners' mode of interaction shifted from one of dominance to one of mutuality, long-standing practices and assumptions began to change. These changes are slow, difficult, and not always welcomed by one or another partner. At times, each partner prefers its former posture. However, these changes are at the same time empowering and allow for greater opportunity to learn from one another, share insights, and be empathic. The changes in assumptions about the community foreshadowed changes that would take place in both the university's and the community's understanding of how the various professions involved in the partnership should collaborate.

*Professionalism*

The partnership created a context that challenged each of the professions to reexamine their usual manner of carrying out their roles. Past understandings of *profession* encourage practitioners to subscribe to an "expert" model that often inhibits collaborative relationships. "Modern professionalism is conceived as a monologue, a one-way conversation in which professionals prescribe and their clients and society merely accept their prescriptions on faith, without recourse to a higher authority" (Skrtic & Sailor, 1996, p. 274). This perspective can lead professionals to gain power over those who require his or her expertise and may lead them to compete for dominance over other professions. Consequently, practitioners sometimes work as if they can solve the problems in their domain of expertise without the input and help of professionals in related disciplines (Walsh, Brabeck, & Howard, 1999).

In the Boston College–Allston/Brighton Partnership, the various professionals came to understand that "there is nothing inherently true about the knowledge that grounds professional practices and discourses, and, moreover, that there is no cognitively certain way to choose among possible alternatives" (Skrtic & Sailor, 1996, p. 274). Professionals increasingly recognize that there are multiple sources and types of valid knowledge: No one profession is the sole broker of knowledge. This shift in thought from the expert model to a more relational view of knowledge is only slowly beginning to impact professional work and training programs (Bay, King, & Chou, 1994; Kaufman & Brooks, 1996), not only at Boston College (Walsh, Brabeck, & Howard, 1999), but also in many academic settings across the country.

For our interprofessional partnership to be successful, all participants have to be willing to cede some of the "turf" that the mindset of professionalism protects. They continuously address the fear that working with others and sharing decision-making power reduces their individual value and importance (Mostert, 1996). The status that the partners, especially university faculty, attribute to collaborating with professionals from other disciplines clearly varied in relation to perceived prestige levels of the professions. For instance, psychologists are generally inclined to value collaborating with "higher status" professionals (e.g., physicians) in contrast to collaborating with traditionally "lower status" professionals (e.g., nurses or teachers). Collaborating with families and community members is valued by few, if any, professions. Attempts to level the professional status hierarchies require significant attitudinal and behavioral adjustments, which emerge out of ongoing reflection on practice.

The subtle but significant differences in the cultures of various professions also serve to discourage collaboration (Walsh, Brabeck, & Howard, 1999). These differences were particularly evident in the linguistic conventions and ethical practices within various professions. Over time, each profession has developed its own technical dialect that helps to facilitate intraprofessional communication, but at the same time can serve as a barrier to interprofessional communication. Similar phenomena are described in different ways across professions. The frequently used example of how to refer to the person receiving services illustrates these differences. He or she is a *patient* to health care providers, a *student* to educators, a *client* to lawyers, and, most recently, a *consumer* to mental health professionals.

*Causes for Celebration: Scholarship Transformed*

Both the university and the community approached the partnership with preconceived and fairly resolute ideas about the relation between research and practice. Although each partner was committed in principle to the necessary connection between research and practice, they often acted in practice as if these two activities were distinct and separate domains. In the early stages of our partnership, both the university and the community assumed that research was the university's forte; practice, whether within agencies or schools, was the domain of the community.

Initially, the university faculty adhered to a traditional approach to research. As the faculty who were engaged in the project conceived of it, research entailed identifying specific questions, collecting data from the community to answer these questions, and analyzing and reporting the findings in scholarly journals. They assumed that the results of their studies would not only advance knowledge in an abstract manner, but also could be applied in practice to the complex problems confronting the human community.

Community members, on the other hand, assumed that although the university was doing some sort of important research, this work probably had little or no relevance to the practical problems that they were trying to solve daily. As they typically made decisions about the types of programs that would be best for their community, they relied more on the pragmatic criteria of cost, word of mouth, and ease of implementation than they did on research findings about the effectiveness of particular programs. Ordinarily, research did not substantially inform the daily decision making of the community. Evidence-driven practice simply did not occur.

However, as the university and the community worked with one another to develop the various projects in the partnership, they both came to new understandings about the relation between research and practice (i.e., between inquiry and the world of action). In developing new models of school–community linkages, they needed information that was not readily available (e.g., community preferences for issues to be addressed, the priority in which program activities should be implemented, and best practices in school–community linkage programs across the country). Faculty recognized that this would require a different kind of research in which the questions were shaped by the parents, teachers, and community members. Furthermore, the answers to these questions would be found in working as collaborators within the community rather than remaining isolated in the laboratories of the university.

As university faculty in the Boston College–Allston/Brighton Partnership realize that the methods of laboratory research will not be effective in capturing the complex interactions of the world of action, they are developing new research methodologies to incorporate the rich resource of parents, teachers, and community members. For example, in the Gardner School Project, the seemingly straightforward task of assessing the community's preferences and needs for particular ESS programs presented significant challenges to traditional quantitative survey methodologies. In assessing the concerns of parents who spoke little or no English and who among them spoke multiple languages, the university researchers were pressed to develop a variety of strategies, such as bilingual focus groups and teacher- or parent-led interviews.

Just as the university came to new understandings of the relation between research and the world of action, the community also came to appreciate the ways in which their practice could be impacted by research. As they attempted to choose among several possible models of school–community linkages, community members became aware of the potential usefulness of research findings. Confronted with multiple options for new programs, community leaders asked the university faculty to "find out the characteristics of effective programs" across a wide range of areas. Their new appreciation of research-based information, for example, left them reluctant to set up an after-school program until the university was able to summarize research findings about best practices in after-school child care. It has now become standard practice in several community agencies to request formal evaluation of any new partnership program.

Over the course of the project, the new understanding of the research–practice relation was reflected in the increasing participation of each partner in the work of the other partner. In sharp contrast to earlier days in which the researchers and practitioners engaged in distinct work activities, the university faculty and community members joined one another in some aspects of their primary work. Working in a partnership led to a deepened understanding of the research–practice relation. The new research methodologies developed to address the community's questions enable the community to participate more actively in the design and execution of more relevant research. The new practices developed by the community have enabled the university to better prepare practitioners across a wide range of professions.

## Conclusion

In the context of conversations about more effective preparation of future professionals, several important shifts in the relation between the university and the community have begun to occur. Community-based professionals and family members are providing their expertise to university faculty who had traditionally considered themselves experts vis-à-vis the community. University faculty are identifying important research questions based on the concerns posed by the community. As the discussions with the community have proceeded, the university and community are both coming to recognize the strong commitment each had to improving the life chances of children and families. It is evident that they share the "compelling ethos" necessary to drive and energize any successful community project (Schorr, 1997).

## References

Bay, M., King, S. H., & Chou, V. J. (1994). Children's services and urban teacher education: Beginning the conversation. In K. A. Levin (Ed.), *Greater than the sum: Professionals in a comprehensive services model* (Teacher Education Monograph No. 17, pp. 127–137). Washington, DC: ERIC Clearinghouse on Teacher Education.

Bibace, R. (1999). A partnership ideal. In I. Sigel (Series Ed.), R. Bibace, J. Dillon, & B. N. Dowds (Vol. Eds.), *Partnerships in research, clinical, and educational settings: Advances in Applied Development Monograph Series* (pp. 275–306). Stamford, CT: Ablex.

Bibace, R., Dillon, J., & Dowds, B. N. (Eds.). (1999). Partnerships in research, clinical, and educational settings. In I. Sigel (Series Ed.), *Advances in Applied Development Monograph Series*. Stamford, CT: Ablex.

Boyer, E. (1990). *Scholarship reconsidered: Priorities of the professoriate.* Princeton, NJ: The Carnegie Foundation for the Advancement of Teaching.

Boyer, E. (1994, March). Creating the new American college. *The Chronicle of Higher Education,* p. A48.

Brabeck, M., Cawthorne, J., Cochran-Smith, M., Gaspard, N., Green, C. H., Kenny, M., Krawczyk, R., Lowery, C., Lykes, M. B., Minuskin, A. D., Mooney, J., Ross, C. J., Savage, J., Soifer, A., Smyer, M., Sparks, E., Tourse, R., Turillo, R. M., Waddock, S., Walsh, M., & Zollers, N. (1998). Changing the culture of the university to engage in outreach scholarship. In R. M. Lerner & L. A. K. Simon (Eds.), *University–community collaborations for the twenty-first century: Outreach scholarship for youth and families* (pp. 335–364). New York: Garland.

Brabeck, M., Walsh, M., Kenny, M., & Comilang, K. (1997). Interprofessional collaboration for children and families: Opportunities for counseling psychology in the 21st century. *The Counseling Psychologist, 25,* 615–636.

Bronfenbrenner, U. (1979). *The ecology of human development.* Cambridge, MA: Harvard University Press.

Chibucos, T. R., & Lerner, R. M. (1999). Serving children and families through community–university partnerships: A view of the issues. In T. R. Chibucos & R. M. Lerner (Eds.), *Serving children and families through community university partnerships: Success stories* (pp. 1–11). Norwell, MA: Kluwer Academic.

Coltoff, P. (1998). *Community schools: Education reform and partnership with our nation's social service agencies.* Washington, DC: CWLA Press.

Corrigan, D. (1996). Teacher education and interprofessional collaboration: Creation of family-centered, community-based integrated service systems. In L. Kaplan & R. A. Edelfelt (Eds.), *Teachers for the new millennium: Aligning teacher development, national goals, and high standards for all students* (pp. 142–171). Thousand Oaks, CA: Corwin Press.

Crowson, R. L. (1998). Community empowerment and the public schools: Can educational professionalism survive? *Peabody Journal of Education, 73*(1), 56–68.

Crowson, R. L., & Boyd, W. L. (1993). Coordinated services for children: Designing arks for storms and seas unknown. *American Journal of Education, 101,* 140–179.

Denham, C., & Etzioni, A. (1997). Community schools. In A. Etzioni (Ed.), *Character building for a democratic civil society* (pp. 104–112). Washington, DC: The Communitarian Network.

Dryfoos, J. G. (1994). *Full service schools: A revolution in health and social services of children, youth and families.* San Francisco: Jossey-Bass.

Dryfoos, J. G. (1995). Full service schools: Revolution or fad? *Journal of Research on Adolescence, 5,* 147–172.

Dryfoos, J. G. (1998, February). *A look at community schools in 1998: Occasional Paper #2.* New York: National Center for Schools and Communities.

Einbinder, S. D., & Sloane, D. C. (1998). Reconceptualizing Mr. Roger's neighborhood: Competing ideas of community and interprofessional collaboration. In J. McCroskey & S. D. Einbinder (Eds.), *Universities and communities: Remaking professional and interprofessional education for the next century* (pp. 36–53). Westport, CT: Greenwood.

Gergen, K. (1991). *The saturated self: Dilemmas of identity in contemporary life.* New York: HarperCollins.

Hammer, M., & Champy, J. (1993). *Re-engineering the corporation: A manifesto for business revolution.* New York: Harper Books.

Harkavy, I. (1999). School–community partnerships. *Universities and Community Schools, 6*(1–2), 7–24.

Holmes Group. (1990). *Tomorrow's schools: Principles for the design of professional development schools. A report of the Holmes Group.* East Lansing, MI: Author.

Howard, K. A., Barton, C. E., Walsh, M. E., & Lerner, R. M. (1999). Social and contextual issues in interventions with children and families. In S. Russ & T. Ollendick (Eds.), *Handbook of psychotherapies with children and families* (pp. 45–66). New York: Kluwer Academic.

Howard, K. A., Thompson, N. E., Warter, E., & Walsh, M. E. (1999). *Final evaluation—MACC After-School Grant to Boston College: An evaluation of the Boston College/Gardner School Service Learning After-School Project.* Unpublished manuscript, Massachusetts Campus Compact, Medford.

Kaufman, D., & Brooks, J. G. (1996). Interdisciplinary collaboration in teacher education: A constructivist approach. *TESOL Quarterly, 30,* 231–251.

Kellogg Commission on the Future of State and Land Grant Universities. (1999, February). *Returning to our roots: The engaged institution* [Brochure]. Washington, DC: National Association of State Universities and Land-Grant Colleges.

Knapp, M., Barnard, K., Bell, M., Brandon, R., Gehrke, N., Lerner, S., Rabkin, J., Smith, A., Teather, E., & Tippins, P. (1998). *Paths to partnership: University and community as learners in interprofessional education.* New York: Rowman & Littlefield.

Lawson, H. A., & Briar-Lawson, K. (1997). *Connecting the dots: Progress toward the integration of school reform, school-linked services, parent involvement and community schools.* Oxford, OH: The Danforth Foundation and the Institute for Educational Renewal.

Lerner, R. M. (1978). Nature, nurture, and dynamic interactionism. *Human Development, 21,* 1–20.

Lerner, R. M. (1986). *Concepts and theories of human development* (2nd ed.). New York: Random House.

Lerner, R. M. (1995). *America's youth in crisis: Challenges and options for programs and policies.* Thousand Oaks, CA: Sage.

Lerner, R. M., & Lerner, J. V. (1987). Children in their contexts: A goodness of fit model. In J. A. B. Lancaster, J. Altoona, A. S. Rossi, & L. R. Sherrod (Eds.), *Parenting across the lifespan: Biosocial dimensions* (pp. 377–404). Chicago: Aldine.

Lerner, R. M., Walsh, M. E., & Howard, K. A. (1998). Developmental–contextual considerations: Person–context relations as the bases for risk and resiliency in child and adolescent development. In T. Ollendick (Ed.), *Comprehensive clinical psychology. Vol. 5: Children and adolescents: Clinical formulation and treatment* (pp. 1–24). New York: Elsevier.

McKenzie, F. D., & Richmond, J. B. (1998). Linking health and learning: An overview of coordinated school health programs. In E. Marx & S. F. Wooley (Eds.), *Health is academic: A guide to coordinated school health programs* (pp. 1–14). New York: Teachers College Press.

Mooney, J. F., Kline, P. M., & Davoren, J. C. (1999). Collaborative interventions: Promoting psychosocial competence and academic achievement. In R. W. C. Tourse & J. F. Mooney (Eds.), *Collaborative practice: School and human service partnerships* (pp. 105–135). Westport, CT: Praeger.

Mostert, M. P. (1996). Interprofessional collaboration in schools: Benefits and barriers in practice. *Preventing School Failure, 40,* 135–138.

Petrie, H. G. (1992). Interdisciplinary education: Are we faced with insurmountable opportunities? *Review of Research in Education, 18,* 299–333.

Pittman, K. J., & Cahill, M. (1992). *Pushing the boundaries of education: The implications of a youth development approach to education policies, structures and collaborations.* Washington, DC: Academy for Educational Development.

Public/Private Ventures. (1999). *An evaluation of Extended Services Schools for the DeWitt Wallace–Readers' Digest Fund.* New York: Author.

Roy, R. (1979). Interdisciplinary science on campus: The elusive dream. In J. Kockelmans (Ed.), *Interdisciplinarity and higher education* (pp. 161–196). University Park: Pennsylvania State University.

Sailor, W., & Skrtic, T. W. (1996). School/community partnerships and educational reform: Introduction to the topical issue. *Remedial and Special Education, 17*(5), 267–270, 283.

Schorr, L. B. (1997). *Common purpose: Strengthening families and neighborhoods to rebuild America.* New York: Anchor.

Senge, P. M. (1991). *The fifth discipline: The art and practice of the learning organization.* New York: Doubleday.

Sherman, F. (1998, June 5). *Leadership and lawyering: Learning new ways to see juvenile justice.* Paper presented at the Meeting of the Law and Society Association, Aspen, CO.

Skrtic, T. M., & Sailor, W. (1996). School-linked services integration: Crisis and opportunity in the transition to postmodern society. *Remedial and Special Education, 17*(5), 271–283.

Stallings, J. A. (1995). Ensuring teaching and learning in the 21st century. *Educational Researcher, 24*(6), 4–8.

Tippins, P., Bell, M., & Lerner, S. (1998). Building relationships between university and community. In M. Knapp (Ed.), *Paths to partnership: University and community as learners in interprofessional education* (pp. 165–192). New York: Rowman & Littlefield.

Waddock, S. A., & Walsh, M. E. (1999). *Paradigm shift: Toward a community–university community of practice.* Manuscript submitted for publication.

Walsh, M. E., Brabeck, M. M., & Howard, K. A. (1999). Interprofessional collaboration in children's services: Toward a theoretical perspective. *Children's Services: Social Policy, Research, and Practice, 2*(4), 183–208.

Walsh, M. E., Howard, K. A., & Buckley, M. (1999). School counselors in school–community partnerships: Opportunities and challenges. *Professional School Counseling, 2,* 349–356.

Walsh, M. E., & Madaus, G. (1997). Evaluation of an extended services school in Boston. *The Evaluation Exchange, 3*(2), 10–11.

Walsh, M. E., & Savage, J. (1995). *Preparing teachers to collaborate with health and human service professionals: Report to the U.S. Department of Education, Fund for the Improvement of Post-secondary Education.* Washington, DC: Fund for the Improvement of Post-secondary Education.

Walsh, M. E., Thompson, N. E., Howard, K. A., Montes, C., & Garvin, T. (2000). The transformative process of action inquiry in a school–community–university partnership. In F. Sherman & W. Torbert (Eds.), *Transforming social inquiry: Transforming social action.* Boston: Kluwer.

Wang, M., & Kovach, J. (1996). Bridging the achievement gap in urban schools: Reducing educational segregation and advancing resilience-promoting strategies. In B. Williams (Ed.), *Closing the achievement gap: A vision for changing beliefs and practices* (pp. 10–36). Alexandria, VA: Association for Supervision and Curriculum Development.

Werner, E. E. (1989). Children of the garden island. *Scientific American, 206*, 106–111.

Werner, E. E. (1990). Protective factors and individual resilience. In S. J. Meisels & M. Shonkoff (Eds.), *Handbook of early intervention* (pp. 97–116). New York: Cambridge University Press.

# Winburn Community Academy: A University-Assisted Community School and Professional Development School

*Sara Delano Moore*
*Sharon Brennan*
*Ann R. Garrity*
*Sandra W. Godecker*

---

SARA DELANO MOORE *is the University of Kentucky Professional Development School Liaison at Winburn Middle School, Lexington.*

SHARON BRENNAN *is Associate Professor and Director of School Collaboration Initiatives, University of Kentucky, Lexington.*

ANN R. GARRITY *is a Fellow of the Commonwealth Institute for Parent Leadership, and former Project Director for the Winburn Community Academy, Lexington, Kentucky.*

SANDRA W. GODECKER *is the teacher outreach liaison at Winburn Middle School, Lexington, Kentucky.*

We thank the many people who helped make this program a success. At the West Philadelphia Improvement Corps replication project, we are grateful for the support of Ira Harkavy, Joann Weeks, and the DeWitt Wallace–Reader's Digest Foundation, especially Laura Pires-Hester. Within the university community, we have received help from Eric Anderman, Harriette Arrington, Luceara Cross, Bob Hemenway, Shirley Raines, and Athletes in Service to America. In the Lexington community, Diane Bonfert, Jackie French, and Anthony Hawkins keep our Parks partnership alive. The Community Action Council; Arts in Action, particularly Sara Holcomb; and the Commonwealth Institute for Parent Leadership, especially Nancy Rogers, make this work possible. At Winburn Middle School, the Ashanti teachers were trailblazers and Virgil Covington our visionary. We also thank Tina Stevenson, Paula Wheeler, and the Winburn faculty and staff. Finally, we thank the parents, students, and neighbors of Winburn.

Requests for reprints should be sent to Sara Delano Moore, Department of Curriculum and Instruction, University of Kentucky College of Education, 315 Dickey Hall, Lexington, KY 40506–0017. E-mail: sdmoore@pop.uky.edu

Winburn Community Academy is a school–university–community partnership that uses win–win collaboration to remove barriers to learning. The primary partners include Winburn Middle School, the Lexington Parks and Recreation Department, and the University of Kentucky. Working together through the Academy, these agencies link with others in the community (nonprofit organizations, businesses, and individuals) to sponsor a school-based recreation and homework center, community learning opportunities both in and out of school, service learning, and a professional development school for the University of Kentucky's middle-level teacher education program. A common thread across all facets of the project is the building of networks—among students, teachers, and parents—to strengthen the community and improve student learning. Our 6-year history shows that developing successful partnerships is a messy but rewarding process. We hope our experiences will be helpful to others.

If we always do what we've always done, we'll always get what we've always got.—Author Unknown

Society mirrors the science of the times. As science refocuses its lens from linear and Newtonian systems to networked and chaotic ones, so does society begin to recognize that schools based on an industrial model do not teach all students well. New science, as Wheatley (1994) described chaos theory (see also Gleick, 1988), shares a world view of a networked system of interrelated people and events. Traditionally, school has been seen as an assembly line where students move from one classroom to the next in a rigid structure, being taught specific content at each point just as cars are moved along an assembly line during production at the factory. This cause-and-effect model, action and reaction, permeates curriculum development (scope and sequence), instruction (share information and repeat it back on the test), discipline (behavior modification), and professional development (24 hr per teacher per year). Myriad data sources (national and state assessments, anecdotal reports) tell us that schools are not working. There are still too many barriers to learning for too many students.

Winburn Middle School serves as the hub of multiple collaborative relations designed to remove barriers to learning. With an ongoing focus on improving education for the sixth, seventh, and eighth graders in the building and for the community as a whole, partnerships and larger networks have grown to focus on different facets of community and school problems. Productive collaboration is the building of relationships that focus on meaningful problems. Like effective cooperative learning, these relationships are ones where all partners can contribute and all partners can learn. If a partner is disenfranchised, the collaboration is not effective and the problem cannot be addressed. Strong personal relationships are required to ensure all partners are heard and valued.

This article is a description of a school–community–university partnership that began in 1993 in the provost's office as an outreach project to an underserved, largely African American community in north Lexington. Over time, with grant support, the partners created a community learning center called the Winburn Community Academy at the middle school. The community school project moved to the College of Education in 1996, where it provided a ready-made platform for the establishment of a professional development school (PDS). Given the crisis of our public schools in teaching all children to high levels, this dual focus on community and school reform provides the organizational structure for systemic intervention, but it requires that education colleges move into a totally new paradigm—the school without walls.

It is our thinking that another group could come into a web like our Winburn collaboration from a number of entry points. Thus, this article emphasizes where we are now—our partners, key players, the connections within the network, and key features of our collaboration—more than the process through which we arrived.

## Evolution of the Partnership

*Institutional Partners*

*Winburn Middle School.* Picture a suburban enclave of 900 small ranch homes and apartments built in the 1960s on the margin between inner city and the farmlands of the Bluegrass 5 miles north of the University campus. Most families are African American, and there are a large number of children and youth. There are three churches, two convenience stores, and a middle school in the subdivision. This idyllic image is in contrast to the neighborhood's local reputation as an unsafe, crime-tainted place. Even though suburban, it shares many qualities with deprived urban environments. There is one road in and out of the subdivision, so it is off the beaten path. It has limited bus service and a mile walk to the nearest shopping area. Drugs are sold on the street outside the two convenience stores. Youth have little to do but "hang out." There is a city park, but crime is a problem there. A recent influx of migrant workers live in the cheapest apartments and draw antagonism because of their different lifestyle and their substandard or nonexistent English.

Due to the fact that Winburn shares a census tract with nearby affluent condominium owners, census tract data is not descriptive. Nearly all residents are employed, but most hold low-end service jobs. Parents often work night shifts or second jobs to earn extra money for clothing, gifts, and the "necessities" their children must have to fit into the youth culture. Younger families often move on when incomes increase. The most stable families are those who are retired and own their own homes; however, these families have no children in school and therefore tend to isolate themselves from the problems facing neighborhood children. Most parents are devoted to their children but are frequently away, working hard to achieve economic stability. In addition, although some parents are high school graduates, some are not. A significant number of children are cared for by foster parents or by grandparents. In this environment, learning competes for attention with survival.

On the positive side, there are a large number of single-family dwellings, including many new Habitat homes, and a school, Winburn Middle School, whose principal had a vision for a community school. Why did he want a community school? With the introduction in 1990 of bussing for racial balance by the school district, this school's character changed. Before bussing, all neighborhood students, plus those in adjoining subdivisions, attended this school and all were African American; after bussing, half of the neighborhood students were sent far from home and were replaced by impoverished, mostly White Appalachian students from the inner city. Not only did this create racial tension within the school, but it also caused a loss of the neighborhood's identity with its school at a time when the neighborhood was aging and the drug trade increasing. The principal knew his students would be best prepared for learning with strong community–school connections. He needed community partners to help make that happen. The University was the answer to his prayer.

*University of Kentucky.* The University of Kentucky is a land-grant institution and one of two public, doctoral level universities in the commonwealth. With 11 colleges, five professional schools, and a graduate school, its Lexington campus and medical center serve more than 24,000 students. It is located just south of downtown Lexington and, although growing, retains a sense of "the campus" that some urban universities lack. As a large institution, the University of Kentucky has a complex administrative structure that must be negotiated to form formal partnerships. It has also had difficulties, as do many universities, being a "good neighbor." Schools and community agencies were (and many remain) wary of university collaboration, afraid of being "done to" rather than "doing with." Large institutions must work to overcome the unequal power balance to be accepted by community residents. Our challenge, entering this partnership, was to create trust and balance.

*Lexington-Fayette County Parks and Recreation.* "Parks" is a division of the municipal government and operates a network of free standing community recreation centers throughout the city. The Winburn Community Academy is their first collaborative partnership in a community learning center based physically at a school. The central staff of the Parks Department allocates special funding for the costs of the school-based recreation center.

*Philosophy*

Our primary philosophy centers on collaboration for mutual benefit. We respect the work of each agency, honor the parameters that organizational structures impose, and try anything we can to meet the needs of the students and community members we serve. As such, mutual benefit, or win–win negotiation, is the hallmark of our work together. Meeting times are held sacred, each player pitches in when needed, and we work to define carefully the responsibilities of each team member in each collaborative effort.

*History*

In the spring of 1993, a local community activist challenged the University to become involved with the community to help with what he saw as growing alienation and hopelessness among our city's low-income, minority youth. The 1960s protester turned youth advocate spoke bluntly: "The University of Kentucky goes all over the state helping people, but it ignores those in its own backyard" (Ronald Berry, personal communication, March 14, 1993). This stinging comment bore truth. Town–gown relations in our city have been cool traditionally. Furthermore, Kentucky's African Americans have suffered outright racism in academics and athletics for most of the 20th century. The provost responded with a promise to see what the University of Kentucky may do to help and organized a task force of faculty, administrators, and the community leader.

After months of brainstorming, trying to match adolescent and family needs with University expertise, the committee concluded that an education intervention was what the University could best offer. Faculty and students would be invited to participate in community and school-based service learning projects that not only benefitted adults and children, but also advanced teaching and research goals. Furthermore, the University would focus on a specific area of the city rather than proceed in its customary "we serve the commonwealth" approach to outreach. The group decided to focus on the declining north end of Lexington, in particular a neighborhood called Winburn Subdivision. The learning intervention would be a school for all called the Winburn Community Academy. Its purpose would be to increase the value of learning as the path to a larger life.

The partners quickly reached agreement on initial activities: community awareness, grant writing to support activities, program support for both school-day and extended school-day activities, participation by neighborhood youth attending other middle and elementary schools, and organization of a college student tutoring corps. The first project occurred that summer. A University of Kentucky intern, the Youth Service Center director, a local artist, and a dozen neighborhood youth organized a mural project for the graffiti-covered wall of the convenience store in sight of the school parking lot. The artist drew the large figures, which were African America historical heroes, and the youth filled in with figures of children. Even the local youth gang contributed and promised, "No one will touch that wall." In 5 years, no one has.

Months later, a project with similar goals came to our attention. A routine news release from the University of Pennsylvania's Center for Community Partnerships in the College of Arts and Sciences described the West Philadelphia Improvement Corps (WEPIC). It looked promising. Further inquiry led to attendance at WEPIC conferences, where several universities developing community partnerships came together. The University of Pennsylvania was awarded a replication grant from the DeWitt Wallace–Reader's Digest Fund, Extended School Service Division. The University of Kentucky submitted a proposal and received a 3-year grant in 1995. This funding was renewed for an additional 2 years and ended in 1999. The financial and technical assistance of the Fund and the University of Pennsylvania proved invaluable from the start (Harkavy & Puckett, 1991).

Shortly after the grant was awarded, the Lexington Division of Parks and Recreation approached the principal about becoming an Academy partner, and since then they have maintained a community recreation center 5 nights a week at the school and codirect the summer camp for elementary children.

In 1995 through 1996, changes in University leadership led to the University staffing for the Academy moving to the College of Education, where it remains. This change allowed the formation of the PDS initiative for the middle school teacher education program. Thus, the College currently manages two distinct but overlapping programs with Winburn Middle School: a community learning center and a PDS. Both focus on achievement, and together they benefit children and families, teachers, teacher education majors, and other university students.

## Program Goals and Structure

As our history suggests, the project began with three goals. First, we wanted to establish a community learning center. Second, we wanted to build networks of students, teachers, and parents in the community, particularly those teachers and families who work at schools linked to the neighborhood high school, Bryan Station. Third, we wanted to establish service learning as a viable and vibrant way to engage students, both K–12 and university, in meaningful community-based learning experiences tied to their academic curriculum. When the Academy moved to the College of Education, a fourth goal, establishing a PDS partnership, was added. The next several sections describe the current status of each of these goals: Where we are, how the key players work together, and what we have learned.

### *Community Learning Center*

As a community learning center, the school serves as a center of community learning and a central element in community development. It has youth development goals, health and social service goals, parent engagement goals, community development goals, and learning goals linked to school day programs (Blank, 1998). As a community learning center, Winburn Community Academy provides academic year programming through Family Nights and school-day assistance with university-based tutors, and summer programming for K–6 students. The Academy also hosts special events throughout the year.

*Family nights.* Parks provides paid staff for a community recreation and homework center 5 evenings each week and every Saturday. This center serves an average of 75 youth each evening and is also open during school holidays. To conserve funding, Winburn's principal staggers the hours of the building custodians, allowing the building to remain open until 9 p.m. for programming without requiring Parks to pay rent to the school division to have the building open after traditional hours. The principal thus waives rental charges for all partners, believing it is in the students' best interest to have safe and supervised learning activities in the building in the evening.

*Tutoring.* One of the first project initiatives was Homework Pals, which brought undergraduate University of Kentucky volunteers to

Winburn during and after school to work with students under teacher supervision. Homework Pals was designed to overcome the community perception that college students tend to be unreliable volunteers. Involving college students in meaningful community experience must account for their first priority: course work. Thus, the Pals commitment was for the 12 weeks in the middle of the semester, once a week for 2 hr. Pals signed a contract that they would honor the 12-week commitment. Homework Pals worked in Extended School Services, another reform act component, under teacher supervision, helping students with homework or remedial assignments. They attended a preservice orientation to middle school tutoring followed by three optional Friday afternoon debriefing sessions over the course of the semester. The program evaluations showed middle school students received the Pals very favorably; all expressed positive regard for the mentoring aspect. Most said working with a Pal improved their grade on a test or paper. Their teachers were extremely positive about the program. They loved having the students around in the afternoon. After a long day of teaching, they said that the Pals provided relief because it helped many students to have someone besides themselves to explain a math concept or review for a test. This modest beginning has grown to include an intensive effort to improve the reading skills of Winburn students through a program called Great Leaps.

Great Leaps is a K–12, direct instruction method that addresses decoding and fluency skills through daily short practice on phonics, sight phrases, and age-appropriate narratives (Campbell, 1996). It is a timed and graphed mastery exercise in which a student competes only with him- or herself for progress. Incorporated as a pilot program for the 1998 summer camp, it was an immediate success with campers and staff. Even the recreation staff noticed the campers' enthusiasm for the program. Although it directly addresses only the skill of fluency, not comprehension, it is a manageable and cost-effective tutoring method for use in community settings by nonspecialists. Following on that success, Great Leaps has been offered in the evening program 4 nights per week with great success. It is a testimony to the power of the program that parents drove their children into the neighborhood from other parts of town 4 nights a week. First they reported renewed enthusiasm for reading at home, and next they reported that the child's teacher was noticing more class participation. Then they noticed acceptance of reading challenges. Finally, they noticed improved classroom grades.

To leverage our grant funding, we have collaborated with AmeriCorps projects in the area, paying $3,000 to $5,000 in exchange for 1,700 hr of assistance during the year. This has proved a valuable exchange. Our workers gain meaningful experience (as program coordinators and Great Leaps tutors) and tuition credits or loan forgiveness, and we have good help for a relatively small investment. The federal AmericaReads initiative also supports our work, paying for work–study students to serve as reading tutors for K–3 students in the evenings without the typical work–study copayment.

*Summer structure.* The summer camp for elementary age children arose from the need to close the space between elementary and middle school for children. Priority enrollment is for neighborhood children with an annual enrollment of 90 to 110 students. The camp integrates four academic periods and two recreation periods into an 8-hr day. The University of Kentucky is responsible for staffing the four academic periods, which are language arts, social studies, life skills, and art. Five weekly sequential themes (Myself, My Family, My Community, My Nation, My World) provide an integrating focus for the hands-on learning activities. Reading happens everyday in most classes. In addition, all children, regardless of reading ability, participate in one-on-one daily reading practice in the Great Leaps Reading Program with an AmericaReads tutor. For the summer camp, all partners contribute staff from program funds. The total cost of the camp, in both hard dollars and in-kind support, is $30,000, or $300 per child. Originally, the camp was free. After discovering the camp's popularity among working families who saw it as cheap child care, the fee was added. It is still modest in recognition that the families who participate are low income in entry-level and service jobs.

*Special events.* To boost community awareness, the Academy sponsors special events each semester. A carnival often is the kick-off event to open fall Family Nights. With other youth agencies, the AmeriCorps workers supervise lock-ins at the school or nearby locations. This year, for the first time, a community health fair was held. The fair had three purposes. It would (a) showcase the spring community school classes, involving University of Kentucky students in preparation and presentation; (b) boost awareness of the Academy in the community; and (c) address the stated need by community members for health information. Twenty agencies provided people, demonstrations, and product samples (mostly food and toothbrushes). Twenty-five University of Kentucky students needing field hours helped organize, set up, and participate in the fair. One hundred fifty children and adults attended the fair, held on a Wednesday evening at the school. It was the most successful public event to date.

*Middle School Service Learning*

The National Society for Experiential Education (1999) defined service learning as any carefully monitored service experience in which a student has intentional learning goals and reflects actively on what he or she is learning throughout the experience. Service learning programs emphasize the accomplishment of tasks which address community issues and include features which foster participants' learning about larger social issues and an understanding of the reciprocal learning and service which can occur between students and community members.

Service learning is a highly collaborative model. Steps include needs assessment, project planning, project implementation, celebration, and reflection. All stakeholders should be present at every step, and consensus is the decision-making method. We have been the most successful when we have been the most collaborative, for consensus allows all parties to commit voluntarily to the plan. Collaboration is a little like fly fishing. You cast many times into the pool before you catch a fish. With collaboration, you cast many ideas into the partnership pool before all partners agree that a given project addresses their self-interest. It is only the mutually beneficial projects that succeed to completion because everyone brings energy and commitment to the project.

A major goal of the project was to introduce service learning into the middle school curriculum. Winburn Middle School organizes its students into seven teams of 100 students and four core subject teachers, each called by a historical derivative of the name of the school mascot, the Warrior, who resembles a Roman soldier. In 1995, the sixth-grade Ashanti Team accepted this opportunity. This team is known for its innovation in addressing barriers to learning. For example, they voluntarily make summer home visits to every incoming sixth-grade student. At the same time that they accepted the University of Kentucky offer to explore service learning, they committed to student–teacher progression or looping, in which they stayed with their students through eighth grade, learning the seventh- and eighth-grade curriculum as they went along. Looping facilitated the incorporation of service learning because projects can continue from year to year, starting small and gradually improving. The favorable community response to the Ashanti Team's successful effort has led to greater participation by other teams. After 4 years of successes and false starts, service learning has been adopted by four additional teams.

Service learning has benefitted these students particularly in their psycho-social development and interpersonal skills. Poverty is not just an income issue. Poverty also limits the range of experiences needed for cognitive development. Children in this school are experience deprived, and community service experiences fill in some of those gaps in real-world knowledge. How these projects directly impact the curriculum is not as well known and is a subject of discussion among teachers who endorse the method and those who do not. The controversy centers around time off strictly academic tasks, which are perceived as more directly related to improving scores on the statewide assessment. It is the task of teachers who endorse service learning to use it as part of the curriculum plan to accomplish learning benchmarks. Following is a teacher education student's comment on middle school service learning after a presentation during a college class held at the middle school:

> The students who came to our class ... were truly exceptional. I think that it is wonderful that they are so involved with service learning. Not only do they learn academics but they also get the opportunity to develop their social skills. I think that service learning is great because I see that it can often give students goals in life. This became apparent to me as I listened to the young person who told us that she knew she wanted to be an elementary teacher someday. She knew this because she had been give [sic] the chance to work with small children during service learning and truly enjoyed it. I find myself now thinking that I cannot wait to become a middle school teacher and try this, if possible, with my own students. (Middle School Teacher Education student, personal communication, March 22, 1998)

*Promoting Networking Through Feeder Pattern Articulation*

Networking has been central to the partnership from the beginning. A strategy to support networking has been linking with elementary schools whose students advance to Winburn and then on to the area high school. Why? To remove barriers to learning, one must consider those that the divisions of K–12 schooling themselves may cause. For example, a very large number of children from one particular elementary school arrive on Winburn's doorstep below grade level in reading. Whose problem is this? Is it the middle school faculty who are challenged to teach? How do they tell the elementary faculty they are receiving unprepared students when they know the high staff turnover in that building? What do the middle school faculty tell the high school faculty about why they are sending forward underprepared students with whom they have done the most they can? Why do parents not demand more, and how do they tell the public school system they expect more? The fact is that it is a systemic problem. Our strategy has been to increase the numbers and types of interactions between levels of schooling—teachers, parents, and administrators. This strategy has been endorsed by school district officials.

*Student networking.* Our early efforts in this area were student networking. We gave priority to students in the feeder pattern for participation in Great Leaps tutoring, reduced rates at summer camp to neighborhood children, and found summer camp group leaders from the middle and high schools. These efforts were minimal in cost, but began to build a sense of community among the children in the area, the Bryan Station High School feeder pattern. The next step was to build connections among the teachers.

*Teacher networking.* We realized that transitions from elementary to middle and middle to high school were quite difficult. The most graphic evidence of this difficulty appears in review of state assessment performance and sixth- and ninth-grade failure rates. Particularly telling are the increasing numbers of students scoring at the novice level on state assessments and the high retention rates at sixth and ninth grades among students enrolled in these grades for the first time. Ninth-grade retention rates are as high as 23% in one school. In addition, some area elementary schools have mobility rates approaching 50%. The larger issue for teachers is a narrow perspective on school as what happens in one building, rather than what happens for students in K–12. We realized that this narrow perspective came in part from our own university preparation programs, which are highly level specific, and sought through this project to inform our own practice as well as impact student achievement.

Through the Seamless Transitions Program, funded by the Kentucky Department of Education, we worked with the eight schools in the Bryan Station High School feeder pattern. These schools serve students at great risk for school failure. Seamless Transitions has three components: (a) alignment of standards within the feeder pattern, (b) a series of seminars designed to provide teachers with the instructional knowledge necessary to teach in a standards-based learning environment, and (c) a university course that provides multilevel teams with a framework for examining systemic issues within the feeder pattern. The schools within this feeder pattern are at various points in the curriculum alignment process. This model focuses on alignment at the seams of the pyramid (Grades 5 to 6 and Grades 8 to 9). The program has served as a turning point in expanding the teachers' thinking from a single building to a K–12 perspective. Seamless Transitions has completed its 2nd year. The project has impacted K–12 student learning, our preservice teacher education program, and the in-service teachers in the buildings involved in the project.

*Parent networking.* The next step was to develop a parent network. To address the chronic problem of parental involvement, the university field coordinator recruited two parents to apply with her as a team of three to the

Commonwealth Institute for Parent Leadership (CIPL). CIPL is a project of the nationally recognized Prichard Committee for Academic Excellence and is designed to empower parents as advocates for their own and all students in their district. One component of the institute is a parent education project conducted in one's local school or district for applying the knowledge and techniques learned. This strategy is proving to be very effective for the Winburn team who met five additional north Lexington parents at the institute. Together, the eight designed Destination Middle School, an educational event for the 500 incoming sixth-grade students and their parents at the two middle schools in the feeder pattern. Separate sessions and speakers for students and parents address early adolescent development, communication, learning styles, peer cultures, academic expectations, and study skills.

*PDS*

Carried to the fullest extent, the PDS concept embodies the idea of school as the center of community revitalization because it assumes that good teaching can be a lever for school success for all youngsters, especially those who are not succeeding. It does so through a careful, analytical process intended to address problems and build scaffolding to improve learning opportunities. Although the name PDS implies that all this is done in a single building, this is a misconception. PDS is a process through which models are designed and tested in school settings: Models that can be generalized to other settings. It is relational in that it depends on the involvement of constituent groups in building, testing, and evaluating models (university and school personnel, families, community members, and students themselves). It is organic in that models change as collaborators reflect and research findings are considered.

If Colleges of Education are to prepare teachers for teaching all children, then they must prepare them for teaching better the nations' poor and minority children. These children form the student body of schools like Winburn–Title I schools, which are challenged to teach the disadvantaged of our society to the same performance levels in the same amounts of time as schools enrolling children of means, the chief difference being parental home support and school involvement. This disadvantage means that teachers must understand their dual role—that of teacher and that of the parent surrogate. This surrogate role must be performed with respect for the parent and recognition that life circumstance of poverty, race, and culture impact the way that each parent will approach the process of schooling. Thus, it is wise for a college of education to invest resources in maintaining community schools at its PDS sites located at Title I schools or similar ones enrolling high numbers of children in poverty.

We have focused our PDS efforts at Winburn on three components: (a) preservice teacher education, (b) professional development for in-service teachers, and (c) research. Other parts of this article suggest that the partnership extends beyond these three into other Academy functions; this assumption is correct.

*Preservice teachers.* Our PDS partnership with Winburn moved the foundation middle school class to meet on-site. This gave the students first-hand experience in the daily life of the school from the beginning of the program. Celebrations such as winning the district math team competition and the county football championship, and tragedies such as the unexpected death of the librarian, became part of the class experience. During this 2nd-year meeting on-site, the literacy course that is paired with the middle school foundation class also met at Winburn. Both classes involve Winburn teachers in presentations, and the students work as teams paired with Winburn teams for their field assignments. The classes have traditionally required the writing of an integrated unit of instruction, teaching model lessons with a literacy focus, and shadowing a middle school student. Due to Winburn's move to a looping model, where teachers and students stay together for 3 years, and because of our learning from our collaboration, class assignments have been extended and new assignments created.

University of Kentucky's College of Education students are required to show evidence of community service as an admission requirement for teacher certification programs, but students are expected to arrange for this on their own. One course is an exception, EPE 301, Foundations of Education in American Culture, in that it requires a community field experience to complement the unit on service learning. The experience must be in the after-school or Saturday program, not during the school day as are most field experiences. For the past three semesters, the instructor of two sections of EPE 301 has taken the requirement one step further by limiting field experience options exclusively to those that support Winburn Community Academy. Due to the fact that the course emphasizes inquiry-based learning, students are taught basic historical and ethnographic methods of community research, which are applied to the field experience. In turn, students are aware that their efforts are benefitting Winburn youth or adults. EPE 301 students are provided several options for completing the 15-hr requirement. There are several benefits to this model. First, Academy participants benefit from the presence of the youthful college role models. The ratio of neighborhood youth to college students is sometimes 1:1, allowing for personal, somewhat sustained interaction over the 8 weeks of the program. Second, mostly White, mostly middle-class college students experience a minority culture. Third, the negative image of the neighborhood as unsafe is proven false in the eyes of those who have a reason to come into this isolated community. Fourth, Academy coordinators can organize programs knowing students will be available to help run things. Fifth, college students have opportunities to create meaningful programs and projects, thereby increasing their own leadership skills.

*In-service teachers.* Our work with in-service teachers has evolved more slowly. Our first step was holding classes in the school so that teachers could participate in professional development activities and fulfill graduate requirements conveniently. Just as we gave priority to feeder pattern children in our programs, scholarship funds were targeted to teachers in these schools. Classes have included action research and organization and supervision of student teaching.

A second model of collaboration that has proven useful is that of minisessions at faculty meetings. The PDS liaison shared basic principles of middle schools and middle school students in brief sessions. A literacy faculty member conducted 20-min strategy sessions monthly to provide the teachers with new ideas. We knew we had success when there was a Venn diagram bulletin board up days after the session on using them.

Finally, we are involved in the professional development of teachers through service by university personnel on school committees, through working with 1st-year teachers on internship committees, and through informal assistance and collaboration.

*Research.* Early research efforts have focused on evaluating the impact of Academy programs on student attitude and motivation through survey research (see, e.g., Anderman, Griesinger, & Westerfield, 1998). In addition, teachers and students are conducting action research projects. Our challenge is to balance the formal research style of the University, with its emphasis (especially for untenured faculty) on rapid production of many publications, with the collaborative nature of our partnership and the slower pace of incorporating meaningful research into educational change. We are still searching for a balance.

## Challenges and Future Directions

*Causes for Celebration*

At the beginning of the grant-funded work, the Academy promised to assess its progress in qualitative and quantitative ways. Qualitative methods and anecdotes have proven to be easier to obtain than quantitative. For example, the ultimate criterion of success is the improvement of Winburn student achievement on the statewide comprehensive assessment test. Winburn's students' scores began increasing the year the University of Kentucky partnership began, 1994. Winburn Middle School's reputation in the state for educating Blacks and Whites equally well is unsurpassed. Their assessment scores show the least disparity between the races. That is also the year the Ashanti team teachers began moving with their students to the next level, and since then several initiatives have caused the teaching faculty to be more collaborative and set specific learning goals. These factors all impact improving test scores. Enrollment in the after-school and Saturday programs is recorded. However, the numbers are often embarrassingly small; sometimes only five people per class attend on a given night (similar to some graduate classes offered on campuses throughout the United States). Is this success or failure? From our point of view, it is a success because personal relationships are the only way to begin to change disenfranchised attitudes toward public schooling. Change happens one by one.

We have regular after-school and community programming, year round. Youth have constructive activities to occupy their time. Participation in all programs is gradually increasing, as is the variety of courses. We are seeing repeat enrollment of families. There are more new homes in the neighborhood; more trees are evident, and there is less litter. The neighborhood association is more active, although we are still seeking a more collaborative relationship. Leadership remains in the hands of a few; the neighborhood remains an enigma even to city officials. Many more Lexington residents come to the school and the neighborhood for school or Academy-sponsored events, thus changing the image of both the school and the neighborhood in this city. An identity and sense of unity for north Lexington schools is in place because there are increased exchanges among parents, teachers, and University of Kentucky faculty through graduate courses, professional development seminars, committee meetings, special events, and proposal writing projects. Additional resources are coming into the school through local businesses, the WEPIC grant, Academy partners, and individuals. Parental involvement is still low, but by building personal relationships, each team has a core of committed parents who help with team field trips.

Service learning is incorporated into instructional practice by about one third of Winburn faculty. Communication between elementary feeder schools and the middle school is more frequent, and activities are planned together. University of Kentucky students have ample opportunities for service learning. Seamless Transitions and Great Leaps show promise for making meaningful change in student achievement.

We are institutionalizing many parts of the program. The teacher outreach liaison is now a permanent staff position. Parks support for the community recreation and homework center is stable. The PDS initiative is well grounded in the college. These are all successes, although we still face challenges.

*Current Challenges*

The research published to date is largely survey-based, correlational research. The teachers see few connections to their daily practice from this work. The move toward action research will help this problem, but it will also slow the research process.

After almost 6 years, we are facing challenges of transitions as well. New players come on board at the University, at the school, at Parks, or in other partners. They must be educated about our work to date and invited to join the conversations. We struggle with the question of formal partnership agreements, even the question of incorporating the Academy, as a way to ensure the programs continue beyond the tenure of current key players.

School-year bussing and poor public transportation systems mean that we struggle to involve in the Academy those children who attend Winburn and its feeder schools but do not live in the neighborhood. We are clearly a community learning center, but who is our community? Those who live in the neighborhood? Those who attend Winburn? These groups are not the same. Related to this is the question of neighborhood buy in. We are still an institutionally driven model working to engage neighborhood members in the leadership of the Academy.

*What's Next?*

We have been least successful in community development and parental involvement. Is this because there are too many other things to do in the provision of programs? Are we acting too much in the place of parents without drawing parents in sufficiently? Or is it, as we surmise, that parents and residents are working at personal capacity, striving to make a living? One approach is to find another partner who can focus on parental involvement. AmeriCorps has helped tremendously in this regard, but leadership development through projects like CIPL may be the answer.

The Winburn example shows what can be done to help schools overcome learning barriers in order to prepare students for productive living in a democratic society. The Winburn story also highlights challenges that are frequently encountered in the process. This work has strengthened our belief that sustained, collaborative efforts are necessary to achieve the aims of educational reform. Indeed, collaborative efforts like the one we have described may offer our best hope to improve educational opportunities for children at high risk for school failure because they involve school families in meaningful ways. As Schorr (1997) pointed out, schools can become "islands of hope in otherwise devastated neighborhoods" (p. 289) as they respond to needs and make allies of families. The Winburn Community Academy represents one example of how to achieve this scenario.

We know we are still laying the foundation at Winburn, and that to have a strong, sustainable community school, we will have to work persistently together on many fronts. We seek to build trust by always focusing on the learning needs of children. Building on our modest successes and keeping student achievement as our focal point, we will continue to modify the school and teacher education curricula, increase family and community involvement, and conduct research to measure success in many dimensions. We will continue to learn from our mistakes and to draw strength from each other. We conclude that time, talk, and tenacity are the keys to win–win partnerships—these principles guide our collaboration.

## References

Anderman, E. M., Griesinger, T., & Westerfield, G. (1998). Motivation and cheating during early adolescence. *Journal of Educational Psychology, 90,* 84–93.

Blank, M. (1998). *Emerging coalition for community schools: A vision for community schools.* Washington, DC: Institute for Educational Leadership.

Campbell, K. U. (1996). *Great leaps reading program.* Micanopy, FL: Diarmuid.

Gleick, J. (1988). *Chaos: Making a new science.* New York: Penguin.

Harkavy, I., & Puckett, J. L. (1991). Toward effective university-public school partnerships: An analysis of a contemporary model. *Teachers College Record, 92,* 556–581.

National Society for Experiential Education. (1999). *Some experiential learning terms.* Retrieved April 6, 1999 from the World Wide Web: http:www.nsee.org/defn.htm

Schorr, L. B. (1997). *Common purpose: Strengthening families and neighborhoods to rebuild America.* New York: Doubleday.

Wheatley, M. J. (1994). *Leadership and the new science: Learning about organization from an orderly universe.* San Francisco: Berrett-Koehler.

# Manufacturing and Production Technician Youth Apprenticeship Program: A Partnership

*Lawrence M. Kenney and Lana Collet-Klingenberg*

For 3 years, a university, a public secondary school, and a manufacturing company have been collaborating in offering an alternative education program to juniors and seniors who are not expected to graduate. The program takes place at the manufacturing site where students who are youth apprentices spend about 20 hr each week in work and another 20 hr in the classroom at the site—all at pay. After 2 successful calendar years in this competency-based program, youth apprentices earn a high school diploma. They are graduating from this program with useful skills, improved behavior, and academic qualifications for higher education. The Youth Apprenticeship (YA) Program meets the manufacturer's demand for skilled high school graduates in a rural area where such candidates are scarce. The program also provides the university with an alternative field site for preparing teachers and conducting research while rendering valuable services in areas of curriculum. Most important, the YA Program adds educational options for the ap-

LAWRENCE M. KENNEY *is Associate Dean and Professor in the College of Education, University of Wisconsin–Whitewater, and is coordinator of the partnership for the University.*

LANA COLLET-KLINGENBERG *is formerly in the Department of Special Education, University of Wisconsin–Whitewater; is currently on staff at the Wisconsin Center for Education Research, University of Wisconsin–Madison; and is program evaluator of the project.*

Requests for reprints should be sent to Lawrence M. Kenney, Associate Dean, College of Education, University of Wisconsin–Whitewater, 800 West Main Street, Whitewater, WI 53190–1790. E-mail: kenneyl@uwwvax.uww.edu

prentices themselves. The program has been recognized regionally and nationally for its design and effectiveness.

The Youth Apprenticeship (YA) Program is an innovative collaboration among a manufacturing industry, a public high school, and a College of Education at a publicly supported state university. Each of these agencies had specific challenges that demanded unique solutions. The privately owned manufacturing firm, recognizing that people are its greatest asset, wanted to offer a manufacturing facility as a school or career site where youth apprentices could begin to make a responsible transition to the world of work. The school district was exploring ways to educate at-risk students in the secondary school through a learning environment and instructional curriculum conducive to their success. The College of Education was looking for opportunities to prepare its preservice and in-service teachers in nontraditional settings. Together, they have created and implemented an award-winning program that can serve as an exemplary model of education to benefit secondary students, school districts, communities, manufacturing companies, and colleges of education throughout the nation and the world.

For some high school students, earning a diploma the traditional way is often difficult, but the YA Program is providing alternative education avenues for students. The program takes juniors and seniors who are not expected to graduate and places them in the world of work. Students spend about 20 hr each week in work and another 20 hr in the classroom at the site—all at pay. Nearly all of their competency-based schoolwork, from English to mathematics, involves some aspect of manufacturing and hands-on involvement. At the end of the program, students receive their high school diploma as well as a list of competency skills they have acquired.

Faculty and graduate assistants in the College of Education have been assigned to the program. There is ongoing research, proposal writing for grant monies, and curriculum development. Free services are provided by faculty, and methods students can receive either lab or independent study credit for their instructional modules. The governor of Wisconsin, the Division on Career Development and Transition of the Council for Exceptional Children, and the Manufacturers Council have all selected the program to receive commendations and awards.

The YA Program meets the manufacturer's demand for skilled high school graduates in a rural area where such a pool is scarce. In addition, the mentor training and morale building opportunities of the program exist for all employees, and the manufacturer has been able to reduce turnover of entry-level employees through the hiring of apprenticeship graduates.

Extent of Need

With increasing numbers of youth with and without disabilities at risk for leaving high school prior to graduation (Wagner, 1993) have come reports of new trends in America's workforce. The Business Council of New York State (1990) reported that by the year 2000, the percentage of jobs in unskilled labor in the United States will have fallen from 60% in the 1950s, to approximately 15% of the total workforce. They also project that many of these remaining unskilled jobs will be part-time employment and at low or minimum wage. It remains a simple projection then to suggest that the American workforce of the 21st century will need to be highly trained in order for this country to participate in continued economic growth, and that most employment opportunities will require high-level skills for high pay.

The Federal School-to-Work (STW) Opportunities Act of 1994 provided a framework to prepare all students for work and further education and increase the opportunities of all students to enter first jobs in high-skill, high-wage careers (U.S. Department of Education, 1994). The three components required to establish a comprehensive STW system are school-based learning, work-based learning, and connecting activities. These components are designed to (a) encourage all students to remain in school and achieve high standards of occupational and academic performance; (b) make education more relevant to students by integrating academic and occupational activities; and (c) enhance students' opportunities for employment or further postsecondary education by building effective partnerships among K–12 schools, postsecondary schools, employers, community agencies, students, and parents (U.S. Department of Education, 1994; U.S. Department of Labor, Education and Training Administration, Office of Work-Based Learning, 1992).

The Wisconsin Department of Public Instruction has established specific guidelines for implementing a STW Opportunities Act Cooperative Education State Skill Standards Certificate Program, which states that in the past, students were provided with opportunities related to STW via academic programs, education for employment initiatives, and vocational education programs. The current guidelines specify that the present direction of STW in Wisconsin is to build on those previous bases of instruction in structuring programs such as cooperative education, youth apprenticeships, paid work experiences, and the continuation of programs such as vocational education, agricultural education, consumer education, and business education (Wisconsin's Model Academic Standards, 1998).

Although many STW models have undergone recent public criticism for poor results in relation to postschool learner outcomes and a low impact on the state's workforce (Borsuk, 1999), one innovative model has received considerable positive attention and shows signs of promising program as well as postschool learner outcomes. The Manufacturing and Production Technician YA Program initiated via a partnership among Watertown, Wisconsin, public schools and the Generac Portable Products Company in Jefferson, Wisconsin. The University of Wisconsin–Whitewater is at the heart of the proposed research because it incorporates many of the desired features identified by the Assistant Secretary for Educational Research and Improvement in the Field-Initiated Studies call for proposals. This YA program is geared toward addressing key educational and employment issues of today. Specifically, it focuses on raising student achievement, providing equitable opportunities for achievement, and addressing the need for workers with high skill levels.

The 2-year Manufacturing and Production Technician YA Program offers a unique approach to youth apprenticeship due to a number of factors. First, it is a collaborative effort among secondary education, postsecondary education, and private industry. This partnership is exploring innovative ways of educating at-risk youth, providing opportunities to better prepare teachers and students to work in nontraditional settings, and modeling industry practices that reflect the belief that people are the greatest asset to any business.

A second unique feature of this YA Program is its full on-site commitment to the apprentices. Each apprentice is paid a wage for a 40-hr work week and is covered by the worker's compensation program. This work week entails 20 hr of on-the-job training and 20 hr of classroom learning centered on a competency-based curriculum. All classroom learning is facilitated on-site at Generac Portable Products by a full-time teacher whose salary is paid 50% by Watertown Schools and 50% by the Generac company. Students are accountable for the same work requirements as other Generac Portable Products employees.

A third notable feature of the Manufacturing and Production Technician YA Program is that students rotate through 14 steps of the manufacturing process during their tenure in the program, with a technical focus on six articulated credits that may be applied toward a vocational technical diploma or a degree program once they have fulfilled their high school graduation requirements. The competency-based curriculum was developed jointly by faculty at Watertown High School, the on-site YA teacher, and (supervised) college students in the Department of Biology and Life Sciences and various departments in the College of Education at the University of Wisconsin–Whitewater.

Program eligibility requirements and standards for student selection also make the YA Program unique. To participate in the program, students must be at least 16 years old, have completed 2 full years of high school, have a desire to work full time, and maintain a satisfactory disciplinary record while in the program. The unique aspect of this is that both the student and his or her parent or guardian must make a commitment to success in the program. Eligibility for the program is determined through the selection process that involves four steps:

1. Students are nominated (by teachers, parents, self).
2. Students and families or guardians attend an informational meeting at which representatives from Generac Portable Products provide information about the company and the YA Program's requirements.
3. Students formally interview with the company trainer and (if selected) with the Human Resources manager.
4. YA Program personnel (teacher, trainer, manager) visit the student at his or her home to confirm student and family commitment to successful program completion.

## History and Development

In December 1995, the Generac Corporation opened a manufacturing plant in Jefferson, Wisconsin, a small town in the southeastern portion of the state. Generac, a producer of emergency generators and power washers, expressed concern about the quality of the labor pool in their rural region. The company expected that high school graduates would be plentiful for their few hundred openings and assumed that a good work ethic and some skills would be a natural profile for most applicants. Instead, the company found that many adults seeking employment did not possess a high school diploma or the desired entry-level work ethic and skill.

At a meeting in January 1996, the principal and STW coordinator at Watertown High School heard the plea for qualified help at a meeting of the Jefferson County Human Resource Managers Association. The existing program at the high school—removing students from the traditional school setting and placing them in the adult world of work—had been successful with many students. However, the principal and the STW coordinator wondered whether they could expand this concept and place students full time at a business site to receive their education. At the next meeting of County Human Resource Managers Association, they discussed Education for Employment and how it had evolved into STW. They explained the types of programs available, from job shadowing to youth apprenticeship, and discussed the possibility of whether a business and a school could work together to benefit at-risk students and improve the quality of the workforce. The principal of Watertown High School offered a challenge to the businesses represented: "Would anyone in the audience care to explore this concept further?" Generac rose to the challenge.

The Vice President of Human Resources and the company's Human Resource Manager expressed a willingness to partner with the Watertown Unified School District located 20 miles away. School personnel toured the Generac plant and were affirmed in their desire to work with this company. The facility was new, modern, and clean. Generac produces generators and power washers for the world and had plans to expand its physical space due to growth potential. The company is also vertically integrated, which means all of the components of its products are made at the plant. The company agreed to provide a training center for instruction on-site, pay for half of the instructor's salary, hire a full-time training coordinator, secure a rider on their workers' compensation insurance, and provide student transportation to and from Watertown and Jefferson.

Watertown, like many other school districts, continually strives to provide at-risk student programming. The at-risk student may be the one who has sporadic attendance or sees little relevance in the way the district conducts business in the high school, but the student still seeks a high school diploma. In the past, companies such as Generac were often able to avoid hiring students who had not been successful in school. With the current labor shortage, however, businesses have begun to tap into the pool that contains at-risk students. These potential workers may be lax in attendance; have few career goals; and, even with a paycheck, see no relevance in the work that is being performed.

By May 1996, Watertown knew that its at-risk student population was the group to target for this partnership program at Generac. The students would be 16-year-old high school juniors. Due to their poor attendance and low academic performance, these students had little chance of graduating under regular circumstances at the high school. Instead, they would be placed at the job site for both work and instruction.

Through meetings of administrators and pupil support staff, a nomination process began to identify students for the program. Generac provided potential youth apprentices with a presentation laying out rules and expectations for the students. The students learned that, as employees, they would need to be at work by 7 a.m. every day, would be allowed only 12 absences per year, and would start with a base hourly wage, but could earn more through regular attendance and good performance both in the training center and on the production line.

Following the presentation, students still interested toured the facility and attended a meeting with their parents. Students and parents were informed that a 2-year successful stay in the program would lead to a high school diploma. Interested students completed an employment application and took a variety of aptitude tests. The students were interviewed, and a team composed of Watertown and Generac personnel conducted these home visits, which proved to be a critical factor in the success of the program.

Watertown and Generac agreed that the total curriculum would be tied to the manufacturing operation and that an academic component would be integrated into every part of the student's experiences—both in the classroom and on the production line. The Wisconsin Department of Public Instruction and the Department of Work Force Development of the Division of Connection Education and Work were consulted, and curriculum development was underway to be in place by the end of September 1996.

Indeed, this program would be unique. The students would be 16-year-old high school juniors who had little chance of graduating under regular circumstances. These students would be placed on a job site for their education and work. The curriculum would be a competency-based program similar to youth apprenticeship. State-approved competencies were correlated with lists from the manufacturing production technician youth apprenticeship, Madison Area Technical College HSED 509 Competencies, the Technical College System Tech Prep Competencies, and the University of Wisconsin Competency-Based Admission Project Competencies.

Meanwhile, prospective students and their parents understood these components of the program:

1. The YA Program is a 2-year plan that occupies the junior and senior years of high school and the summer between those years.
2. Each apprentice is paid a wage for a 40-hr week and is covered by the company's worker's compensation program.
3. The YA Program is divided into two parts: on-the-job training and classroom learning consisting of a competency-based curriculum.
4. There are approximately 14 rotations within the company that the apprentices complete during the program.
5. Students are held to the same expectation and requirements as other company employees during the work and training portion of the day.
6. Youth apprentices spend approximately 20 hr in apprenticeship training each week.
7. The technical focus of the curriculum consists of six articulated credits that can be applied toward a vocational technical diploma or degree program.
8. Supplemental instruction is also provided through field trips, guest speakers, and training in order for apprentices to meet the competency requirements of the program.

Seven students were selected to begin the program in September 1996.

*Curriculum*

The YA curriculum was completed in October 1996. The curriculum consisted of two parts: Blueprint Reading (15 units) and Manufacturing Processes (20 units). These courses made up six articulated credits that apprentices earned through the program. The curriculum integrated English, science, math, and social studies. Learning in the classroom directly relates to the real world (i.e., the apprentices' worksite). For example, as part of the literature component, apprentices read a novel *HeroZ* (Byham & Cox, 1994), which takes place in a manufacturing setting.

Apprentices were provided with several methods to attain information in each of the curriculum units. Each unit has a packet of questions referenced to specific competencies. Each unit also has accompanying videotapes that explain the unit and use diagrams and pictures to further explain the chapter concepts from related readings and texts. For the auditory learner, cassette tapes of the text are also available. Each unit and videotape include specific questions that pertain to the company. The apprentices were required to move from one physical area to another and to confer with the experts at the worksite to obtain necessary information.

Once selected for the program, students were interviewed to determine their likes and dislikes. Students also took a learning-styles inventory. Terminology was carefully chosen, too. For example, the word *classroom* is associated with *school*, so the term *training center* was selected for its association with industry. The days of the week and times during the day mattered, too. Mondays were less productive for students, so the training was transferred from Monday, Wednesday, and Friday to Tuesday, Thursday, and Friday. Also due to the fact that afternoons were less productive, all training was conducted in the morning, while the hands-on work, being more active, was conducted in the afternoon and on the remaining weekdays.

There were critical factors contributing to the immediate success of this program. These included the fact that all of the personnel of the manufacturing company, from the line people to the CEO, were considered instructors. Second, students were never told that they had to work alone; they soon discovered that they could work in teams. Third, a rating system was used with students, and a target board was designated for their assignments. Instead of a report card, there was a weekly competency report. Lastly, parent communication occurred on a weekly basis, both written and oral.

In January 1997, the College of Education at the University of Wisconsin–Whitewater was invited to join the Generac–Watertown partnership.

The College provides a full-time graduate assistant, faculty expertise, and undergraduate and graduate assistance through projects and independent study or field experience credit. The college students have provided literacy testing, student and family counseling, minilessons in biology (from the College of Letters and Sciences), and reading and writing instruction in having students transform their required novel into a play.

About 2 years ago, a portion of the Generac company was sold, resulting in a name change for the manufacturing site where this program takes place. The new name for this site is Generac Portable Products.

*Achievement*

Within months, success was felt. Students who had been absent 2 to 3 days per week were now absent only 2 days during a 10-month period. Several who had earned only one half credit by the start of the junior year were now moving successfully toward a high school diploma. Students who were withdrawn were now taking lead positions as a result of their training, and test scores in math and reading on the Wide Range Achievement Test (WRAT) began to soar. All apprentices made gains in both areas. One student improved from a seventh-grade level in math to a postsecondary math level, and another student improved from a sixth-grade reading level to a postsecondary reading level. Students began to take control of their own learning. Also, students began to view their full-time teacher as a mentor as well as an instructor.

Watertown High School compared the YA students' achievement scores to those of a similar group of at-risk students who remained at the high school in a competency-based program. The Generac students' gains in math and reading were three times as great. Some students were doing trigonometry and calculus in relation to gears and blueprint reading at Generac, whereas students in the more traditional high school were failing basic math. These results affirmed the direction of the program. Data being compiled and analyzed on WRAT results from the subsequent 2 years suggest continued high performance in math for most students and a low growth in reading for most students.

Of the seven students who began in September 1996, four graduated in June 1998. In September 1997, another six students began the program with four of them graduating in June 1999. Four additional students began in January 1998, and six students began in September 1998. For disciplinary reasons, nine students have been dropped from the program since September 1996. Plans call for a total of 24 apprentices in the fall of 1999, including four students from outside the Watertown School District, who will enroll on a tuition-basis sponsored and supported by their own school districts. In addition, a more extensive evaluation is planned.

*Mentoring*

The production-line supervisors are key mentors in the program. These supervisors mention the importance of training the mentors who work with the youth apprentices. Mentor training is one opportunity Generac provided the supervisors and line leaders. According to one supervisor, the mentor training alleviates a lot of questions employees may have when working with the YA Program. Supervisors frequently rely on observation and information from production-line leaders or other workers when assessing the progress of the youth apprentices. In many departments, the production-line leaders have more interactions with the apprentices than supervisors. Therefore, the production-line leaders handle many decisions and problems on their own.

Supervisors felt communication was essential when assessing the progress of the youth apprentices on the production floor. Mentors felt sitting down and talking with the apprentices were the best solution to any problems that arose. Supervisors met individually with apprentices and explained the problem and what needed to change. They try to head off the problem before it escalates. When apprentices make mistakes on the production line, they are shown the correct procedure and how to prevent making the mistake again.

Supervisors may ask other employees to spend more time with a struggling apprentice. Supervisors have to be fair, correct the apprentices if necessary, and set the conditions for success. Having patience with the apprentices is also very important. Apprentices go through many adjustments when they first start the program, and supervisors need to assist with these adjustments. One supervisor commented that you have to keep the apprentices under your wing and make sure they are being treated fairly by all employees.

*Cost*

A frequently asked question is: How much does this program cost? The company and the university have direct costs, as does the school district, in sharing salary costs with the company and by providing materials. However, the school district estimates that its real costs approximate $3,000 per student for a 12-month instructional year versus the average cost of $7,000 per year for traditional students in a 9-month program. The university pays graduate student assistants about $9,000 per calendar year.

*Program Visibility*

This pilot program, now in the 3rd year, has generated a great deal of interest locally, regionally, and even nationally. Other area school districts (e.g., Fort Atkinson, Jefferson, Janesville, Oregon, and Whitewater) have toured the facility and expressed an interest in replicating the program in their communities. In the fall of 1998, Wisconsin's Governor Tommy Thompson awarded a certificate of commendation to Generac for its commitment to the state's YA Program. Also in the fall of 1998, the international Organization for Economic Cooperation and Development (OECD; including a team of four international experts and Tom Edwards, representing STW programs in the Department of Labor) visited the program to gain a better understanding of how young people's transition from school to adult life is changing in the United States. An overriding goal of the OECD tour was to identify effective policies and programs throughout the international community that help young people learn and succeed to ultimately engage in productive and meaningful work. Also in 1998, a 21-member team from the state of Alabama visited the program to gain ideas for launching a similar program throughout their county. Representatives included school board members, superintendents of schools, principals, teachers, business leaders, and members of chambers of commerce. More recently, the program was selected for an award from the Wisconsin Council of Administrators of Special Services Division. A student was awarded Student of the Year and Generac Portable Products received the Business Community Award. In April 1999, Generac Portable Products was presented with the Employer of the Year award from the Division on Career Development and Transition for Exceptional Individuals (DCDT).

The YA Program was presented as "Pathways to Learning for a New Century: The Changing Face of YA in Wisconsin" for the DCDT at the 10th International Conference of the Council for Exceptional Children in October 1999 in Charleston, South Carolina. The YA Program was also presented by representatives of the partnership at the European Reading Conference in Stavanger, Norway in August 1999.

*Benefits to Participants*

The benefits and successes of this YA Program are shared, but each group realizes unique and specific rewards as well.

The benefits for Generac are: (a) the YA Program continues to build a qualified, quality workforce with a reinforced work ethic; (b) the mentor training and morale building opportunities of the program exist for all employees; and (c) Generac Portable Products is able to reduce turnover of entry-level employees through the hiring of apprenticeship graduates.

The benefits for the Watertown Unified School District are: (a) the YA Program adds educational options for high school students; (b) this program provides an integrated, authentic curriculum in partnership with business and industry; and (c) parental involvement is increased as parents take pride in the accomplishments of their son or daughter.

The benefits for the University of Wisconsin–Whitewater are: (a) university students from all licsensure areas in teacher education as well as students majoring in other programs have a nearby site from which to gain meaningful field experiences, internships, independent studies, symposia, and student teaching practica; (b) faculty members are provided a rich venue for research demonstrating educational theory and practice in a manufacturing workplace; (c) faculty members are able to assist in the building of a curriculum library on a regular and systematic basis for College of Education faculty and students; and (d) university personnel (faculty, undergraduate and graduate students) are able to gain ongoing staff development training as a result of their involvement in the program.

The benefits for the youth apprentices are: (a) the ability to earn a Certificate of Occupational Proficiency while acquiring a Watertown High School Diploma; (b) the opportunity to demonstrate enhanced self-esteem, improved citizenship, and self-motivated ownership of learning; (c) gainful employment with steadily increasing responsibilities; and (d) the chance to learn about various career opportunities.

Summary

The YA Program at Generac is appropriately named Pathways to Lifelong Learning, as stated on the cover of the public relations booklet developed by the company, the school district, and the university. At Generac, the students are given the opportunity to explore, first hand, career options from entry-level assembly to job-shadowing management positions. Students learn the skills necessary to acquire those jobs on graduation. The training at Generac prepares the students for successful careers beyond entry-level jobs. Although traditional schooling tends to emphasize visual and auditory learning and offers limited real-life situations in which learning can occur, this YA Program fosters an approach to accommodate a different learning style in an environment where students can and do succeed. YA students complete competencies in core coursework and earn credits toward a vocational technical degree. They also rotate through a variety of manufacturing work roles and earn a full-time wage. At the close of the 2-year program, a student has his or her high school diploma, a competency-based transcript, vocational credits, and a YA certificate in manufacturing and production.

During the next 3 years, the company, school district, and university plan to improve, expand, and replicate this successful model program that is the first of its kind in Wisconsin and perhaps in the nation. We will strengthen the program by developing new, readable instructional materials and integrating technology. We will expand the program by increasing the number of youth apprentices and by adding qualified teachers licensed in alternative education. We will replicate this model at new worksites in southeastern Wisconsin by adding industry mentors, school district participants, and university faculty and their students. Finally, we will continue promoting Pathways to Lifelong Learning by presenting the program before local, regional, national, and international groups. This community-based program is a creative solution for serving the needs of at-risk youth who were failing to succeed in the traditional school setting.

## References

Borsuk, A. J. (1999, January 20). School-to-Work gets poor grade in study. *Milwaukee Journal Sentinel*. Retrieved August 8, 1999 from the World Wide Web: http://www.jsonline.com/news/ian99/0119work.asp

Business Council of New York State. (1990). *Schools for the future*. Paper presented for the 1990 Business-Labor Education Symposium, Albany, NY.

Byham, W. C., & Cox, J. (1994). *HeroZ*. New York: Harmony Books.

U.S. Department of Education. (1994). Federal school-to-work opportunities act of 1994, Pub. L. No. 103-239, 108 Stat. 568 (1994). Retrieved January 15, 1999 from the World Wide Web: http://www.stw.ed.gov/factsht/act.htm

U.S. Department of Labor, Education, and Training Administration, Office of Work-Based Learning. (1992). *School-to-work connections: Formulas for success*. Washington, DC: Author.

Wagner, M. (1993). *Trends in post-secondary youth with disabilities: Findings from the national longitudinal transition study of special education students*. Paper presented at the meeting of the Transition Research Institute at Illinois Project Directors' Eighth Annual Meeting, Washington, DC.

Wisconsin's Model Academic Standards. (1998). Madison, WI: Department of Public Instruction.

# Creating the 21st-Century School of Education: Collaboration, Community, and Partnership in St. Louis

*Charles D. Schmitz, Susan J. Baber, Delores M. John, and Kathleen Sullivan Brown*

Creating 21st-century schools of education requires a new way of working in collaborative partnerships. In this article, we describe 3 key factors in restructuring the University of Missouri–St. Louis School of Education. Collaboration, partnerships, and community building helped shape the nature, pace, and outcomes of that restructuring. We assert that if education, and especially

CHARLES D. SCHMITZ *is Dean of the School of Education and Professor of Educational Leadership and Policy Studies, University of Missouri–St. Louis.*

SUSAN J. BABER *is Institutional Advancement Officer for the University of Missouri–St. Louis School of Education.*

DELORES M. JOHN *is Associate Dean for Continuing Education and Assistant Professor of Special Education for the University of Missouri–St. Louis School of Education.*

KATHLEEN SULLIVAN BROWN *is Assistant Professor of Educational Leadership and Policy Studies at the University of Missouri–St. Louis School of Education and a member of the Board of Directors of The Holmes Partnership.*

Requests for reprints should be sent to Charles D. Schmitz, Dean, School of Education, University of Missouri–St. Louis, 201 Educational Administration Building, 8001 Natural Bridge Road, St. Louis, MO 63121–4499. E-mail: charles_schmitz@umsl.edu

teacher education, does not heed the signals issuing from the workplace and the public, those who prepare professional educators run the risk of being late for a very important date: the dawn of the 21st century. How well educators are prepared to collaborate, develop partnerships, and make effective use of technology directly correlates with how well regions can meet workforce and community needs—and how schools of education themselves will fare in the 21st century.

Schools and colleges of education, and those of us who work in them, possess the power to change lives, neighborhoods, communities, cities, and even nations. We do so when we shoulder the responsibility to prepare education professionals. They, in turn, educate our future citizens. Those students whose lives we touch indirectly through our graduates are the people who will ensure the peace, pay our Social Security, build our cities, solve pressing social problems, and drive our economy in the future. In our increasingly connected world of global interchange, the potential influence of schools and colleges of education, and their faculty and graduates, is more far reaching than ever before in educational history.

Yet, it is difficult to pick up a journal or newspaper, or to hear a radio or television broadcast, and not learn about e-commerce, technology, the information age, and related concerns for "where in the world are the highly skilled workers going to come from?" Newscasters interview the policy analysts who fret and worry about tomorrow's economy becoming more competitive, and the media describe a national fear that schools are letting us down. Unless our schools today can change and adapt to this new world and produce a qualified workforce for a changing workplace, the solutions to these challenges will not emerge in our schools of education. The great opportunity we have could be lost.

The federal government acknowledges the depth of this problem as Bachula, Acting Under-Secretary for Technology, U.S. Department of Commerce, has indicated tremendous growth is expected in jobs requiring highly skilled workers. Yet, the supply of info-tech workers appears to be declining (Bachula, 1997).

Professional groups such as the American Electronics Association (AEA) are not waiting around for the United States or our schools to produce a qualified workforce. In its 1998 appeal to Congress, the AEA called for an expansion of the current annual immigration cap of 65,000 people to fill the growing demand for engineers and computer scientists. To support this request, AEA noted that there has been a 16% decrease in the number of Bachelors of Science engineering graduates from 1985 to 1997, and a 29% decrease in the number of people with computer science and math degrees from 1985 to 1995 (AEA, 1998).

If education, and especially teacher education, does not heed these blatant workplace signals, those who prepare professional educators run the risk of being late in the proverbial Mad Hatter's words: late for a very important date. In this case, it is the date with the dawn of the 21st century. How well educators are prepared directly correlates with how well regions can meet future workforce and community needs (Schmitz, 1998). U.S. Secretary of Education Riley (1996) explained the problem this way in an address to the St. Louis education community:

> Today, too many of our young people see no connection between what they learn in school and the skills they need to function in real life. And too many business leaders rightly complain that high school graduates come to them without the skills for today's jobs. We need to redesign our schools for success and place more attention on the forgotten middle—the average kids with untapped potential who are still looking for direction. Today's young people will be tomorrow's paramedics, emergency room nurses, Army helicopter pilots, and the skilled technicians who build the NASA rockets. There is no point in preparing our young people for jobs in a widget factory.

In the information and technology age, all our students need is to become knowledge workers with strong symbolic–analytic and collaborative skills (Wirth, 1992). They must learn to partner with others and to find answers and apply them to a specific problem. This means that teachers take the role of researchers alongside their students. Faculty in educator preparation programs must model and teach along the same lines. We need to teach more interactively, to reach out to diverse learners, to lecture with the aid of visuals and worldwide connectivity, and to question more purposefully for critical thinking. The teachers and administrators we prepare must also model in their classrooms and schools the specific behaviors and skills that their students will require as they move from school to a knowledge-based workforce and a technology-dependent world. Children need to see teachers and school principals as learners who research on the Internet, find information to support hypotheses, look up facts and ideas, and share their findings with others. When they set this type of example, teachers and administrators will automatically become research advisors or guides, assisting and collaborating with their students as information-gathering and fact-finding sleuths. Students will have the task of sorting through their findings, making judgements on what it means, analyzing information for accuracy and usefulness to their intent, and then reporting. These are the critical thinking skills that will be rewarded in the 21st century.

Lamentably, however, classrooms designed for the 19th century, with their neatly cultivated rows of desk-bound children, still prevail in too many of our schools. In the classroom of the future—which must be created today—instructional technologies will be applied in new and unconventional ways to improve learning, create new knowledge, and especially provide access to the worlds of information that technology can bring to less mobile, rural, and inner city students. Research in technology as it applies to how we learn is still in its infancy. This poses challenging opportunities for schools and colleges of education as well as business and industry (Schmitz, 1998).

Need for New Vision of Connectivity

This new world of education hinges on two types of connectivity. The first is electronic connectivity to give our students the ability to command the new communication technologies. The other kind of connectivity is the desire and capacity to be meaningfully connected to others, from classmates to coworkers in a pluralistic, ever-changing society. Advanced social skills in collaboration, communication, and democracy are needed to connect people and their ideas.

Students must connect to the world of discovery as it applies to their present and the world of work in which they will live their adult lives. Teachers must be prepared to use "contextualized teaching and learning" (Sears & Hersh, 1998) to enhance student success in and beyond school. Integrated approaches to learning science, math, reading, social studies, and geography are needed. We as university faculty and K–12 classroom teachers must understand the skills our employers seek and our communities need so that curriculum can be relevant to students' lives and to students' ultimate success as productive members of their communities. By the same token, employers must be realistic in their expectations and gain a deeper understanding of the issues teachers face in today's classrooms.

Therefore, the new model for our schools will need to expand our connections and extend far into the community (which, with technology, reaches well beyond mere political borders). The evolving new model depends on collaboration among the schools, educator preparation programs, corporations, museums, zoos, science centers, and cultural and social service institutions. Partners in the 21st-century schools of education will include practicing teachers, preservice teachers, counselors, principals, university faculty, employers, parents, employees, senior citizens, volunteers, and more. New teaching models from K–12 and in educator preparation models must include the school-to-work concepts—tying real-work experience and real-life skills to student learning. Today's newly designed school-to-work programs not only include access to high-tech learning environments for students, but also offer opportunities for practicing teachers, counselors, and other education leaders to spend time in corporations learning firsthand the variety of job skills needed. Educators move out of the island classroom to shadow employers and employees at their work sites, or they go online with employees and community members who volunteer as classroom mentors. In turn, corporate or small-business volunteers spend time in schools to show students how the concepts they learn are applied in business, professional, or manufacturing situations. While in the classrooms, these volunteers see the possibilities as well as limitations of teaching children in a classroom setting. They come to appreciate the dimensions of education that go beyond schooling to a deep appreciation of what it takes to make a community.

Technology is driving much of this interchange and collaboration. On-the-job engineers now correspond with science classes through E-mail mentoring projects. Teachers now set up chat rooms for students and professionals and entrepreneurs to discuss specific careers. CD-ROM videos show scientists, accountants, or stockbrokers talking about how they apply concepts that ninth graders are learning in chemistry, algebra, or calculus. Virtual job fairs, Web-based classified ads, and interactive video interviews help people find employment anywhere in the world. Professional learning and job skills assessment that corresponds to specific job analysis, with on-the-spot training, are widely available today via the Internet (Schmitz, 1998). This is not something that is going to happen; it is here.

How must schools of education respond to this brave new world? How can we learn to partner and use the new technologies and the power we have to connect learners? In what new ways can we collaborate to lead this transformation of learning for the knowledge workers of the future? In St. Louis, we are in the process of addressing these questions and creating this new model of education. It is not in any sense a finished product. It is definitely a work in progress. In this article, we describe our partnership, its ambitious goals, and its complex agenda. We follow the 3-year journey from strategic planning and internal restructuring to the unfolding of several creative new initiatives and newly germinated ideas. The article also takes this as an opportunity to reflect on problems encountered and new skills and attitudes we discovered were needed to collaborate successfully. We call our broad-based partnership "Creating the 21st Century School of Education."

### A Regional Example: The University of Missouri–St. Louis

As an urban institution, the University of Missouri–St. Louis plays an important role in its regional economy. Other urban-based schools of education share a similar responsibility, especially in maintaining economic health by providing a continuous stream of well-qualified, employable workers. More than 2.5 million people live in the Greater St. Louis region, making it the 18th largest metropolitan area in the United States. Home to 19 Fortune 1,000 companies, Greater St. Louis ranks sixth in the United States as a headquarters location for Fortune 500 companies, and these companies represent more than 50% of the state of Missouri's payroll (St. Louis Regional Commerce and Growth Association, 1998). The region must stay healthy to retain these key companies, and the companies need skilled workers to run their businesses and keep our communities vital.

For all of its pluses, the region shares many of the same issues and concerns experienced by other urban communities. The City of St. Louis is one of the poorest in the United States, with one in four city residents and approximately 60% of the children living in poverty. Urban sprawl saps diversity and energy from the city. Regional and racial polarization remains a growing concern. Adding to the difficulty is the fact that the St. Louis region includes 12 counties, 95 separate municipalities, and 771 units of government (Peirce & Johnson, 1997, p. 1B).

The fragmentation permeates the metropolitan area's 48 public school districts located in the city and county of St. Louis and serving over one third of all Missouri school-age children. Urban spread and its political and cultural fragmentation hamper the region's ability to progress educationally and economically. In fact, the St. Louis region is proving that psychological or cultural distance can sometimes be greater than geographic distance. The gap between the educational and technological haves and have nots can only widen without conscious intervention.

Fortunately, the region has become proactive and is heading toward an economic and political renaissance. Community leaders are coming together on many regional issues and initiatives. One of them, St. Louis 2004, is a group of leaders and representatives from education, business, and cultural and social service institutions convened to foster collaboration, understanding, education, and economic health and growth throughout the area. As a result of these community development initiatives, institutions are realizing that survival, vigor, and community renewal demand the best efforts of all, which means collaboration. The School of Education at the University of Missouri–St. Louis has been an active member of these community development efforts—for example, by assisting in the development of policy reports and recommendations for teacher preparation and professional development (St. Louis 2004, 1999).

Collaborations within the community (not only within K–12 systems or education colleges) can create a powerful infrastructure for increased accountability and resources for teaching and learning. Businesses, unions, government agencies, and community-based organizations can all contribute. Due to the fact that preservice and in-service teachers need to learn about the worksite, the "simultaneous renewal" (Goodlad, 1994, p. 235) of schools and educator-preparation programs can be effective only if they are actively connected to the world of work and community. As society places more demands on those entering the workplace, it is imperative that both educators and students have firsthand knowledge of employer expectations, community resources, and needs.

The interval between stating that a community or an institution will build itself through collaborative efforts and the actual process of collaboration is a rocky ravine—narrow in spots, gaping in others. Collaboration can be messy, filled with ambiguity, uncertainty, and confusion (Fullan, 1993; McGowan, 1990). Moving schools of education to change is proving to be a daunting challenge as Fullan (1993) warned: "The school change process is uncontrollably complex, dynamic and in many circumstances unknowable" (p. 19). Successful professors and instructors generally learned through a didactic approach to teaching and learning (lecture, memorize, and recite). It is difficult then to dispute a highly accomplished academician who has a "well, it worked for me" attitude and ask them to venture into the unknowable. Also, we need to be careful to recognize and celebrate the historic successes of our educational system while we continuously try to improve what we do and increase the number of people who are successful in our schools and higher education institutions. For the School of Education at the University of Missouri–St. Louis, faculty resistance to change has been relatively mild. However, when even moderate resistance is coupled with the very nature of change and the fragmented climate of the region, the challenges grow quite formidable. This is how we began.

Setting the Wheels in Motion

As the first step, the faculty of the School of Education addressed fragmentation within its own ranks. In 1996, the School of Education faced a transition period with the appointment of a new dean. As often happens during a leadership transition, we began a strategic planning process. A crucial difference in this case was that, instead of just an internal planning task, the process was collaborative in its intent and makeup, with representatives from the faculty, school districts, businesses, and university students. Following many meetings and conversations, drafts and documents, the result was a new vision for the University of Missouri–St. Louis School of Education "to become a national leader in education research and scholarship that supports education professionals within an expanding collaborative community" (University of Missouri–St. Louis, 1997, p. 8).

*Ambitious and Achievable Goals*

Over the last 3 years, the School of Education at the University of Missouri–St. Louis, under the leadership of the new dean and the reorganized faculty, has been steadily implementing the changes that this strategic planning process identified. A new pair of eyes, taking in the local scene, could see what was in place and could discern a new pattern. This was graphically translated into the University of Missouri–St. Louis Solar System (see Figure 1), a visual representation that aided in the understanding of complex ideas about new ways to work. The other partners in our universe helped the University of Missouri–St. Louis create a new role for the state land grant institution in "connecting the dots" that were scattered across the region. Each partner within this solar system could, to some extent, determines its own orbit, place, and relation to the other planets.

Visionary, participatory, and strategic thinking like this now needed to be operationalized into tactics for implementation. The School of Education faculty moved into the next phase, looking at life on our own "planet." Faculty decided that four main characteristics that emerged from the vision statements would produce the backbone of the program, creating the 21st-century School of Education. The four themes require us to design programs that (a) are field based, (b) are technology rich, (c) promote lifelong learning, and (d) stress collaboration with the wider community.

*Field Based*

The formal preparation and continuing education of classroom teachers is a collaborative effort involving many committed partners. Our preservice students and majors spend less time in lecture halls and more learning time in K–12 schools, working with practitioners in Professional Development Schools (PDSs), and collaborating with the community in ways that are relevant to the future workplace and the current needs of the community.

*Technology Rich*

Technology is the glue that connects our School of Education with the community partners and the rest of the world. Technology must be used to

*Figure 1.* University of Missouri–St. Louis solar system. Copyright: University of Missouri–St. Louis School of Education.

reach—not further alienate—at-risk learners: "Computing is not just about computers anymore—it's about living" (Negroponte, 1995, p. 6). Telecommunications linkages are in place, and two-way audio and video technology is a planned component of PDSs. These links will create stronger connections between the University of Missouri–St. Louis School of Education faculty and practicing professionals. They also provide multipoint connections between the School of Education, its PDSs partners, and the other educational and cultural institutions in St. Louis.

*Lifelong Learning*

The notion that a teacher can be prepared for a lifetime in a 4- or 5-year preservice program is no longer educationally sound. Combining preservice and in-service professional development will strengthen school-improvement goals. With the use of technology links and interactive communication, more efforts are being made between the School of Education and community partners to offer professional development to all teachers.

*Collaborative*

The University of Missouri–St. Louis School of Education is an active part of the St. Louis community. By enlisting the help of community resources and building partnerships and collaborations, the School of Education will become more responsive to the needs of this region—the future workforce needs, the education needs, the social needs, and the career-preparation and learning needs of children (University of Missouri–St. Louis, 1997). We have become engaged in praxis, the real work of helping K–12 students be successful in our schools.

Organizational Structure

With these four foundations for positive change in place, the next implementation step was to organize the School of Education in a manner that complemented the new goals. Through a process of faculty input and continuous review and approval, four new units were created: (a) teaching and learning; (b) counseling; (c) educational psychology, research, and evaluation; and (d) educational leadership and policy studies.

To encourage continuous information sharing and collaboration in scholarly research, service, and teaching, faculty members selected a primary division where most of their work would occur. Most also selected a secondary and, in some cases, even tertiary division, in which they had particular and shared interests. The largest division is the teaching and learning group with 38 faculty. The structure has been in place for more than 2 years.

Unique among colleges and schools of education is the University of Missouri–St. Louis School of Education's exceptional number of endowed professorships. More important than quantity, however, is the scope and relevance of these new positions in the university and the school's commitment to becoming a community leader in collaboration. Nearly all of the 10 professors hold formal joint appointments between the School of Education and area cultural institutions, informal science education centers, youth service organizations, an inner city school district, or a technical college. Many hold joint appointments between the College of Arts and Sciences and the School of Education, a relation that is gaining increased importance and visibility. There are endowed professorships in citizenship, science, art, music, tutorial education, character education, urban education, and technology and learning. These are located all or in part in the School of Education and illustrate the collaborative nature of the organization:

- The Teresa M. Fisher Endowed Professorship in Citizenship Education (connected to the Citizenship Education Clearinghouse, which offers precollegiate programs in citizenship education).
- The E. Desmond Lee and Family Fund Endowed Professorship in Science Education (connected to the St. Louis Regional Institute for Science Education and provides professional development in K–12 science education).
- The E. Desmond Lee and Family Fund Endowed Professorship in Science Education II (connected to the St. Louis Regional Institute for Science Education and provides professional development in K–12 science education).
- The William R. Orthwein, Jr. Endowed Professorship in Life-Long Learning in the Sciences (connected to the St. Louis Science Center and provides professional development in K–12 science education).
- The E. Desmond Lee and Family Fund Endowed Professorship in Art Education (connected to the St. Louis Art Museum and provides professional development in K–12 science education and programs for informal science education).
- The E. Desmond Lee and Family Fund Endowed Professorship in Music Education (connected to the St. Louis Symphony Orchestra and Opera Theatre of St. Louis, providing music enrichment programs for K–12 students).

- The E. Desmond Lee and Family Fund Endowed Professorship in Tutorial Education (connected to the E. Desmond Lee Regional Collaborative Institute for Tutorial Education and 10 United Way Youth Service agencies, providing volunteer and staff training in tutorial education).
- The Sanford N. McDonnell Endowed Professorship in Character Education (connected to the Sanford N. McDonnell Leadership Academy of Character Education, providing principals and superintendents with leadership training in character education).
- The E. Desmond Lee and Family Fund Endowed Professorship in Urban Education (in conjunction with the St. Louis Public Schools Project Renaissance, developing PDS partnerships in K–12 urban schools with University of Missouri–St. Louis and other institutions of higher education in the region).
- The Emerson Electric Company Endowed Professorship in Technology and Learning (in conjunction with Ranken Technical College in St. Louis, providing professional development for Ranken faculty, as well as a Technology and Learning Center at the University for research, educator preparation, and professional development in effective use of technology in the teaching and learning process).

These professorships were the result of creative policy and legislation at the state level. The Missouri Legislature in 1993 established the Missouri Endowed Chair and Professorship Program, thus offering a national model that other states and institutions could adopt. A combination of private and public resources is used to establish endowed chairs and professorships in the University of Missouri system, of which the University of Missouri–St. Louis is a part. The program requires three funding sources: (a) a gift from a private donor, (b) a match from the State of Missouri, and (c) a funded position from the participating campus. The minimum contribution to endow a professorship was $550,000. Through a formula, the state appropriates a 100% match of the donor's gift. The position is permanently located on the campus and must be filled by a qualified individual who is not working in the university system. This incentive model was critical for the University of Missouri–St. Louis to build new and solidify existing partnerships within the community and the university.

Now that the infrastructure has been set in place, and these new partnerships with other area educational and cultural institutions have begun to develop projects, the school is poised to redesign curriculum and teaching methods. A curriculum redesign project is underway to move the program toward performance-based, authentic teaching and learning. As faculty have understood the need and value of self-assessment and collaboration (even though our voices of frustration with the process can be loud at times), the school needed to continue sending a strong message to potential partners while the internal reorganization took shape. Top-level administration of the School of Education met one-on-one with leaders and staffs of businesses, civic groups, human service agencies, cultural and scientific institutions, and school districts. Everyone received (and continues to receive) a clear message:

> We will have a well-prepared workforce only through a good education system, and a good education system will not be possible without good teachers. The entire community must be involved. The University of Missouri–St. Louis wants to be your partner.

It was important during this outreach effort to get people together physically, not just virtually. In this sense we could not rely on high tech alone. It took several attempts with each partner, but eventually people began talking to each other. Trust began to develop, and each partner felt empowered. We have learned that working with potential partner organizations calls for us to pay close attention to some key issues: (a) helping each partner understand that partnering enhances, not diminishes, everyone's opportunities; (b) guiding and facilitating, not controlling; (c) finding common-ground locations and meeting regularly; (d) starting your relationship with easy-to-accomplish projects; (e) developing trust by making a commitment and sticking with it; (f) finding ways to give up something to make the partnership work; and (g) combining resources to create joint appointments (Schmitz, 1999).

### Finding Funds and Resources

All collaborations seek new resources. Collaboration is effective, but it also takes dedicated time and resources. Although most partners have limited funds, collectively they can have a stronger impact. Schools of education need to attract resources, but they can also contribute resources in the form of influence, reputation, and intellectual capital and stability. The 10 University of Missouri–St. Louis School of Education endowed professorships were instrumental to the collaboration process because they connect members of the School of Education with important scientific, cultural, and human service agencies in the greater St. Louis community. They represent a commitment to collaboration that is high on potential external funders' priorities. They provide a tremendous basis for collaborative learning and information sharing by working on the real work, reducing the isolation for which many criticize the academy.

A development officer within the School of Education devotes time to locating new funding sources and assisting faculty with applications for private grants as well as state and federal funds. Local and national donors are approached with ideas that fit their philanthropic missions. As faculty were reorganized into the four divisions, projects that seemed disparate previously became more convergent, making more effective use of available resources. Risk taking and hard work produced early successes, which led to other opportunities and more successful ventures.

Early Success and Two New Initiatives

One of the first collaborative successes of this broad-based partnership has been the creation of the Regional Education Park in a facility adjacent to the campus. The park is a collaboration formed in 1997 among various education and teacher resources and professional development programs. Current partners in the Regional Education Park include five entities: (a) St. Louis Regional Professional Development Center, (b) the Missouri Department of Elementary and Secondary Education Initiatives Programs, (c) the Cooperating School Districts Staff Development Division, (d) the St. Louis Regional Institute for Science Education, and (e) the St. Louis Professional Development Schools Collaborative.

An idea long aborning in St. Louis, the Education Park is now a reality, and it continues to grow and expand into additional programmatic directions. A new initiative is now underway to round out the existing Education Park, adding a workforce analysis, skill analysis, and training resource to this already potent mix. WorkABLE St. Louis is the regional Work Keys Alliance of business, labor, and education, a partnership utilizing ACT's national Work Keys system to profile, assess, and teach critical workplace skills. Another broad-based partnership, this one is part of the School of Education and will be housed in the Education Park as funding becomes available. WorkABLE brings to the Regional Education Park education and professional development collaboration two powerful partners: the Regional Commerce and Growth Association (a regional "chamber of commerce") and the St. Louis Labor Council, AFL–CIO.

This growing collaborative effort will be called the Regional Center for Education and Work and will become an educational resource center for workplace skills assessment, training, and guidance. Action-oriented programs among the collaborators on site and their networks will effectively address workplace skill preparation. The Regional Center for Education will be able to provide professional development for teachers, counselors, and education leaders in design and implementation of school-to-work reforms. At this same site, partners will be able to study, research, and report best practices in collaborative school-to-work initiatives. Finally, the center will provide policy research and analysis regarding labor market information as to future job trends, expected wages, areas of growth, and expected job skill requirements to meet future labor market demands.

A second new initiative is the Technology and Learning Center. Plans for developing this next collaboration are nearly complete. The E. Desmond Lee Technology and Learning Center is being designed to reach diverse school districts from inner city to rural. The center will serve both preservice and in-service professional educators with new approaches to education that incorporate technology, lifelong learning and professional development, and career preparation for students and adults. The key goals of the Technology and Learning Center are to (a) establish a model classroom environment for hands-on practice in managing new methods of teaching through technology and for helping teachers become proficient with technology; (b) research and develop new technology-enhanced teaching methods and approaches to engage students from disadvantaged backgrounds; (c) create programs that connect school classrooms with the workplace, show theoretical concepts applied in the workplace, and encourage students to communicate with on-the-job professionals and labor force employees; and (d) develop with education and school administration professionals innovative ways to create attractive, modern, well-equipped, and technologically advanced learning environments.

The Technology and Learning Center itself is a unique partnership between a technical school, Ranken Technical College, and the University of Missouri–St. Louis School of Education. Ranken Technical College has a rich history of providing the St. Louis area workforce with highly skilled technicians. As technology becomes more sophisticated, so must the workers' basic skill levels. Ranken was seeking ways for its faculty to keep pace with the increased technical skill requirements that industry demands.

The partnership between Ranken Technical College and the University of Missouri–St. Louis will complement each institution's comparable goals to provide qualified graduates to meet workforce needs. An endowed professorship at the University of Missouri–St. Louis was established to serve the Ranken Technical College and the University of Missouri–St. Louis partnership. Through the Emerson Electric Company Endowed Professorship in Technology and Learning, and the new partnership that it creates, the University of Missouri–St. Louis and Ranken Technical College will share resources, programs, and knowledge. We work in concert to (a) enhance and provide mutually beneficial certification and graduate degree programs in emerging technologies, (b) develop technology-based curriculum and programs to meet the education needs of preschool to postsecondary students and lifelong learners in the work place, and (c) conduct research in the ways people learn and how technologies can enhance and assist in the learning process.

Ranken Technical College will benefit from this partnership because Ranken students will have new technology course offerings available through the University of Missouri–St. Louis. Ranken faculty will have more professional development opportunities, and the college will choose new faculty from a better-prepared, more advanced pool of educators. From its strategic, inner city location, Ranken will have access to new markets—regionally and worldwide. Its students will have increased options to continue their studies at a 4-year institution.

For its part, the University of Missouri–St. Louis will benefit from this partnership because current and future educators will have hands-on experience in developing educational programs with teams of faculty paired with technicians. Education faculty and students will gain a deeper understanding of technical education (e.g., the program at Ranken Technical College) and other educational choices as integral to educating for workforce needs. School of Education faculty and the educators we prepare will have access to cutting-edge, emerging technologies that are used in instruction and learning. The School of Education will have the ability to expand its instructional technology curriculum, and Ranken will provide computer laboratory instruction at the University of Missouri–St. Louis.

Ultimately, the benefits of this alliance will accrue to the entire region, as Ranken Technical College and the University of Missouri–St. Louis provide another crucial link between the world of work and education. Through this partnership will emerge a "new social equity that looks for opportunity doors for everyone—Instead of looking at college as the only ticket to prosperity, the new focus [will be] on lifelong learning, career training and retraining for every economic class" (Peirce & Johnson, 1997, p. 1A).

## Problems Encountered

Attempting to invent a new model of education is not without its painful moments. The two major stumbling blocks we encountered arose from the lack of trust between people and institutions that had not previously partnered and the competitive nature of some of our work. St. Louis has nine teacher education programs in the immediate area and another large number within a 100-mile radius. In addition, the region is rich in professional development resources, although services, while abundant, are uncoordinated. The University of Missouri–St. Louis is sometimes seen as an overwhelming presence as the largest preparer of teachers in the state.

When the University of Missouri–St. Louis said, "we want to be your partner," many heard "we want to be the boss."

Creating a sense of trust and common mission was critical to these efforts within the School of Education and between the School of Education and its community partners, including other teacher education programs. Doing that required us to work together in new ways.

### New Skills and Approaches Required

How have these barriers been overcome? First, they have not all magically disappeared after a few sessions of bagels and coffee. However, there is evidence of a new level of collaboration and synergy that will benefit all of us as individual programs and the region as a whole. For example, the University of Missouri–St. Louis participates with four other area universities and colleges with K–12 school partners on a Goals 2000 project. In this effort, preservice teachers, school- and university-based teacher educators, and arts and science colleagues work together to improve teacher preparation in social studies. Jointly, they examine current practices, review standards in the field, and share observations and resources across sites. We learned through this and other efforts to use a great deal of patience and inclusiveness. Teams of participants held many conversations with open-ended agendas and concentrated on process, buy in, and brainstorming rather than defining solutions too early. Listening is a critical skill for collaboration. Some participants in this process have spent hours learning to listen to the content as well as the affect embedded in the messages we receive from colleagues. We paid attention to the learning community as we began to build it.

Facilitative leadership is another new skill that we have begun to practice. The dean and the school principal are no longer the only ones up front and visible when we get down to crafting strategies and solutions. Sometimes, those who are good at administration and organizing need to step back and let the creativity, energy, and leadership of the entire group emerge. Those who have not been up front and visible have also stepped up, taken risks, and found opportunities to lead. This lesson is one of the more difficult ones we have learned because so many of us are passionate about the urgency of our task to educate our children for a democratic society. For good reasons, we feel that we have so little time to accomplish so much, to meet so many critical needs. Futrell (1993) wrote about this frustration when K–12 schools and universities try to partner and the going is slow. By strategically investing time, however, at the beginning of the partnership in both product and process, we have gained effectiveness and creativity while nurturing leadership within all of the partners. In some instances, personnel changes or transitions have occurred, yet our partnership has been able to deal with these because we have been developing collaborative leadership along the way. New leadership can move into a project that is well designed and documented and that does not exist inside one person's head.

Communication is another important skill. We have learned to communicate better but also more quickly and more openly with electronic conversations, listservs, and other ways of sharing information broadly. Information has always constituted power. Now—by using the new technologies available to us—we are sharing the power of the information and decision making.

Our technical communication skills (using E-mail and listservs) had to be augmented with attention to listening to others and to articulating our own ideas clearly and cogently. We needed to learn to listen to our critics, not dismiss either their feelings or their ideas. Strategies and solutions that emerged became more powerful when they were tested by the pull of opposing ideas.

Finally, St. Louis has a deep tradition of action research and professional development that goes back to the days of Susan Blow, the pioneer early childhood educator who held Saturday classes for kindergarten teachers (Brown, 1999). This tradition of inquiry has continued, and it has enabled participants in this collaborative process to learn new skills and evaluate strategies. The critical friend model, shared teacher action research, and structured reflections and retreats helped us think about the work we do. As our values and priorities became clarified, we began to define personally and interpersonally what we really meant by good teaching.

## Plans for the Future

Over the next 4 to 6 years, the School of Education will pursue development of 15 to 20 new PDS partnerships. Currently, we have four PDSs affiliated with the St. Louis Professional Schools Collaborative, an umbrella group that includes 18 PDSs with seven local universities. We are holding preliminary conversations with several other school districts to begin building new partnerships. Our understanding has grown that a PDS is and will always be a work in progress.

A major goal in forming these new partnerships is to increase field-based experiences for students. Missouri is implementing a set of knowledge and performance standards for beginning teachers. Teacher preparation programs in the state will be evaluated based on their effectiveness in helping their graduates meet these new standards. This move to standards-based teacher education also galvanized the School of Education to engage in another step of its reorganization, one that is still underway. That is a curriculum redesign project that will eliminate course-by-course compartmentalization and move the program toward a coherent, competency and standards-based approach. Field-based experiences are key to meeting this new threshold of authentic teacher performance. Expanding field-based experiences would be impossible, however, without increasing the number and the depth of our partnerships with schools and using new technologies to keep the students, campus, and faculty connected. This goes hand-in-hand with the need for teachers to understand and effectively use technologies in the classroom to help their students connect with the world at large. It also introduces new challenges such as the distribution of faculty resources to support our PDSs. We need to work differently.

On the drawing board is one last example of a different approach to our work. As part of the St. Louis Regional Virtual Learning Center in Instructional Technologies, the School of Education is crafting a plan to develop and offer a unique web-based Master's in Teaching with Technologies (MTTs). The School of Education is accredited by the National Council for Accreditation of Teacher Education (NCATE) and will use NCATE standards recommended from the International Society for Technology in Education National Educational Technology Standards project in this design effort. This degree program will be patterned after the innovative University of Missouri–St. Louis MBA online program in the School of Business. In early ideas for design and delivery, 50% of the graduate education course will occur on campus, with students attending the first class as a face-to-face session for 8 hr. The second session (also a full 8-hr day) occurs in the 4th-week period. The final session (4 hr) occurs in the 8th week. When not attending classes, students will be connected to faculty and to each other online in professional conversations over their subject matter. For efficient time use, breakfast and lunch will be provided during these sessions, and these meals will be used as opportunities to build the learning community and facilitate electronic communications between class meetings. The cohort program will set up study groups or learning teams based on their professional backgrounds as teachers, counselors, or administrators. These learning teams of five to seven students become an important program component for intellectual, networking, and professional development purposes. The cohort itself adds to the quality of the students' learning experience through enhanced identification and commitment to the program.

The MTTs program will include E-mail discussions and Web-based bulletin boards so students can participate in numerous groups or create their own. Students will perform Internet and site-based research of best practices, and they will lease laptop computers. Endowed scholarships will be available for teachers from low income schools to pay for tuition, laptop leasing, and other fees.

Experience has shown that those who are not interested in using instructional technologies, even if they have access to computers and other instructional media, rarely take the initiative to explore the possibilities. Therefore, the MTTs program will develop small networks of educators in the schools in which these graduate students identify at least one partner teacher (preferably a team of several) in their school. (If they are not teaching in a building, they will select a teacher in another K–12 school.) They will be connected to the E-mail listserv and become involved in the Web site, using it as a teaching resource. By involving more than one teacher or counselor in a school, the chances will grow for increased teaching with technologies because the graduate students will have school-based support and a forum for trying out their new skills and resources.

Working in the ways described in this article is challenging, exciting, and productive—and a little scary and also inevitable. Our window of opportunity for schools and colleges of education to lead the transformation of learning is probably just the next 3 to 5 years. At the University of Missouri–St. Louis, we have begun (and continue to do) the self-assessment, restructuring, and rethinking necessary to launch ourselves into this new direction. Reaching out to partners has expanded our knowledge base, creativity, and opportunities.

Conclusion

We began this article by asserting that schools and college of education possess the power to change the lives of individuals, neighborhoods, communities, cities, and even nations. We do this by preparing educators who will help form the members of our democratic society. We do this by connecting people and ideas in rich learning environments, although those environments have historically changed and will continue to change. The most important power, however, is one we often overlook, even though it is the core principle of education. We have the power to change ourselves through learning, experience, and reflection. Our partnership experience over the past 3 years in Creating the 21st Century School of Education in our community has shown that we can also change ourselves and achieve our overarching mission through collaboration, partnerships, and community.

## References

American Electronics Association. (1998). *Report before the House Judiciary Committee Subcommittee on Immigration.* Retrieved June 15, 1999 from the World Wide Web: http://www.aeanet.org/aeanet/public/search/pub.index.asp

Bachula, G. R. (1997). *Information technology and electronic commerce.* Retrieved June 15, 1999 from the World Wide Web: http://www.ta.doc.gov/Speeches/eleccomm.htm

Brown, K. S. (1999). Susan Blow. In J. A. Garraty & M. C. Carnes (Eds.), *American National Biography* (Vol. 3, pp. 63–64). New York: Oxford University Press.

Fullan, M. (1993). (Ed.). *The complexity of the change process.* New York: Falmer.

Futrell, M. H. (1993). K–12 education reform: A view from the trenches. *Education Record, 74*(3), 6–14.

Goodlad, J. (1994). *Educational renewal: Better teachers, better schools.* San Francisco: Jossey-Bass.

McGowan, T. M. (1990). Reflections of an experienced collaborator. In H. S. Schwartz (Ed.), *In collaboration: Building common agendas* (pp. 41–47). Washington, DC: American Association of Colleges for Teacher Education.

Negroponte, N. (1995). *Being digital.* New York: Knopf.

Peirce, N., & Johnson, C. (1997, March 9). The Peirce report. *St. Louis Post-Dispatch,* pp. 1A, 1B.

Riley, R. W. (1996). *U.S. Secretary of Education, Third Annual State of American Education Address.* Retrieved March 21, 2000 from the World Wide Web: http://www.ed.gov/Speeches/02-1996/secretar.html

Schmitz, C. (1998, September). Are we late for a very important date? *St. Louis Commerce,* pp. 44–46.

Schmitz, C. (1999). University schools of education as partners. In D. Hull (Ed.), *Tech prep: The next generation* (pp. 397–414). Waco, TX: CORD Communications.

Sears, S. J., & Hersh, S. (1998). *Preparing teachers to use contextual teaching and learning strategies to enhance student success in and beyond school: A framework for further study of contextual teaching and learning in teacher education preservice programs.* Retrieved March 21, 2000 from the World Wide Web: http://www.contextual.org

St. Louis Regional Commerce and Growth Association. (1998). *Economic development facts and figures.* Retrieved March 21, 2000 from the World Wide Web: http://www.stlrcga.org/aboutstl.html

St. Louis 2004. (1999). *Attainment of excellence in teaching: Teacher preparation and professional development.* St. Louis: Author.

University of Missouri–St. Louis. (1997). *University of Missouri–St. Louis futures strategic planning report.* St. Louis: Author.

Wirth, A. G. (1992). *Education and work for the year 2000: Choices we face.* San Francisco: Jossey-Bass.

# Florida Early Literacy and Learning Model: A Systematic Approach to Improve Learning at All Levels

*Cheryl Fountain and Janice Wood*

The University of North Florida, in partnership with educational, business, and community agencies, has established the Florida Early Literacy and Learning Model (ELLM) to improve literacy among over 1,000 4-, 5-, and 6-year-olds in the region. The ELLM initiative is founded on the concepts of collaborative restructuring, reading research, high-performance learning environments, and family involvement. It has been found to be effective in increasing literacy and reading achievement of young children who have come to school underprepared.

The most important job of the elementary school program is to teach children to read and write. Although children do not usually learn to read until the age of 5 or 6, the years from birth through Age 5 are the most important for literacy development. We now know that when we design liter-

---

CHERYL FOUNTAIN is Executive Director, Florida Institute of Education, and Assistant to the Chancellor for Education Policy, University of North Florida, Jacksonville.

JANICE WOOD is Professor, Division of Curriculum and Instruction, College of Education and Human Services, University of North Florida, Jacksonville.

Requests for reprints should be sent to Cheryl Fountain, College of Education and Human Services, 4567 St. Johns Bluff Road, South, University of North Florida, Jacksonville, FL 32224–2645. E-mail: Fountain@unf.edu

acy programs for the first few years of formalized schooling, we must consider the early literacy skills and concepts that children possess (International Reading Association and the National Council of Teachers of English, 1996). To reach children prior to the age of entering school requires a community-wide effort. This article describes an early literacy program founded on collaboration among many community partners.

## A University–School–Community Partnership

The Florida Early Literacy and Learning Model (ELLM), an alliance among educational, community, and business agencies, proposes to improve literacy and reading achievement among 4-, 5-, and 6-year-old children, particularly those who come to school underprepared or who are considered at risk. The ELLM initiative (a) builds on current collaborative restructuring efforts; (b) takes advantage of recent advances in research related to learning to read; (c) helps to create, support, and sustain high-performing learning environments that provide multitiered curricular and instructional support; and (d) leverages community resources to enhance children's literacy success by helping children and families acquire the literacy and readiness skills they need to help children learn to read.

To help meet the challenge of improving the emergent literacy skills of young children in urban schools, the University of North Florida's College of Education and Human Services (COEHS) and the Florida Institute of Education established a comprehensive community-based partnership. Both the University and the COEHS have long and rich histories of collaboration with the public schools. This collaborative tradition provided the foundation for expanding the partnership and the creation of the Florida Early Literacy and Learning Partnership. This partnership included members of several civic, governmental, and private organizations; Head Start Centers; public and private child care centers; and two public school districts. The leadership of these partner agencies, along with their public school counterparts, was committed to improving reading among young children, particularly those children who come to school underprepared. Figure 1 is a graphic representation of this partnership.

During the 1998 through 1999 school year, the Florida Department of Education funded a collaboratively designed grant developed by the community-based partnership: the Early Literacy and Learning Partnership. The Florida Institute of Education (FIE) serves as the fiscal agent and sponsors the project director. FIE, housed at the University of North Florida, is one of several Type I Centers charged with a statewide mission to

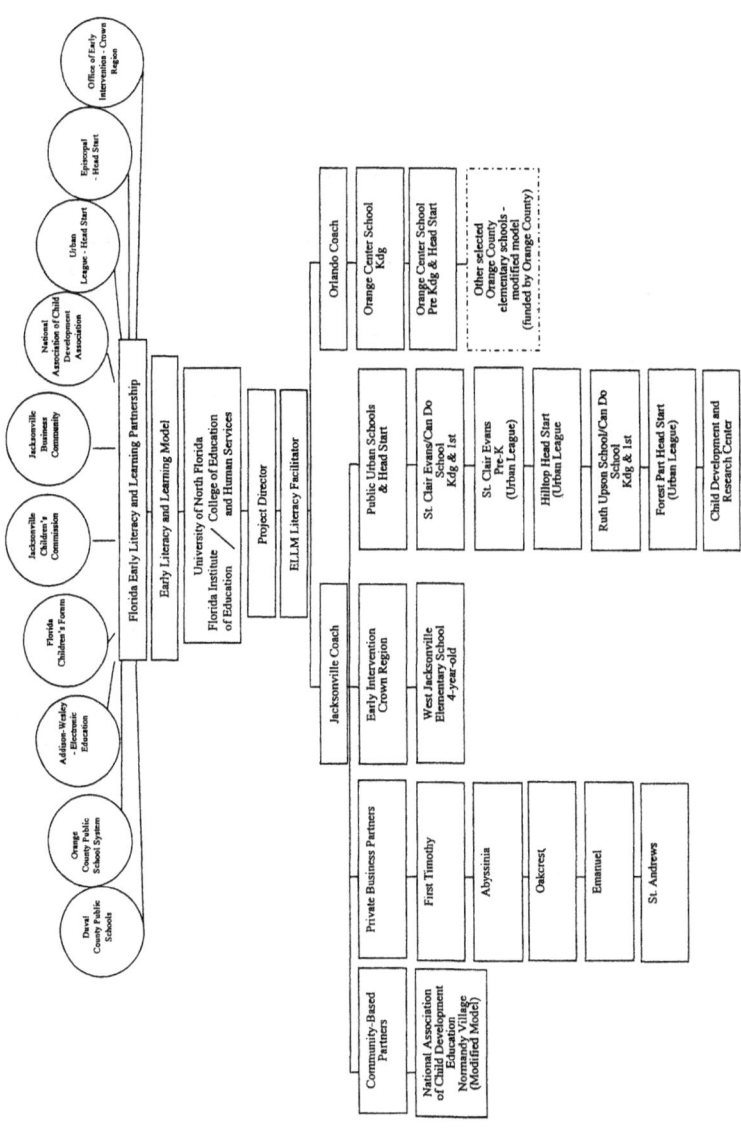

*Figure 1.* Florida Early Literacy and Learning Partnership.

strengthen and improve Florida's prekindergarten through university learning system.

## Collaborative Agenda for Change

National and state reform agendas are demanding new ways of thinking about readiness, schooling, achieving challenging education outcomes, and creating stronger links between education and emerging workplace competencies. For the first time, early learning is seen as a vital link to educational success and economic prosperity. Dramatic changes in practice—at all levels—are needed to successfully manage the array of technological, political, cultural, and informational changes sweeping across local, state, national, and international landscapes.

If the challenges are to be conquered, increased levels of innovation, more sources of information, differing perspectives on the problem, and new ways to bring together human and material resources will be needed. Knowledge access, management, and innovation are becoming central strategical features for improvement.

No single educational organization, public agency, or private enterprise will succeed in achieving desired visions or goals working in isolation. The issues are complex. New mind sets, knowledge, tools, structures, and strategies are needed and are most likely to come about through collaboration because each partner brings a critical perspective to the relationship needed to produce results.

Successful collaboration relies on the ability of the individuals involved to continually negotiate the separate norms, beliefs, and cultures of their respective organizations and come together to create new organizational structures designed to achieve specific purposes. This kind of cross-institutional collaboration requires developing trust and a sense of respect for differing ideas; parity among the partners; support from top leadership; long-term commitment; an understanding of the change process; and multiple opportunities at multiple levels for collaborative work, problem-solving, and inquiry.

Using these guiding principles, the Florida Early Literacy and Learning Partnership developed the Florida ELLM to achieve important and shared goals that can be used by other stakeholders as a blueprint for a systemic improvement process. This process rethinks ideas about creating new kinds of collaborative relationships; designs strategies to improve literacy and reading skills of children (a shared and pressing goal); and increases policymakers' understanding and support for the new knowledge, tools, and structures.

As knowledge is gained and used to address shared problems, practices within the project have evolved and changed. Through collaborative actions, we have been able to instigate organizational as well as individual learning and tap other partner resources to bring more to the shared venture. Collaborative actions are focused on achieving shared goals (improving literacy skills of at-risk children) as well as integrating changes in practice (using research-based curricular materials and coaching model) and in structure (use of collaboration as a preferred operating mode and use of the ELLM guiding principles) into the infrastructures of each of the partner organizations.

## ELLM Purposes

The ELLM partnership is committed to dramatically improving the levels of literacy and reading achievement among 4-, 5- and 6-year-old children, particularly those who come to school underprepared or who are considered at risk. The purposes of the ELLM program are:

1. Design, implement, and evaluate promising community, family, school, and university collaborative strategies to help 4-, 5- and 6-year-old children acquire and use the literacy skills needed to become eager and proficient readers.
2. Translate research findings into usable information and guidance for families, educators, and others involved in the care and instruction of young children.
3. Establish literacy and learning networks among educators, community and governmental agencies, and families.

The ELLM partnership designed and is testing models that bring together powerful research-based elements and lessons learned from other collaborative reform initiatives into a cohesive delivery system.

To increase family and community involvement in early learning experiences of children, the ELLM seeks to connect and reinforce literacy activities taking place in the schools and in homes. This is accomplished by (a) modeling successful literacy strategies that are known to influence and enhance reading success; (b) providing regular and ongoing coaching sessions that develop and model effective early literacy instructional strategies; (c) providing monthly literacy packets and children's books for classroom use; (d) promoting family and community partnerships; (e) offering classroom book lending libraries, family literacy calendars, and regular family and school activities; and (f) identifying key competencies needed to be included in preservice primary education preparation programs, child care provider programs, and professional development programs for urban teachers.

Research shows that children who enter prekindergarten classes with prereading experiences become more skilled readers than those who enter school with limited at-home literacy experiences. It is clear that learning patterns are established in the very early years, usually prior to beginning formal school experiences. Parents are encouraged to provide literacy-rich home environments developed by exposure to books, printed materials, songs, poems, nursery rhymes, and through talking and interacting with others.

## ELLM Work and Learning Teams

The Florida ELLM collaborative team-based design draws from the learning organization research from business and reform and professional development literature from education (Chawla & Renesch, 1995; Darling-Hammond, 1994; Fullan, 1993; Marquardt & Reynolds, 1994; Mohrman, Cohen, & Mohrman, 1995; Murphy, 1991; Nonaka & Takeuchi, 1995; Senge, 1990; Zeichner, Melnick, & Gomez, 1996). The ELLM project is designed as a collaborative team-based organization that uses a number of different kinds of teams (e.g., action teams, managing teams, coaching teams, teacher teams) to carry out project activities. Some teams focus on coordinating efforts, whereas others focus on accomplishing a particular task.

ELLM team members are drawn from the partner organizations. A team's authority is determined by the scope of its responsibility. Teams are given parameters and direction, based on shared goals and desired outcomes, but have the latitude to plan, implement, learn, and assess their own collaborative actions and their contributions to overall project goals. The ELLM teams are charged not only with carrying out specific tasks and responsibilities, but also with developing the expertise of its members through ongoing learning and professional development. Team members model individual and team learning as they work to enhance the learning and achievement of the children. Two examples of ELLM teams are illustrated later.

### ELLM Implementation Team

Central to the project is the ELLM implementation team. It functions as the "managing team" for the project. It consists of key decision makers from each of the partner institutions. The implementation team focuses on three goals. First, it focuses on increasing literacy readiness for children by helping to overcome barriers as project activities are implemented. Second, partners share with other Florida child care professionals and educators successful practices developed by the ELLM initiative. Third, the implementation team brings policymakers, educational leaders, and other stakeholders together to develop methods that can support intensified efforts to improve literacy and reading skills of children.

The Implementation Team meets monthly using the principles of: unity of purpose, ongoing inquiry, assuming responsibility for decision making, and commitment to change and risk taking. A number of agencies and schools are members of the ELLM Partnership and therefore members of the implementation team. They include (a) two large school systems in the State of Florida: Duval County (Jacksonville) School District and Orange County (Orlando) School System, (b) the Florida Department of Education, (c) the Florida Children's Forum, (d) the Fernside Service Center–Crown Region, (e) the National Association of Child Development Education, (f) the Jacksonville Children's Commission, (g) representatives from the Jacksonville business community, (h) the Jacksonville Urban League Head Start, (i) the Jacksonville Episcopal Head Start, and (j) Pearson Digital Publishing Group–Electronic Education Division.

*ELLM Coaching Team*

ELLM builds an ongoing support network of professional development that encourages action learning, collaboration, and capacity building to improve students' learning. The coaching component is grounded in clinical supervision and peer coaching literature related to developing professional expertise (Berliner, 1994; Hall & Hord, 1987; Leithwood, 1990; Lieberman, 1995; Mayer & Brause, 1991). The professional development model used by the ELLM coaching team is based on the following assumptions: (a) professional development should be long term and performance based; (b) equal attention needs to be placed on learning processes and content; (c) learning should be problem based and active rather than passive; (d) learning is a cyclical process that involves planning, implementing, assessing, and reflecting; (e) learning takes place individually as well as collaboratively among peers; and (f) coaching accelerates learning by focusing on ongoing improvement, thinking critically, and helping others to do so as well.

The coaching team is led by the ELLM facilitator. Other members include the literacy coaches, classroom teachers, and site liaisons. The project-wide ELLM coaching team coordinates the work of the site-based coaching teams located at child care centers and public schools.

*ELLM Facilitator*

The ELLM literacy facilitator provides the supervision for the literacy coaches and content knowledge for literacy activities. The literacy facilitator is a faculty member in the College of Education and Human Services with expertise in the area of literacy and early reading. The literacy facilitator models effective coaching strategies and works collaboratively with the ELLM literacy coaches to establish teacher networks. Just-in-time training is presented through work sessions, demonstrations, practice with children, and opportunities for discussion and problem solving.

The literacy facilitator takes the lead in developing learning materials for use in both the classroom and the home, translating research findings into usable information and guidance for families, educators, and others involved in the daily instruction of young children. The facilitator coordinates the activities of the ELLM project and its partner institutions and establishes literacy and learning networks among educators, community and governmental agencies, and families to share "best practices" and address academic and nonacademic barriers to literacy and learning. The facilitator coordinates the planning of the summer training conferences for literacy coaches and ELLM teachers and facilitates sharing results of the ELLM project at state and national meetings.

*ELLM Literacy Coaches*

Literacy coaches are hired to work in ELLM classrooms on a regular basis throughout the school year. Teachers from Head Start centers, early intervention prekindergarten programs, private child care centers, and public kindergarten and first-grade classes were selected to work in the ELLM program. There are a total of 60 teachers working with 1,062 urban children.

The ELLM coaches are highly qualified master classroom teachers who meet and plan with teachers on a regular basis. They observe classroom instruction and help teachers reflect on their practices. They assist teachers in the translation of research findings into practical instructional practices by demonstrating teaching in the classrooms on a regular basis. The demonstration lessons are designed to model strategies for successful literacy instruction using monthly benchmarks identified for each grade level to plan the focus of the lessons.

*ELLM Site Liaisons*

A liaison contact person is selected at each school to help the ELLM program run smoothly. This person is a master level teacher who is an ELLM classroom teacher in the school. He or she serves as the primary contact for the literacy coach and helps solve literacy and technology-related problems at the school site. This person meets weekly with the literacy coach.

## ELLM Coaching Team Activities

### Classroom Visits

ELLM coaches visit classrooms weekly. Demonstration lessons, first conducted by the ELLM coaches, model strategies for successful literacy instruction. Coaches work collaboratively with preschool and elementary ELLM teachers in implementing student-centered lessons and activities using monthly literacy packets. The coaching cycle begins with the demonstration lessons. Following the demonstration lesson, a debriefing meeting is held in which coaches and teachers jointly develop next steps toward emerging expertise.

### In-School Meetings

The literacy coaches hold monthly on-site meetings at each of the child care centers and public schools. The literacy coaches demonstrate the use of the monthly children's books, share instructional ideas to go along with each book, and highlight the benchmarks and coaching strategies that have been emphasized for the month. The on-site meetings provide time for the teachers to share effective literacy strategies with one another and discuss issues related to the implementation of the ELLM program. Finally, the meetings allow the literacy coaches to gain feedback on the effectiveness of the classroom visits and gain insight on how to better meet the needs of individual teachers.

### Teacher-Get-Togethers

All of the ELLM teachers are invited to monthly Teacher-Get-Togethers. These meetings provide the teachers with an opportunity to build professional networks and share ideas with other educators. The meetings are held after school on the third Monday of every month. Each month, the meeting locations rotate to a different ELLM site. Guest speakers are brought in to discuss reading and writing strategies. Teachers take turns sharing at least one literacy idea. The Teacher-Get-Togethers conclude with a tour of the primary classrooms. This allows teachers to share literacy activities that have been used in the classrooms at the various ELLM sites.

## The ELLM Classroom Model

The ELLM classroom teachers are committed to increasing literacy instruction in the classrooms by providing children with the readiness skills they need to learn to read. The ELLM classroom model builds on critical elements needed for literacy and reading success. Each ELLM teacher receives a monthly literacy packet and corresponding books that provide sample literacy activities. The classroom model is depicted in Figure 2.

The ELLM classroom instructional approach emphasizes (a) reading aloud with discussions following the reading, (b) alphabet and word recognition, (c) independent reading and oral-language development, (d) vocabulary, (e) phonenic awareness, (f) phonological awareness, (g) print awareness, and (h) daily drawing and writing. This is accomplished through a wide range of methods including the use of computer programs.

## The ELLM Family Involvement

Getting families and parents involved more effectively in their children's learning is a top priority among educators, governmental officials, community leaders, and the ELLM project. Past experiences tell us that getting parents and families involved in their children's learning is hard work and time consuming, but a critical condition if children are to succeed.

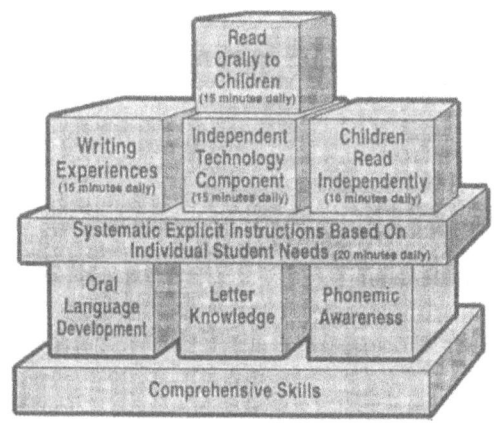

*Figure 2.* ELLM: Daily classroom activities.

*Florida Early Literacy and Learning Model*

There is research evidence (e.g., Epstein, 1995; Snow, Burns, & Griffin, 1998; Snow & Tabors, 1996) indicating that family involvement leads to improved student achievement and has significant long-term benefits on reading. An important predictor of a child's achievement in school is not income or social status, but rather the extent to which the student's family has become involved in their child's education (Henderson & Berla, 1994). Programs that assist families in initiating cognitive stimulation in early literacy activities in the home have positive benefits for reading achievement (Maxwell & Eller, 1994).

The ELLM focuses attention on three barriers to family involvement: (a) lack of knowledge on the part of both teachers and family members about what works in helping children learn to read, (b) lack of skill on the part of both teachers and family members about putting literacy information into practice, and (c) lack of opportunity when other factors vie for attention (e.g., time and energy on the part of both teachers and family members).

To overcome theses barriers, ELLM approaches include families reading together, literacy calendars, family literacy get-togethers, and regular family and school activities. The ELLM Family Involvement Model is depicted in Figure 3.

The ELLM literacy coaches work with teachers to develop more family-friendly communication strategies and design ways to restructure and reschedule learning initiatives and activities to meet the needs of working, urban family members. The family component of the ELLM recommends that families read to their children and to talk and interact with their children daily. To facilitate this reading and conversation, the ELLM teachers distribute literacy-related materials to the parents on a regular basis, including an annual family literacy calendar. Also, each ELLM classroom has been equipped with a book lending library for family members and children to check books out for reading together as a family. In addition,

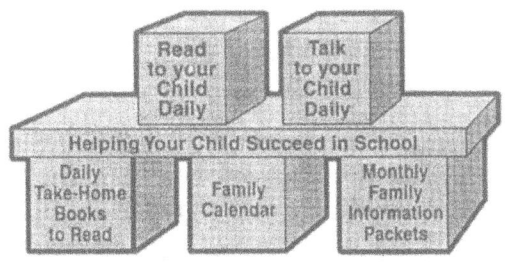

30 minutes daily = 90 hours of literacy instruction each school year

*Figure 3.* ELLM: Family and home activities.

each ELLM classroom teacher designs four family workshops or family activities throughout the school year. These workshops seek to offer family members opportunities to receive information on child development and provides parents with hands-on literacy activities.

## Evaluation Component

An external evaluator designs and implements the evaluation plan. ELLM expected outcomes include: (a) mastery of critical prereading skills by all ELLM children; (b) increased attendance of preschool, kindergarten, and first-grade students; (c) increased family and community involvement in children's learning; and (d) increased collaboration among Early Literacy and Learning partners organizations that results in more effective delivery of services by preschools, schools, community, and higher education institutions.

Evaluation emphasis is placed on using specific standardized instruments, supplemented with the construction or adaptation of criterion-referenced tests. A standardized test with known reliability and validity is used for two purposes: to quantify the level of the treatment effect and to assess the magnitude of change. Specific outcomes are compared with national norms. Depending on the implementation time line, either a pretest–posttest design or a posttest-only treatment group versus a control group design is used. Qualitative methodologies are used to assess use of specific curriculum and instructional strategies and the achievements and competencies of participants. Computer software usage for each student is collected and analyzed, as is individual student progress as measured by the embedded evaluation protocols in the technology component. Teacher interviews are held to determine level of use and variation of project components. Ongoing formative feedback is provided to the ELLM literacy coaches, the literacy facilitator, the site liaisons, and members of the ELLM implementation team.

## Summary

The ELLM initiative builds on current collaborative restructuring efforts and takes advantage of recent advances in research related to learning to read. It forms partnerships with community agencies and schools to enhance children's literacy success and uses collaborative work and learning teams to carry out activities. ELLM children are given opportunities to develop skills that are prerequisites to beginning reading.

All successful literacy programs should start by supporting and encouraging rich literacy experiences in the home and school. Classrooms in which the Florida ELLM has been used have increased literacy and reading achievement of 4-, 5-, and 6-year-old urban children for the past 3 years, particularly for those who come to school underprepared or who are considered at risk. The ELLM initiative found that preschool programs enriched with literacy experiences are beneficial for children who experience limited learning opportunities in their home.

The ELLM is one strategy that can be used by other interested stakeholders working toward similar goals. It provides a structure for working together to create multiple and diverse learning teams and networks that change perceptions of and expectations for families, schools, and communities to improve at-risk students' learning, literacy achievement, and success in school.

## References

Berliner, D. (1994). Expertise: The wonder of exemplary performance. In J. Mangieri & C. Black (Eds.), *Creating powerful thinking in teachers and students* (pp. 161–185). Fort Worth, TX: Harcourt Brace.

Chawla, S., & Renesch, J. (Eds.). (1995). *Learning organizations: Developing cultures for tomorrow's workplace*. Portland, OR: Productivity Press.

Darling-Hammond, D. (1994). *Professional development schools: Schools for a developing profession*. New York: Teachers College Press.

Epstein, J. (1995). School/family/community partnerships. *Phi Delta Kappan*, 701–712.

Fullan, M. (1993). *Change forces: Probing the depths of educational reform*. London: Falmer.

Hall, G., & Hord, S. (1987). *Change in schools: Facilitating the process*. Albany: State University of New York Press.

Henderson, A. T., & Berla, N. (1994). *A new generation of evidence: The family is critical to student achievement*. Washington, DC: National Committee for Citizens in Education.

International Reading Association and the National Council of Teachers of English. (1996). *Standards for the English Language Arts*. Urbana, IL: Author.

Leithwood, K. (1990). The principal's role in teacher development. In B. Joyce (Ed.), *Changing school culture through staff development* (pp. 71–90). Alexandria, VA: Association for Supervision and Curriculum.

Lieberman, A. (Ed.). (1995). *The work of restructuring schools: Building from the ground up*. New York: Teachers College Press.

Marquardt, M., & Reynolds, A. (1994). *The global learning organization: Gaining competitive advantage through continuous learning*. Burr Ridge, IL: Irwin.

Maxwell, L. L., & Eller, S. K. (1994, September). Children's transition to kindergarten. *Young Children*, pp. 56–63.

Mayer, J. S., & Brause, R. S. (1991). The never-ending cycle of teacher growth. In P. S. Brause & J. S. Mayher (Eds.), *Search and research: What the inquiring teacher needs to know* (pp. 23–44). London: Falmer.

Mohrman, S., Cohen, S., & Mohrman, A. (1995). *Designing team-based organizations: New forms for knowledge work*. San Francisco: Jossey-Bass.

Murphy, J. (1991). *Restructuring schools: Capturing and assessing the phenomena*. New York: Teachers College Press.

Nonaka, I., & Takeuchi, H. (1995). *The knowledge-creating company: How Japanese companies create the dynamics of innovation.* New York: Oxford University Press.

Senge, P. (1990). *The fifth discipline: The art and practice of the learning organization.* New York: Doubleday.

Snow, C. E., Burns, S., & Griffin, P. (Eds.). (1998). *Preventing reading difficulties in young children.* Washington, DC: National Academy Press.

Snow, C., & Tabors, P. (1996). *Intergenerational transfer of literacy. Family literacy: Directions in research and implication for practice.* Washington, DC: Office of Educational Research and Improvement, U.S. Department of Education.

Zeichner, K., Melnick, S., & Gomez, M. (1996). *Currents of reform in preservice teacher education.* New York: Teachers College Press.

# Springfield College Collaboration With the Springfield Public Schools and Neighboring Community

*Dale Lucy-Allen*
*Dennis Brunton*
*Jenny McDade*
*Jennifer Seydel*
*Dennis Vogel*

DALE LUCY-ALLEN *is the Director of Community Relations at Springfield College and serves as the Program Director for the Springfield Community Outreach Partnership Center, Springfield, Massachusetts.*

DENNIS BRUNTON *is a science teacher at Bridge Academy, Springfield Public Schools, Springfield, Massachusetts.*

JENNY MCDADE *is currently a 1st-year student at New York College of Osteopathic Medicine, Old Westbury, New York.*

JENNIFER SEYDEL *is the Director of the Springfield College Authentic Graduate Programs in Education and the SAGE Project, Springfield, Massachusetts.*

DENNIS VOGEL *is the Director of Alternative and Collaborative Programs for the Springfield Public Schools, Springfield, Massachusetts.*

Requests for reprints should be sent to Dale Lucy-Allen, Student Volunteer Programs, Springfield College, 263 Alden Street, Springfield, MA 01109–3797. E-mail: Dale_Allen@spfldcol.edu

For the past 7 years, Springfield College (Springfield, MA) has reinvigorated attempts within the divisions of academic and student affairs to develop collaborative efforts with the Springfield Public Schools and the neighborhoods that are adjacent to the college. The humanics philosophy of the college emphasizes provision of opportunities that will challenge and educate our student in spirit, mind, and body to be of service to others. This philosophy provides the foundation for the expansion of curricular and cocurricular activities that are the components of small to large collaborative efforts with the community. This article provides an overview of the college's humanics philosophy, the history of the college's recent outreach, a description of the development of the broad spectrum of college–community collaborative efforts, and the results of these efforts. Also included is a description of the infrastructure and logistical support that has been institutionalized among the collaborators to sustain these activities.

Springfield College was founded in 1885 as the international training college for Young Men's Christian Association leaders. The college is a private, coeducational, nonsectarian institution that has changed to meet the needs of society in its 115 years while maintaining its commitment to helping people. Today, the college is comprised of 3,500 students from every state and 20 foreign countries, pursuing undergraduate and graduate study in 39 fields.

The mission of Springfield College is to educate students—in spirit, mind, and body—to excel in service to others. The unique humanics philosophy infuses every aspect of the College's interdisciplinary curriculum and inspires the extensive service involvement of our students, faculty, and staff. The commitment to academic excellence and our practical, service-oriented curriculum prepare our undergraduate and graduate students for careers in the human-helping professions. Springfield College students learn to analyze and communicate ideas, to judge what is of value, and to further their sense of social responsibility so that they can contribute at the highest level to meeting the challenges of an increasingly complex world. The entire college community—students, faculty, and staff—is committed to volunteer community service, especially in local communities throughout Western Massachusetts. These efforts are supported institutionally by the college's Office of Student Volunteer Programs and by the many service learning courses offered that are designed to meet community identified needs.

In 1992, a confluence of events occurred that allowed a new standard of collaboration to develop. The timing was right for the partnership between the Springfield Public Schools and Springfield College to evolve. Although Springfield College has had longstanding ties to the Springfield Public

Schools, city departments, and community-based organizations, the strength of these relations fluctuated at different times during their tenure. In 1992, a new president had been appointed at Springfield College and a new superintendent had recently been named for the Springfield Public Schools. Over the coming years, these two individuals provided the administrative leadership and vision to bridge the gap between higher education and community issues. Under the new president, the college renewed its institutional commitment to local community outreach. At the same time, the superintendent of schools was initiating one of the most comprehensive strategies for school reform in the nation. With the symbolic rebirth of the humanics mission in our adjacent community, Springfield College's faculty and students became key players within the education reform strategy.

Springfield Public Schools is a system comprised of 45 schools that educate 26,000 students of very diverse racial, ethnic, and socioeconomic status. Close to 98% of public school students qualify for free or reduced lunch. The K–12 student population is composed of the following: 30% African American, 25% White, 40% Hispanic, and 5% Asian. Within the neighborhoods directly surrounding Springfield College, there is a growing population of Russian and Vietnamese immigrants.

The City of Springfield, Massachusetts, is the financial, commercial, and industrial center of Western Massachusetts. As noted in the 1990 federal census statistics (U.S. Census Bureau, 1999), it is the fourth largest city in New England, with a population of 156,983 and a regional population of over 500,000. Once the heart of Connecticut River Valley, Springfield is now a city that has been facing a dramatic economic decline. With the statistics noted, the city, public schools, and neighborhoods provide a unique opportunity for the college's students and staff to learn from and be of assistance in a real-world setting.

The college president and the superintendent of schools had strong beliefs about the relations of their respective institutions to the community and to each other. This belief stretched beyond the boundaries of a college and school system of utilizing each other for placement of student teachers and normal interactions. This vision opened the doors to the collaborations that followed. Both Springfield College and the Springfield Public Schools were committed to the utilization of service activities and the pedagogy of service learning, which proved to be the catalyst for reform and laid the foundation for trust between the two institutions. A significant turning point occurred in March 1993, when the Springfield Public Schools was hosting a statewide "Youth HERO'S Conference." Two weeks before the conference, they lost their site and turned to Springfield College for help. The staff and students of Springfield Public Schools and the staff and students of Springfield College began working together, and, as a result, the conference for 700 young leaders throughout the state of Massachusetts was a huge success.

Shortly before that event Springfield College and Springfield Public Schools had started to work on a joint endeavor that would improve the lives of the students at both William N. DeBerry Elementary School and Springfield College. DeBerry School is located approximately one half mile from the campus and in the Enterprise Community. A collaborative grant application was submitted to support the start-up of the program. This grant was denied funding. The college decided to continue to develop and implement the program during the next semester without external support. This decision proved pivotal in improving relations with DeBerry School and the neighborhood community. External support was provided to the program in the next semester by the Nellie Mae Foundation, and this became known as the Partners Program. As a result, trust deepened and territorial issues began to slowly dissipate. This allowed for the mutual sharing of resources and the clear identification of needs by both parties and gained the attention of the local community.

The Partners Program has evolved to be a nationally recognized tutoring and mentoring program that pairs college students one to one with local youth for academic enrichment and social and cultural activities. The pairs meet once a week for 3 hr and monthly at large social events that involve all the college students, the youth, their parents or guardians, and their teachers. Faculty within the Education Department and Recreation and Leisure Services assisted with program design and implementation of the program into their courses. For example, the Program Planning course from the graduate program of Recreation and Leisure Services worked with the student leaders and staff at DeBerry School to assess the plans for the program. One faculty member from the Education Department utilized the program as a service learning component of Child Growth and Development course that he was teaching.

At the time that the Partners Program was just getting off the ground, the City of Springfield was in financial crisis, and the summer park program—operated by the Springfield Parks and Recreation Department—was in danger of collapse. The college assisted by bringing additional community partners to the table to identify what was needed to ensure the reopening of six city parks with qualified recreation staff at each site. The Springfield Public Schools, Mayor's Office, New England Farmworker's Council, Community Foundation of Western Massachusetts, and the college developed and implemented the Summer Enrichment Program in 1993 to provide trained high school and college students to staff and ensure access to summer programs for youth and families. The

Summer Enrichment Program provided educational, cultural, recreational, and service-related activities at six parks in 1993 and worked with 2,000 youth. In 1999, this program provided trained staff at nine parks.

The administration, teachers, neighborhood residents, and parents saw good things happening for children involved with the Partners Program and the Summer Enrichment Program. Springfield Public Schools pushed for replication and expansion of the Partners Program. At Springfield College, faculty and administrators associated with the Office of Student Volunteer Programs worked with other community partners in meeting the challenge to involve two additional city colleges to collaborate on Colleges Serving the Community. Colleges Serving the Community was designed by (a) students, faculty, and administrators from Springfield College, American International College, and Springfield Technical Community College; (b) representatives of three neighborhood public schools: DeBerry, Brookings, and Homer Street; and (c) Springfield Public Schools. In 1995, Colleges Serving the Community was funded by Learn and Serve America: Higher Education to (a) expand the Partners Program to the three schools; (b) increase the utilization, training, and support for sustained service learning at each college; and (c) provide monthly one-day service events for large numbers of students and community members.

In 1996, Springfield Public Schools recognized a pressing need that required new solutions and collaboration. The number of special education students requiring out of district placements had escalated, and the number of middle school and high school youth returning to the system from the Department of Youth Services had increased dramatically. Springfield Public Schools felt the need to incubate a teaching staff that had the expertise and training to teach these high-risk students. Discussions began between Springfield Public Schools, Springfield College, and the Western Area Office of the Massachusetts Department of Youth Services to develop a program to address these needs. As these discussions unfolded, additional community partners became involved, including the District Attorney's Office, Springfield Police Youth Bureau, Corporation for National Service, and other social service agencies. After a year of discussions and planning, the SAGE (Springfield Adolescent Graduation Experience) Project was developed and operationalized. The SAGE Project and all its components continue to be a joint venture of both institutions.

The SAGE Project is a city-wide effort to reclaim youth who are at risk of criminal involvement and dropping out of school. The Department of Youth Services and Springfield Public Schools have partnered with the college to establish the following components: (a) the Springfield College Authentic Program in Education Program that prepares secondary school teachers to meet the academic, social, and emotional challenges of students in Springfield's Public Schools and leads to secondary teaching and school adjustment counseling certification; (b) the SAGE Secondary School, an alternative public high school that provides a school-based component with a comprehensive prevention strategy to address the needs of high-risk youth; (c) the SAGE Partnership for Reclaiming, Intervention, and Developmental Education (PRIDE) Center, an after-school and summer program that provides computer training, sports and recreation activities, vocational exploration, academic tutoring, and psycoeducational programming; and (d) the Springfield College Authentic Graduate Program in Education (SAGE) AmeriCorps Program, which provides mentors, tutors, and case managers for the alternative school and provides supervised field experience for students in the Master's of Education program.

The discussions and effort that resulted in the Partners Program, Colleges Serving the Community, and the SAGE Project have had many unexpected yet pleasant spin-offs, including opportunities for joint professional development, training, and presentations. In addition, the partners continue to work collaboratively on numerous efforts, including the America Reads Initiative, which places college tutors in the public schools to work with the students on reading skills and countless one-day service events that bring the community together in meeting shared needs. These initiatives would not have been possible without the strong relation that has developed among Springfield College, the Springfield Public Schools, and numerous community-based organizations and entities.

In 1999, the College leadership underwent a transition to a new president, who has provided his enthusiastic support and talents to this effort. As the senior management team and the deans of the five academic schools at the college, and all program directors, principals, and supervisors within the Springfield Public Schools, have accepted collaboration as an important part of their organizations, administrative structures and support have been created to increase collaboration in all areas.

Goals

As suggested by Lucy-Allen and Seydel (1999), an urban institution of higher education must relate its educational activities to four objectives: (a) living and teaching the mission of the institution; (b) preparing students to meet the demands, expectations, and commitment to civic responsibility needed for the 21st century; (c) striving to meet the identified needs of urban neighbors and community organizations through collaborative efforts; and (d) making a positive impact on the quality of life of students, staff, youth, and families within the urban environment. In the past 7 years, Springfield College has reconnected with the city of Springfield by focusing on efforts in the surrounding neighborhoods and with the Springfield Public Schools. The transition from separate entities to trusting collaborators reflects a learning curve with peaks and plateaus along the way. To establish the college as a true neighbor, and not as a self-serving entity, a priority on building trust, respect, and commitment through long-term projects has been necessary. The perception of "Here comes the college again, what do they want from us now?" or "What can we ask the college to pay for?" had to be replaced through hard work, long-term commitments, and egalitarian relations.

As the college and community partners examined options, they began by setting goals that they felt confident could be achieved. Research conducted by Springfield College students and community-based organizations provided the data that was utilized to support the need for programs and therefore increased the probability for success of the original efforts. The use of trained college students as paid staff members and the leaders of the day-to-day operations has been utilized whenever possible with support and direction provided by faculty, administrators, and community members.

Successful community and college ventures have led to a shift in the view of community outreach and collaboration as an expectation, not an addition. The willingness of the college and community to work together as equals and commit to the long-term success of initiatives has made the collaborative efforts truly successful.

## Organizational Structure

The organizational structure of each of the collaborative projects described varies. All of the projects, however, strive to maintain a process that includes clearly identified roles and systems of shared responsibility for program planning, implementation, and accountability. All projects also have a representative body that meets regularly to set goals, review process and product outcomes related to those goals, evaluate the programs, and plan for sustainability. A detailed description of the structure that has been developed to support the SAGE Project is provided as one example, among the collaborative ventures described.

The SAGE Project brought together three organizations with distinct structures, needs, resources, and desired outcomes. To manage the project and maintain broad community input, the SAGE Project oversight is provided by a six member Executive Committee and a 25-member Advisory Board. The SAGE Executive Committee meets once a month to receive updates on the five programs and advise project staff. They also hold two retreats per year to work out major concerns, establish benchmarks for the upcoming 6 months, and plan for long-term sustainability. The Advisory Board meets on a quarterly basis to receive updates on the five programs and provide guidance for future program development. Members on the Advisory Board and Executive Committee also act as liaisons for program staff within their respective agencies, departments, communities, and organizations. Due to the fact that all constituents are kept well informed of the project goals and needs, they are able to act as resources for potential funding.

Up to this point, Springfield College acts as the fiscal and oversight agent for the SAGE Collaboration, the SAGE Master's of Education Program, the SAGE AmeriCorps Program, and the SAGE PRIDE Center. Staff members responsible for the day-to-day management of these programs are Springfield College employees and work directly under the supervision of the SAGE Project Director, who is supervised by the Director of Teacher Preparation and Certification. The Springfield Public Schools organize their schools around a principal. Due to the size of the SAGE Secondary School, it was decided to hire a supervisor for the program who would work directly under supervision of the Director of Alternative Education. The SAGE School Supervisor and the Project Assistant Director share supervision responsibility of the Springfield College AmeriCorps members placed at the secondary school. There is a continuous improvement philosophy at all levels of the SAGE Project that requires feedback that is seamless and multidirectional. Each organization needs to know what the constraints and difficulties are so that each can adopt and develop the capacity to meet new challenges. The SAGE Secondary School Supervisor and the Director of Alternative Schools work cooperatively with the SAGE Project Director from Springfield College to implement any recommended or needed alterations of the program design within the Springfield Public Schools structure.

## Funding

As recent as 1992 through 1993, there was no college budget to support collaborative outreach efforts with the community. This is not to say that there was no interaction between the college and the community or support for these efforts by the college. Internship placements, student teaching, small amounts of service learning, and volunteering by student groups did occur, but were not promoted as a priority. In August 1994, the college funded the Office of Student Volunteer Programs to increase the participation of students and faculty in service and service learning activities. This original funding of $35,000 to support one professional staff member and a programming budget was leveraged with community partners to meet the needs of the college and the community. Each year the college's financial support for collaborative ventures has increased with the growth of collaborative efforts. The total amount of funding provided in cash and through in-kind contributions is difficult to calculate due to the number of different initiatives managed by academic and student affairs divisions of the college. It is not difficult, however, to identify the funding secured by the college for collaborative efforts through federal, state, and local governmental entities and foundations. In the past 6 years, the collaborative ventures of the college have secured over $2.2 million in grant support. These grants have been matched on the local level by over $2 million in cash and in-kind contributions from the college and community partners. The scope of support is evident from the following list of financial partners: (a) Office of Juvenile Justice and Delinquency Prevention, (b) Massachusetts Service Alliance, (c) Corporation for National Service, (d) Bell Atlantic, (e) Davis Foundation, (f) Gardiner Howiland Shaw Foundation, (g) Massachusetts Department of Education, (h) U.S. Department of Education, (i) Learn and Serve America: Higher Education, (j) Nellie Mae Foundation, and (k) Community Foundation of Western Massachusetts. This listing is representative of the grants secured and managed by the Office of Student Volunteer Programs and the SAGE Project since 1993. Additional support for collaborative efforts related to the Education Department at the college have been provided to develop district standards, recruitment of minority teachers, and innovative professional development training for teachers within the Springfield Public Schools.

As previously noted, the college and collaborators have secured substantial external support. More important, all of the ventures that have been successful at receiving grant support have been designed with the following imperatives: (a) to base the programs on the needs and input of the community partners and college constituencies, (b) to support the mission of the college, (c) to develop an administrative and oversight structure to sustain the effort, and (d) to commit matching resources from all partners for a predetermined amount of time. These elements have proven successful. The Office of Student Volunteer Programs, since 1993, has submitted or been a collaborator on behalf of the college on 14 grant applications—13 of which were funded. The SAGE Project, since 1996, has maintained an 86% success rate on grant applications.

## Activities

Beyond the Partners Program, Summer Enrichment Program, Colleges Serving the Community, and the SAGE Project, the college is involved in many other initiatives. The following list provides examples of just a few of these programs:

- Under the joint sponsorship of the college, the Springfield Public Schools, and a community-based agency called The Learning Tree, Project SPIRIT was designed. The goal of this program is to significantly increase the number of Springfield Public School teachers of color to reduce the number of students of color who drop out and heighten the educational aspirations of all students.
- Organized by students and community residents, one-day service events bring together anywhere from 50 to 2,000 volunteers for day-long, intensive work that meets identified community needs. On September 10, 1998, Springfield College canceled classes and closed offices for Humanics in Action in conjunction with the local United Way's "Day of Caring." Over 1,500 students, faculty, and staff worked with neighbors on over 85 community improvement projects, including educational projects in neighborhood schools, clean-up and painting projects, and business-plan meetings. Humanics in Action was repeated on September 9, 1999, and included more than 2,000 college and community members participating at 75 service locations.
- In conjunction with the City of Springfield, Time Out for Communities provides recreational, educational, and cultural enrichment opportunities for youth. More than 200 Springfield College student athletes conduct 15 sports clinics per year, as well as substance abuse prevention workshops at city schools.
- The Babson Library Youth Orientation Program provides a safe and fun, educational setting for neighborhood youth to learn more about Springfield College's Babson Library and to develop and improve computer skills. College students train neighborhood children to use Springfield College's resources to access information and enhance computer skills.
- The Junior Achievement Program allows Springfield College students to work with Junior Achievement volunteers in teaching business concepts to elementary and junior high students. Together the college students and volunteers present economic-based curricula and help the youth learn business concepts through hands-on activities and role playing.
- Service learning fuses theoretical concepts presented in class with work done in the community. Approximately 44% of faculty at Springfield College who responded to a recent survey use service-learning techniques, and at least 56 courses were identified as incorporating service learning during the 1997 through 1998 academic year.

## Development of Volunteers

As each program has developed, success has rested on the attention paid to the collaboration as well as to the project. We have found that it has been important for all partners to have equal input into program planning to ensure a sense of shared responsibility and lateral accountability. This level of cooperation has required each institution participating in the program to develop an increased level of ownership, involvement, and trust of the other partners.

All projects have had key faculty, administrators, and community partners that have been able to facilitate and manage the college–community collaboration. These college and community members have identified four essential elements in their leadership roles: (a) respecting the traditions and structures of all partners, (b) maintaining the integrity of the collaboration over loyalty to any one partner (including the employer), (c) ensuring that all partners have a voice, and (d) maintaining a visible and vocal role in the community and college.

There have been many lessons learned from the development of these college–community collaborations and the rapid expansion of community outreach at Springfield College. The most crucial of these include (a) the importance of open communication between the college and community, (b) the importance of flexible program leadership that allows the college–community collaborations to evolve and change as the partnerships strengthen, and (c) the necessity for centralized coordination and clear communication within the college community by the leadership of community outreach programs. By responding to these three lessons internally, Springfield College has become a more responsible partner in community revitalization.

Open communication between the college and community has been a key to the success of the collaborative programs discussed in this article. This factor has allowed members of the college community to work closely with neighborhood partners. Relationships are based on honesty, trust, and genuine respect. As these peer relationships have developed, not only does commitment to the program become a value, but also commitment to the healthy professional and personal development of each person involved becomes a value. Within this atmosphere of collaboration, open communication allows the partners to clarify roles, share resources more readily, and build on the strengths of the program and individuals while managing areas of concern. Students, faculty, community members, teachers, and principals involved are empowered to be the leaders who provide the formation and direction for the programs.

## Faculty Involvement

At Springfield College, utilizing our humanics philosophy as the foundation for the outreach has been the driving force for increasing the involvement of our faculty and students. These individuals, collectively, select the college in part because of the belief in educating students to be leaders in service to others. Empowerment of and support for students and faculty to be creative in their involvement with and learning from our shared community provided an initial increase in participation in collaborative ventures. However, the spark ignited when the Partners Program, the Summer Enrichment Program, and other efforts implemented in 1993 were successful and began to rebuild the trust with the community. By being mission driven, it should be logical for the college and its constituents to sustain and support the learning opportunities and challenges that are provided by our community partners.

The Committee for the Advancement of Service Learning is provided as one example of building an infrastructure that increases faculty involvement and ownership of community involvement in fulfilling their three roles of teaching, research, and community service. As a component of Colleges Serving the Community, a faculty governance committee, the Committee for the Advancement of Service Learning, was created in January 1997 to explore and recommend ways that service learning can be integrated into and across the academic curriculum. The Committee is also responsible for ensuring that faculty will be rewarded and provided support for utilizing this approach to meet our surrounding communities' needs. During the 1998 through 1999 academic year, this committee provided funding as a standing subcommittee of our Faculty Curriculum Committee. This is the structural unit within the Faculty Senate that approves all changes and additions to the course offerings of the college. The committee has supported release time for faculty members to redesign existing courses to include service learning. Additional support is provided by committee members as peer mentors, with support and technical assistance provided by the Office of Student Volunteer Programs.

The Community Council Steering Committee was created during Fall 1998 to identify and assess the College's current outreach efforts. This committee is comprised of students, staff associates, administrators, and faculty who volunteered to represent their respective governance group. The representation of all groups on campus was vital to ensuring that the participants in outreach efforts were being heard. The charge of this committee has been to develop a comprehensive plan with the community to address the needs of collaborative efforts. It is the desire of this committee, our surrounding neighborhoods, other colleges, and the city to develop a centralized access point for college and community collaborations.

## Factors Contributing to Success

There are a number of factors that have contributed to the success of each of these projects. Four of the key reasons include (a) administrative support from both the president of Springfield College and the superintendent of the Springfield Public Schools; (b) development of a shared vision and identified needs, resources, and benefits for each institution involved; (c) the organizational structures previously described; and (d) the tireless commitment of the individuals involved within each collaboration to make things work.

Within the Springfield Public Schools, the educational philosophy of the superintendent has played a key role in both the success of the collaborations and education reform within the community. When the superintendent of schools came to Springfield in 1989, his agenda of opening the schools to parents, to the community, and to all agencies and services that interact with students was unveiled, the ultimate goal of this agenda being that everyone work together for the good of students. Organizations that previously worked under strained conditions (e.g., the police and Springfield Public Schools, Department of Youth Services and the schools, Department of Social Services and the schools, the local colleges and the schools, etc.) all sat together to strategize ways to work together. Springfield is now the only city in the Commonwealth of Massachusetts where information from Probation is shared with the schools. This is possible because Springfield Public Schools has agreed not to expel students to the street when they would have the right to do so. The superintendent's commitment to educate all children, and his desire to balance zero tolerance for school violence with zero tolerance for expelling or suspending kids to the streets, has played a major role in the success of the SAGE Project. His attitude that "if it is not illegal, not immoral and helps children, it should be tried" has opened the door for the success of the Partners Program. He has also identified individuals who are willing to "think outside of the box" to guide and lead these projects. In addition, the superintendent has not shied away from an open dialogue about the shortcomings of the Springfield Public Schools.

These attitudes have led to a number of institutional shifts within the Springfield Public Schools. School-centered decision-making teams have led to an open invitation to community members to participate in the reform of the Springfield Public Schools. Within this process community members are invited to bring both resources and needs to the partnerships that are developed. Throughout the system, educators, parents, and community members are reminded to leave loyalties behind and focus on what works for kids. This shift has led to the development of partnerships among systems and agencies who have never worked together and often competed for funding and clients.

As noted by Lucy-Allen and Seydel (1999), these working relationships, in all collaborative programs described, have allowed each program to grow and change as the partnerships have strengthened. When this occurs, it has been important for the leadership at the college to be flexible and responsive to becoming an active community partner. The entire college community needs to be more aware of the impact its decisions and actions have on these partnerships. What may appear to be nonthreatening decisions by the board of trustees, administrators, or faculty can seriously impact college–community collaborations if they do not involve the community partners in the decision-making process.

As community outreach increases, additional institutional, community-based, and external support is necessary. Leadership from the college and community must respond positively to these needs to enhance a trusting relationship within the community. Securing this support is directly correlated with the degree of success in initiating and sustaining our outreach efforts.

## Future Plans

Springfield College is committed to being a true neighbor within the community. The transformation that has occurred over the past 7 years has brought the faculty, staff, and students closer to living our humanics philosophy. The walls of separation between the college and the community are disappearing quickly. The efforts of the last 7 years have reestablished the trust, respect, communication, and understanding that collaborative efforts will meet our collective needs. It is not always an easy path, but the results will continue to transform the college and community culture of collaboration. By overcoming these obstacles, the trust and commitment increases for everyone's benefit.

In an effort to assure continuity of support at Springfield College, the responsibility for coordination of collaborative activities has recently been moved to the president's office. In addition to the internal efforts of coordination, Springfield College is leading an effort to formally link the outreach activities of American International College, Springfield Technical Community College, the City of Springfield's Planning and Community Development Departments, and three neighborhood councils that lie between the three colleges in a long-term, strategic initiative to utilize shared resources and expertise to meet our collective needs. The transformation of separate cultures over the past 7 years has enabled these discussions to reach this historic precedent. By unifying our efforts through a Community Outreach Partnership Center, we will attract and leverage our shared resources to meet any need that is present or may arise. In addition, these resources will be utilized to attract resources that would not have been secured without our collective power. Each institution of higher education and the City are committing cash and in-kind resources for a minimum of 3 years to support this Center, regardless of external funding. The first collaborative grant application was submitted to the Office of University Partnerships at the Department of Housing and Urban Development for initial funding to be provided. In September 1999, notification of award was received to begin implementing the research and outreach activities identified in the Springfield Community Outreach Partnership Center proposal.

By January 2000, this Center will be in the beginning stages of operation. The City will provide the structure to house this Center. The neighborhood councils and residents will contribute their individual expertise to assist with all efforts. In addition, they will be linked via technology with each college and the Center and will be a driving force on the advisory committee. The computers and technology support will be provided by Springfield Technical Community College. The colleges will involve their students, faculty, and staff through the use of service learning in courses, providing 1-day service events that mobilize all of these groups, designing research projects that meet the needs of the community and colleges, and expanding outreach programs to be led by college students and young adults from the community.

The research projects will be codirected by an equal number of community and faculty members who will serve as team leaders for each project. The method of research will vary depending on the needs of the community, but is designed to be participatory action research. Each research team will be comprised of an equal number of college students and community residents who will work side by side in their training and data collection.

## Conclusion

The collaborative ventures described in this article vary in their size, impacts, and operational methods. The differences of how to develop, operate, and sustain similar programs on other campuses may be great. Recommendations from those involved in Springfield College's collaborative efforts include (a) alignment with departmental, college, and university missions; (b) early involvement of key stakeholders (i.e., faculty, students, community residents and leaders, public school personnel); (c) pursuit only of those initiatives that support learning and research opportunities for constituents; and (d) flexibility in tapping the talents of those from the institution and the community.

## References

Lucy-Allen, D., & Seydel, J. (1999). Revitalizing the community through neighborhood and institutional partnerships. In T. R. Chibucos & R. M. Lerner (Eds.), *Serving children and families through community–university partnerships: Success stories* (pp. 163–171). Norwell, MA: Kluwer Academic.

U.S. Census Bureau. (1999). *1990 census data*. Retrieved June 1999 from the World Wide Web: http://venus.census.gov/cdrom/lookup/953568034

# Twenty-Five Years of Collaboration for Interprofessional Education and Practice at The Ohio State University

*Steven A. Harsh, Jilaine W. Fewell, and R. Michael Casto*

As a society, we realize that the profound issues facing us cannot be addressed by any individual or profession alone. By tracing the 25-year history of the Interprofessional Commission of Ohio at The Ohio State University, this article illustrates how collaboration among the helping professions, academics, individual citizens, and community agencies and organizations offers the best hope for meeting the challenge of improving human conditions in our increasingly complex world. This article chronicles the development of the Commission from its inception as a vision to its present form, describes the evolution of the program from a client-centered focus to one that now em-

---

STEVEN A. HARSH *is Associate Director of the Interprofessional Commission of Ohio and the Campus Collaborative at The Ohio State University, Columbus.*

JILAINE W. FEWELL *is a Graduate Administrative Assistant for the Interprofessional Commission of Ohio and the Campus Collaborative, and a doctoral candidate in Adult Education at The Ohio State University, Columbus.*

R. MICHAEL CASTO *is Director of the Interprofessional Commission of Ohio and the Campus Collaborative at The Ohio State University, Columbus.*

Requests for reprints should be sent to Steven A. Harsh, Interprofessional Commission and Campus Collaborative, 1501 Neil Avenue, Suite 020, The Ohio State University, Columbus, OH 43201–2602. E-mail: harsh.1@osu.edu

braces a community-based approach, and concludes with a brief look at some challenges facing collaborative programs in the new millennium. Web site addresses are included.

The concept of interprofessional collaboration on the issues facing a complex society may not remind us of the late 1960s and early 1970s as much as flower power, free love, and disco music. It was, however, a vision for several in the central Ohio area. The author of the dream for us was the Dean of the Methodist Theological School in Ohio, Van Bogard Dunn. He envisioned professions such as medicine, law, theology, social work, nursing, allied medicine, education, psychology, and others joining together to study the societal issues that are too complicated to be addressed successfully by any one profession. His vision was of collaboration in professional education and practice for the sake of those in need of the services of helping professionals (Dunn & Janata, 1987).

Dunn was joined by others who shared the dream: the Director of Medical Education at Columbus Riverside Hospital, The Ohio State University's (OSU) Dean of the College of Education, a representative from the Ohio Bar Association, and the president of the newly formed Academy for Contemporary Problems. These individuals met with others, including representatives from the Pontifical College Josephinum, Trinity Lutheran Seminary, other deans of colleges for the helping professions at OSU, and corresponding state professional associations. The idea of a commission, made up equally of academics and practitioners, emerged in the early 1970s. A partnership between state professional associations and higher education was constituted as the "Commission on the Role of the Professions in Society," later to become the "Commission on Interprofessional Education and Practice," and currently the "Interprofessional Commission of Ohio" (ICO). The ICO offered continuing education opportunities for professionals throughout Ohio and credit courses for preservice graduate and professional students at OSU and the Columbus Cluster of Theological Schools. Topics for conferences and courses would focus on ethical issues common to the helping professions, changing societal values and the professions, and clinical cooperation between professionals. With assistance through a grant from the Ohio Board of Regents—the state coordinating board for postsecondary education—the Commission on Interprofessional Education and Practice became a reality in the fall of 1974 (Browning, 1998).

During the next 18 years, the ICO moved toward meeting its mission. Continuing education programs and conferences dealt with issues ranging from genetic screening and counseling to privacy and confidentiality and drug and alcohol abuse. An "Interprofessional Assembly" was formed for the purpose of bringing together representatives from other Ohio colleges and universities who wished to replicate the ICO model. With guidance from the Assembly, Public Policy Panels were convened for up to 2 years for the study of difficult public policy issues (e.g., family violence and health care cost containment). Visionaries from the Ohio-based ICO also worked to form a parallel national organization, the National Consortium on Interprofessional Education and Practice. During this period numerous books, articles, and other resources were published, hundreds of practitioners attended accredited continuing professional development conferences, and thousands of students participated in interprofessional credit courses.

In 1992, a change in structure and a new name reflected the changing climate in which the ICO found itself. The Commission on Interprofessional Education and Practice became the not-for-profit corporation known as The ICO. Shortly thereafter, the Dean of OSU's College of Education asked the ICO to take on the formidable task of involving the faculty, staff, and students of OSU with the residents of the neighborhoods adjacent to OSU in improving the quality of life in the university district. This initiative came to be known as the Campus Collaborative (Browning, 1998).

Involvement in the Campus Collaborative has added a new dimension to the work of the ICO. In addition to continuing to offer interprofessional credit courses, the ICO now brings a more diverse constituency together to learn from and teach each other. The goal is the creation of a learning-serving community through the identification and enhancement of assets and strengths residing within the university neighborhoods. The Collaborative hopes to assist with improving the quality of life of all residents as it works to create a model for university and community partnerships that can be replicated elsewhere.

Throughout its nearly 30-year history, the goals, organizational structure, funding activities, and partnerships of the ICO have evolved to meet the challenges of the dynamic institution, community, and culture in which it finds itself. This article explores these and a number of other equally fluid dimensions of the life of the ICO, including faculty involvement, outcomes, factors contributing to success, causes for celebration, and problems encountered. We review these issues and what was learned during several distinct periods in the history of the ICO. We begin with the formative period prior to 1973 and follow with the initial developments that occurred from 1973 through 1980. The period from 1981 through 1990 was one of rapid growth followed by diminishing resources; 1991 through 1994 found the organization in a holding pattern, focusing on defining and sustaining its most basic features. Finally, 1995 to the present has been a period of an expanded vision and new directions. A look at some challenges for the future completes the article.

From the beginnings of the dream in the late 1960s through the expanded mission of today, the ICO has suffered and rejoiced, waxed and waned, grown and adjusted. It is our hope that the telling of our story and what we have learned over nearly 3 decades will provide some insight into what we believe to be one of the best hopes for addressing the difficult and complicated issues that we face as a society. That hope is the collaboration, understood in its broadest sense, of several helping professions, academics, individual citizens, and community agencies and organizations working together to improve the human conditions of our complex world.

## Pre-1973

In the last years of the 1960s, OSU and the Columbus Cluster of Theological Schools (known today as the Theological Consortium of Greater Columbus) were involved in a number of cooperative ventures, each of which could be seen as paving the way for what was to become the Commission on the Role of the Professions in Society and later the Commission on Interprofessional Education and Practice. These initial cooperative endeavors involved students and faculty working together in areas of mutual interest and were most often presented as credit courses open to all for the normal fees charged by the student's home institution. For example, in one course offered in 1969 students from Medicine, Education, Law, Nursing, and Theology met on the OSU Campus with faculty from these areas to explore contemporary applied ethical issues. There was no formal organizational structure and no ongoing support other than through the cooperating institutions and their agreement that such courses should be included among their credit offerings. Funding for the program was not an issue because faculty taught as part of their regular course load. Administrative supports were, however, minimal, and this is one factor that led to developing a more structured and systematic approach to collaboration across professional and institutional boundaries. It was difficult for faculty to come together in a sustained and organized way to plan interprofessional courses, and it was not feasible to produce professional development activities across professional lines without an administrative structure to support and sustain activities.

From these early efforts at collaborative work between institutions and across professions, it became apparent that an organization needed to be developed to facilitate the activities that all agreed were desirable and effective. Out of these initial limited efforts and with this kernel of an idea, the

ICO began to take shape among the leaders of the institutions, organizations, and faculties engaging in interprofessional education and thought.

## 1973 Through 1980

Although critical issues such as funding and organizational structure were certainly key concerns in the infancy of the ICO, references in the primary sources as well as the observations of the ICO's first Director, Robert L. Browning, suggest that partnerships and program content were the organizing principles around which the original organization took shape (Browning, 1998). A 1974 grant from the Ohio Board of Regents secured funding for the 1st year of the ICO's official organization and subsequently nurtured multiple cross-organization partnerships. The organizing principle for each of these partnerships was the mutual need of the various constituencies to respond to increasingly complex issues facing professionals. As Houle, Cyphert, and Boggs (1987) noted, the demand for interprofessional practice and hence interprofessional education stems from the awareness that "it is increasingly difficult to compartmentalize the needs of people in modern society" (p. 92).

During these early years the basic organizational structure of the ICO was established. It consisted of dual governing bodies: a Board of Directors with responsibility for policy development and general oversight of the activities of the ICO, and a Committee of Deans with responsibility for credit academic programs. The Board was made up of representatives from each participating professional association, college, and theological school, as well as representatives from the university's central administration and other constituent bodies. Each of these administrative structures was designed to give the ICO a unique shape and set of partnerships as well as to facilitate what Snyder (1987) described as "horizontal activity in a vertical world" (p. 96). Even in its earliest form, the ICO provided a context in which individuals were able to bridge the vertical structures that institutions create and naturally support. Indeed, this continues to be a primary function of the ICO and may be its most significant organizational and structural contribution.

Following the initial year of state funding, which was awarded through a special program to foster collaboration between state and private institutions of higher education, support was secured on a shared basis from the participating academic units and associations. Each college included faculty time as part of routine teaching loads. In addition, the colleges contributed cash to support the central organization of the program, administrative support to publicize the courses, and time to carry out the work of the Board and Committee of Deans. The state professional associations provided funding as well as representation on the Board and Continuing Education Committee, assistance with securing relevant continuing education accreditation, and mailing lists to publicize continuing education events. Each academic unit and professional association provided support at the level at which they were comfortable in light of their individual constituency and budget. A "Memorandum of Understanding," addressing faculty, was prepared for each contributing unit and reviewed annually.

The Office of Academic Affairs provided financial and administrative support. Office space was provided initially by the Academy for Contemporary Problems and later by the Mershon Center, a research center at the university. The ICO continues to enjoy the hospitality of the Mershon Center. Equally important, it was during the early life of the ICO that the College of Education assumed responsibility as the fiscal and hiring agency for the ICO. This allowed the staff to focus on program development rather than being absorbed by many of the administrative responsibilities associated with a large academic institution. As with administrative structure, programming for the ICO developed its basic shape during this period and provided a number of contexts through which individuals and associations were invited to think and act across professional boundaries.

Three basic courses were developed during this time period, each of which has continued to be taught throughout most of the life of the ICO. The Seminar on Ethical Issues Common to the Helping Professions provided a context in which students and faculty explored ethical dilemmas facing an increasingly technological society. The Seminar on Interprofessional Care provided students the opportunity to develop the skills necessary for interprofessional practice, and the Seminar on Changing Societal Values and the Professions allowed students to consider the social context of the professions and its effect on professional practice.

The structure for each of these courses was similar. They all used cases from professional practice to illustrate and explore the principles being taught. The concept of case presentations—based as nearly as possible on actual situations—persists in the courses today. Weekly sessions included theoretical and contextual insights, student evaluation, professional groups in which a faculty member met with up to 12 students from their own profession, and interprofessional groups in which an individual faculty member met with a group of students representing a cross section of the participating six to eight professions.

During this time, professional development conferences began to be held once or twice a year on topics determined by the Board and Continuing Education Committee. After identifying a topic and developing beginning goals and objectives, the committee would identify a group of consultants from the sponsoring professions. The consultants would be invited to use their expertise in the topic to give shape and substance to the conference and would often provide leadership for the event. Each conference was accredited for continuing education units by the relevant bodies to provide an additional incentive to professionals for their participation.

This period in the life of the ICO was characterized by thoughtful and measured growth, including hiring a part-time executive director and an office associate. The emphasis was on securing the engagement and commitments of the many partners necessary to undertake the complex mission that the ICO had established for itself. The primary challenges of identifying sustained funding and creating a functional organizational structure were effectively addressed. Like all efforts, the creativity, insight, and most of all persistence of the ICO's leadership during these formative years must be cited as the critical elements in creating this opportunity for success.

One of the key names that must be mentioned in considering developments during this period is Van Bogard Dunn, founding Dean of the Methodist Theological School in Ohio, to whom the basic ideas about interprofessional collaboration and the concept of a "commission" must be attributed. Dunn, recognized as the Founder of the ICO, served as its first Board chair (1973–1980). Another key name is Mary M. Janata, the second director, who served from 1976 to 1987. It was under her leadership that the ICO experienced its most significant growth. Two Deans of the College of Education during this period, Luvern L. Cunningham, who became chair of the Board in 1980 and later served as Executive Director (1987–1992), and Frederick R. Cyphert, who taught in the interprofessional courses and served on the Board, provided a fiscal home and significant administrative support for the ICO during this important period. Richard Snyder, Director of the Mershon Center, provided equally important support by encouraging the ICO to move to the campus of the university by offering office space in the Center. Many other individuals also played critical roles to ensure the success of the ICO in these early days, which is to say that the sustained success of the program and organization of the ICO must be attributed primarily to the encounter of a group of capable, creative, insightful, and persistent individuals with an irresistible concept.

## 1981 Through 1990

This period in the life of the ICO is characterized by remarkable growth in the partnerships and programs that were at the heart of the organization in the 1970s. This growth was facilitated through the generosity of the W.

K. Kellogg Foundation in 1981 when it awarded two grants totaling over $1.2 million to the ICO to expand its work in a number of areas. Throughout this period, the organizational structure remained constant. Funding patterns varied near the end of the period while activities, partnerships, and patterns of faculty involvement developed very rapidly in a number of new and exciting directions.

Browning (1998) identified several areas in which significant program development occurred during this period. The continuing education program received awards from the National University Continuing Education Association for innovative and creative approaches to professional development activities. Semiannual statewide conferences on such topics as genetic screening, privacy and confidentiality, stress, human sexuality, aging, adolescent mental health, and AIDS brought internationally recognized speakers to Ohio, as well as local experts and thousands of practitioners. Together with state professional association leaders and practicing professionals, faculty were intensely involved in the planning and production of these professional development activities.

The Interprofessional Assembly brought faculty from other institutions of higher education in Ohio together twice each year to explore interprofessional issues. The Assembly was home to intensive professional development activities in the form of the ICO's Public Policy Panels. Teams of 16 professionals—an academic and a practitioner from each discipline—came together every 6 weeks over a 2-year period to develop legislative study documents, educational initiatives, and other creative approaches to help shape emerging policy issues in the state legislature. Panels explored health cost containment, artificial modes of human reproduction, and family violence, as well as stress (Cunningham & Dunn, 1987).

Rigorous program and organizational evaluation and assessment also occurred during this period. In 1984, the ICO participated in a comprehensive qualitative evaluation. Among the most significant of the findings was the general acceptance of the concept of interprofessional collaboration as essential for effective professional practice. In addition, the development of a long-range program and development plan for the ICO was encouraged. Unfortunately, these plans were never developed, and in the next period of its development, the ICO experienced the consequences of limited long-term organizational planning.

One doctoral dissertation was developed during this period (Spencer, 1983). Spencer's research determined that interprofessional education assists professionals in being more explicit and articulate about the interprofessional dimensions of their practice. Interprofessional education seems to provide professionals with a conceptual and theoretical framework for understanding interprofessional practice that other professionals lack. Professionals educated in the OSU interprofessional courses reported more interprofessional contacts and interactions and a greater ease of establishing such relations.

Numerous books and articles were published during this period. Several conferences lead to publications, many of which have made significant contributions to knowledge in their field. Specifically, Arnold (1983, 1985, 1990) prepared a series of books based on interprofessional conferences that dealt with family and child issues. In addition, proceedings of the three meetings of the National Consortium were also published (Casto, Lyons, & Rosenberger, 1990; Lyons & Casto, 1990; McLaughlin, 1988). A number of curricular resources and programmatic descriptions were also published during this time (Casto & Macce, 1990; Cyphert, 1987).

Additional interprofessional credit graduate and professional courses were also developed during this period: Interprofessional Seminar in the Family Dynamics of Chemical Dependency, Seminar in Interprofessional Clinical Practice, Interprofessional Seminar in Child Abuse and Neglect, and Seminar in Interprofessional Policy Analysis were all fully developed and taught annually during this period. Each summer the ICO assisted with the development of a credit summer institute on an interprofessional theme. These courses used a similar approach and methodology including case studies, professional and interprofessional analysis of issues, and development of collaborative solutions and plans. Each course provided an additional path through which to expand, deepen, and sustain faculty involvement in interprofessional education (Casto, 1987).

Another significant development during this period was the formation of the National Consortium on Interprofessional Education and Practice. The National Consortium brought together the national professional associations and their counterpart educational associations in each of the disciplines with which the ICO worked on the state level. The purpose of the National Consortium was to consider the national implications of the development of interprofessional education and practice and its impact on professional education and practice. The National Consortium sponsored three national meetings of leaders of the professions as well as a number of planning sessions and publications (Casto et al., 1990; Lyons & Casto, 1990; McLaughlin, 1988). OSU faculty, faculty from other institutions, and leaders of state professional associations participated fully in these national symposia.

Outcomes during this period included not only the growth in program and activities previously described, but also the dissemination of the concept of interprofessional education and practice through numerous presentations at state and national professional association meetings. Refinement of the concepts occurred as educational activities increased, developed, and matured as well as through the increasing number of publications. These successes can be attributed to a number of factors: outstanding leadership from the ICO's staff and Board; significant funding from the W. K. Kellogg Foundation, as well as a $400,000 grant from the National Center on Child Abuse and Neglect; increasing national interest in interprofessional collaboration as a path toward solving some of society's most distressing and complex problems; and state and national requirements for professional development.

Subtle forces worked against sustaining the significant organizational and programative gains previously discussed. Chief among these was a failure to view the long-term future of the ICO, especially in the context of a nearly universal reality of higher education: Grant support for program development does not carry with it any assurance of continuity. The ICO did not prepare for the end of its substantial external support, and university resources were not available to replace this support.

Growing interest in accredited professional development lead to competition and specialization among professional development providers as well as increasingly focused and narrow standards for accreditation. Both of these conditions meant that by the end of the decade the ICO was working in an environment in which it had difficulty competing. It could no longer receive some forms of profession-specific accreditation for its programs because of its very nature as an interprofessional organization. It also could not compete with larger and more targeted professional development providers and activities. At the same time the statewide character of the ICO was undermined because funds for travel for professional development were being reduced, resulting in an increasingly higher concentration of ICO participants from central Ohio. Toward the end of this period, university resources were becoming increasingly scarce because of substantial cuts in state funding. Programs like those of the ICO were increasingly seen as extraneous to the basic mission of the university. Unhappily, these forces began to converge near the end of this period, setting the stage for the difficulties described in the next period in the ICO's development.

### 1991 Through 1994

The mission and vision of the ICO remained constant at the beginning of the 1990s. The commitment to preservice and continuing interprofessional education held firm even as the organizational structure and staff underwent major changes. The mission to advocate for, implement, and achieve interprofessional education, practice, and research captures the essence of what has always been the purpose of the ICO. However, the overarching de facto goal of this period was to preserve the organization and its potential for addressing complex issues in our society.

The very existence of the ICO was at risk in the early 1990s as both external and internal sources of funding became extremely limited. Some of this change was predictable (e.g., support from the W. K. Kellogg Foundation ended in 1988), and some was not. Due to decreased state funding for OSU, the major university funding of the program through the Office of Academic Affairs evaporated after nearly 20 years of continuous support. By definition, interprofessional programs cannot have the institutional security of belonging to any one college or department. So, like other interdisciplinary programs, the ICO was orphaned in a sea of university-wide financial cutbacks in the late 1980s and early 1990s.

However, the ICO's unique structural nature (i.e., having a board of directors that was in but not completely of the university) provided strong supporters who were not dependent on or accountable to the university administration. Therefore, when it was suggested by the university that it was time for the ICO to fold its tent, the Commission Board was free to say, "We do not think so." The vision that gave birth to the ICO in the early 1970s was still embodied in board members and staff who set about the task of finding a way to continue the organization and programs.

With strong leadership from the Dean of the College of Education, the direction chosen was for the ICO to incorporate as a not-for-profit organization known as the ICO. Board membership was streamlined and designed to restore the scope of work to a statewide constituency and was no longer based on academic or professional association representation. Ties to OSU were maintained in this new structure through the commitment of three successive deans of the College of Education who have maintained their college's role as the fiscal agent for the ICO to the present day.

Staffing for the ICO reflected the restricted resources of the organization during this time. For several years (1991–1994), the staff consisted of one full-time director, one half-time graduate administrative associate, and a part-time student employee as office support staff. OSU funding from participating colleges and from the theological schools and professional associations continued on a reduced basis during this period, and the Janata Fund and another significant fund started at the Columbus Foundation by Henry and Ruth Leuchter also provided critical support during this transition period. To meet financial needs, a prime motivation in seeking nonprofit status was to have the freedom to seek funding through grants and services in the name of the ICO. Although having two identities (as an OSU program and as a nonprofit corporation) and dual fiscal arrangements has complicated the life of the staff and the Board, this arrangement was essential for the ICO's survival.

S. A. Harsh, J. W. Fewell, R. M. Casto

Given the ICO's long-time interest in public education, a natural opportunity for a mutually beneficial partnership with the Ohio Department of Education arose in 1992. The ICO was invited to develop resources and training materials on collaboration in community education and service learning. From 1993 through 1995, a major program initiative and source of funding came from development of the Ohio Collaborative for Community Involvement in Education. ICO staff time was devoted to development of a resource guide and implementation of those resources in a series of train-the-trainer events cosponsored by ICO and the Ohio Department of Education.

Adjustments in program and other activities were made during this period to correspond to funding and staff levels. Course offerings were reduced to two per year. Continuing education conferences were refocused to include an increasing emphasis on community practice and state and national relations. The fall 1993 conference was a national conference on Integrating Services for Children and Youth cosponsored with the National Consortium on Interprofessional Education and Practice, and the spring 1994 conference, Communities that Work: Service Learning Partnerships for the Well-Being of Families, was held on the campus of cosponsor Ohio Wesleyan University. Both of these events were reflections of a national trend in interprofessional education toward university–community partnerships that has become central to the work at OSU in recent years.

This era was typified by a decrease in the number of traditional partners affiliated with the ICO. The difficult spiral of funding cuts and staff reductions meant fewer opportunities to nurture existing partnerships. At the same time, new partnerships were formed through consultative relationships and by virtue of an expanding vision of community collaboration. Commitment by both the Board and key leadership within the university opened the way for the rapid expansion of partnerships.

Funding cuts from within the university meant decreased faculty involvement in courses and in student–faculty conferences, which had to be discontinued in 1993. Changes in the Board and organizational structure also eliminated two key avenues for faculty involvement. One was membership on the board, and the other was the important input and contact with faculty through the Council of Deans, which ceased to exist in the new structure. A dedicated core of five faculty and four adjunct faculty maintained the two interprofessional courses through this period. The Theological Consortium continued to supply a faculty member for each of the courses, rotating this responsibility among the three schools. Nursing and Medicine withdrew from one or both of the courses during part of this time to conserve on faculty expense. The low faculty to student ratio for the interprofessional courses (maximum of 1:12 from each college) is a continuing challenge for maintaining college involvement.

One of this period's most significant new involvements of faculty came from the team that collaborated to produce the first text book on interprofessional collaboration, *Children and Youth at Risk: Interprofessional Care and Collaborative Practice* (Casto & Julia, 1994). Ten faculty from six professions coauthored this work, which has been used as the textbook for the Interprofessional Care course every year since it was published.

A key factor in sustaining the success of the ICO during this transition period was the 20-year history of successful interprofessional education that engendered long-term support from a few key OSU leaders, a support that has shown that depth of commitment in the university context may be more critical than breadth. That depth was grounded in a solid theoretical, theological, and pragmatic vision that interprofessional education and practice are not luxuries in the 20th century, but necessities for any ethical or effective professional response to society's complex problems. That vision on the part of board members, staff, and the new dean of the College of Education was critical. However, equally important was the flexibility to adapt to changing institutional and societal demands. Those elements led to the paradigm shift described in the next section. As this transition period came to a close, the new structure began to mature and new visions of university–community partnerships were emerging, while the focus on interprofessional education was maintained. New disciplines and players began to come to the interprofessional table at OSU, and that was possible only because the ICO was able to adapt to new circumstances and emerge as a stronger voice for collaboration.

The problems experienced in this period were ultimately related to the fact that the ICO was never an institutionalized part of the university. We have acknowledged the advantages of that mode of operation and would not argue for a traditional niche on the university flow chart for interprofessional education (Casto, 1994). It is obvious, however, that some innovative "home" needs to be provided for such programs that will free staff and board members to direct fewer resources to basic survival and more energy to the purpose and mission of the organization.

## 1995 to the Present

The most recent chapter in ICO history began in 1993, but its evolving shape did not become clear until 1995. At that time several critical factors came together to create a major expansion of the scope of ICO's structure and mission. A university restructuring effort was underway, an Interprofessional Leadership Task Force (ILTF) was convened, and conversations with community leaders and the president of OSU were taking place, with the result that Campus Partners for Community Urban Redevelopment, Incorporated was established. The ILTF offered its services to work with Campus Partners in studying and addressing the needs in the university district (Casto, Harsh, & Cunningham, 1998).

Goals for this period were shaped by an emerging need for interprofessional collaboration in a specific urban community and have evolved to include implementation of recommendations developed by the four action teams of the ILTF. Working with Campus Partners, community partners, and OSU faculty, staff, and students interested in the university's outreach and engagement mission as a land grant institution, the goals for this aspect of ICO's work are: (a) integrate the academic work of faculty, staff, and students into the Campus Partners programs to improve the university neighborhoods; (b) support faculty participation, stronger schools, improved student quality of life, health, and well being, and economic development; (c) create a model for university–community partnerships; (d) develop collaborative, community-based teaching, learning, and inquiry; and (e) build on community assets.

These goals have not replaced the ICO's basic purpose of doing interprofessional education, but they have redefined the context and form in which that education is carried out. Existing courses have taken on more community-based and service learning dimensions. An inactive course on interprofessional clinical practice has been redesigned and expanded as a course on interprofessional community practice. Continuing education conferences have become annual forums on university–community partnerships. Public policy research now focuses on "Civility and Community Building in America."

In 1996 the ILTF, now expanded to include 35 academic units at OSU, adopted a new name, the Campus Collaborative (CC). The CC was, and continues to be, a voluntary, ad hoc organization of university and community organizations and individuals interested in the improvement of the university district neighborhoods through a university–community partnership. The CC was chaired by Dean of the College of Education, Nancy Zimpher, until her departure from OSU in 1998 to become Chancellor of the University of Wisconsin at Milwaukee. Since its inception, the Campus Collaborative has been staffed by the ICO. Over the last 4 years, through CC-generated grants and increased university support, the staff has grown to three full-time persons (director, associate director, and office associate), one part-time program manager focusing on urban schools, and two half-time graduate administrative associates. Other staff and graduate administrative associates are provided by participating colleges, specific grant-funded projects, or both as needed to implement CC programs and goals.

In 1997, the CC was directed by the university president to report on its activities to David Williams II, Vice-President of Student and Urban–Community Affairs, who also chairs the Campus Partners board. In 1998, key leaders of the CC and Vice-President Williams agreed that to diversify the leadership of CC, cochairs would be asked to assume leadership. The interim dean of the College of Education was asked to accept one of the cochair roles to provide continuity with that college as fiscal agent for ICO and CC. The dean of the College of Arts, a relative newcomer to the CC, accepted the other cochair position, and that arrangement continues to the present. Given the fluid nature of the structure, however, it should come as no surprise that the organization and funding of CC, and therefore by association of ICO, is currently under discussion by a high-level university outreach steering committee. This group is charged with developing a plan and a more efficient structure for coordinating all of the outreach and engagement activities at OSU.

In response to the new focus on community, the ICO Board now includes several members who are related to the CC project. The new Board structure adopted in 1998 calls for a 20-member board of trustees. Recruitment and election of the full compliment of board members was phased in gradually and completed in the fall of 1998. Of the 20 trustees, 6 were chosen because of their relation to OSU, the CC, or both. Several steps have been taken to reinvest the Board in advising and supporting the staff, including increasing frequency of board meetings from four to six per year, reactivating the executive committee, and appointing subcommittees to address organizational and programmatic dimensions.

As in previous periods, funding for the now-joined efforts of the ICO and CC comes from three sources: (a) expanded donations from supporters, including establishment of a professorship in interprofessional education; (b) university support from several colleges, the Office of Academic Affairs, and the university trustees (University funds support some of the operational expenses and include $50,000 to $80,000, which is awarded annually by CC to faculty and staff for university neighborhood seed grants); and (c) grants ranging from $3,000 to $1.7 million for various program initiatives. Since 1985, the ICO and CC have generated over $4 million in nonuniversity funds. Funding patterns for ICO and the CC still need to be stabilized, and that is part of the discussion underway by the outreach steering committee mentioned previously.

Current activities include (a) Interprofessional Credit Courses, (b) annual university–community forums, (c) a Community Outreach Partnership Center, (d) networking and dissemination, and (e) University Neighborhood Seed Grants. Interested readers may visit www.osu.edu\ico and www.osu.edu\campuscollab for a more complete discussion.

The number of partners involved in the work of ICO and CC soared during this period due to the interest in university–community partnerships. From the eight original and constant professions that were part of the ICO's first 20 years, the number of partners around the CC table has grown to 16 of OSU's 19 colleges; 26 schools, departments, and other offices; and four community affiliates. In addition, community partners include religious organizations, a variety of community organizations, social service agencies, and the public schools. An estimated 180 such community groups exist in the university district, and most have been involved in some way with the CC–Campus Partners project. Beyond the university district, partners include other institutions of higher education (both 4-year and 2-year schools), the three theological schools that have been a part of the ICO from the beginning, and continued relationships with some of the state professional associations.

With increased partnership has come a new influx of faculty participation through attendance at monthly CC planning meetings, as recipients of seed grants, as codirectors on grant projects, through teaching in the interprofessional courses, and as members of the ICO board.

The following is a sampling of the most significant outcomes from this period. A more comprehensive list appears on the CC and ICO Web sites.

- The North Education Center Community Computer Center, in operation since 1996, provides residents access to computer technology and the Internet, as well as computer access through a joint project with Indianola Middle School.
- University Neighborhood Seed Grants have produced a variety of outcomes, including a booklet describing the university district public schools and a school Web site (www.coe.ohio-state.edu\tlb), a Web-based resource to assist students and families making the transition from middle school to high schools (www.Grade9.org), health screening and referrals for residents, the creation of a half-day geriatric dental clinic at the College of Dentistry, and the creation of new service learning courses at OSU and a service learning faculty roundtable.
- Six hundred forty-five K–12 students participated in career experiences on the OSU campus hosted by 103 OSU faculty and staff. Seven career teaching units were created and printed, and 38 teachers and school administrators attended professional development workshop on the OSU campus.
- The Community Outreach Partnership Center (COPC) program has helped to produce a monthly newspaper for the Weinland Park neighborhood written by Indianola Middle School students, a 6-week job training program in the construction trades, a community garden and market, recruitment and training of block watch leaders, and hiring two residents as

community liaisons. Most important, the COPC project has produced a more valuable but intangible outcome—a university–community partnership that seemed impossible in 1996.

- The Interprofessional Community Practice course in the spring of 1999 produced an updated resource guide for residents, service providers, and agencies and community organizations in the university district, and a study of one neighborhood in the district as a model for meeting the goals of the Campus Partners improvement plan.

The success achieved in this period has been based on a continuation of factors developed over the life of the ICO: a sound philosophy of collaboration and a track record of successful implementation of that philosophy, and a timely convergence of an awareness of the university and the community of the necessity for a visionary and far-reaching collaborative effort to both address community needs and maximize community and university assets.

## Future Challenges

The history of the ICO is one rich in peaks and valleys, successes and disappointments, and lessons to be pondered. It is our hope that in this open and frank presentation of our more than 25 years the reader may find some common ground for a shared vision of interprofessional collaborative education and practice.

We conclude with some challenges that face our future and, we suspect, those of similar initiatives:

- Establishing a university-wide structure for coordination and support of outreach and engagement activities.
- Providing for a more stable financial situation for interprofessional education.
- Overcoming the reluctance on the part of some university departments and colleges to value applied, community-based inquiry and teaching.
- More effectively communicating about the shifting paradigm for interprofessional education from individual client-centered collaboration to community partnerships.

## References

Arnold, L. E. (Ed.). (1983). *Preventing adolescent alienation: An interprofessional approach.* Lexington, KY: Lexington.

Arnold, L. E. (Ed.). (1985). *Parents, children, and change.* Lexington, KY: Lexington.
Arnold, L. E. (Ed.). (1990). *Childhood stress.* New York: Wiley.
Browning, R. L. (1998, February). *Retrospective.* Unpublished presentation prepared for the 25th Anniversary of the Interprofessional Commission of Ohio, Columbus.
Casto, R. M. (1987). Preservice courses for interprofessional practice. *Theory into Practice, 26,* 103–109.
Casto, R. M. (1994). Defining, supporting and maintaining interprofessional education. In L. Adler & S. Gardner (Eds.), *The politics of linking schools and social services* (pp. 153–155). Washington, DC: Falmer.
Casto, R. M., Harsh, S. A., & Cunningham, L. L. (1998). Shifting the paradigm for interprofessional education at The Ohio State University and beyond. In J. McCroskey & S. D. Einbinder (Eds.), *Universities and communities: Remaking professional interprofessional education for the next century* (pp. 54–64). Westport, CT: Praeger.
Casto, R. M., & Julia, M. C. (1994). *Interprofessional care and collaborative practice.* Pacific Grove, CA: Brooks/Cole.
Casto, R. M., Lyons, J. P., & Rosenberger, J. M. (Eds.). (1990). *Children and youth at risk: Interprofessional approaches to their problems: Proceedings of the second national leadership symposium on interprofessional education and practice.* Columbus, OH: The National Consortium on Interprofessional Education and Practice.
Casto, R. M., & Macce, B. R. (1990). *A model interprofessional curriculum in child abuse and neglect: Interprofessional education and practice occasional papers* (No. 2). Columbus, OH: The Commission on Interprofessional Education and Practice, The Ohio State University.
Cunningham, L. L., & Dunn, V. B. (1987). Interprofessional policy analysis: An aid to public policy formation. *Theory Into Practice, 26,* 129–133.
Cyphert, F. R. (Ed.). (1987). Interprofessional education. *Theory Into Practice, 26,* 86–156.
Dunn, V. B., & Janata, M. M. (1987). Interprofessional assumptions and the OSU commission. *Theory Into Practice, 26,* 99–102.
Houle, C. O., Cyphert, F., & Boggs, D. (1987). Education for the professions. *Theory Into Practice, 26,* 87–93.
Lyons, J. P., & Casto, R. M. (Eds.). (1990). *Interprofessional education applied: Children and youth at risk. Proceedings of the Third National Leadership Symposium on Interprofessional Education and Practice. Interprofessional Education and Practice Occasional Papers* (No. 1). Columbus, OH: The National Consortium on Interprofessional Education and Practice.
McLaughlin, R. T. (Ed.). (1988). *Proceedings of the first national leadership symposium on interprofessional education and practice.* Columbus, OH: National Consortium on Interprofessional Education and Practice.
Snyder, R. C. (1987). A societal backdrop for interprofessional education and practice. *Theory Into Practice, 26,* 94–98.
Spencer, M. H. (1983). *Assessing the impact of interprofessional education on the attitudes and behaviors of practicing professionals.* Unpublished doctoral dissertation, The Ohio State University, Columbus.

# Collaborating to Promote Effective Elementary Practices Across Seven School Districts

*Sheri Rogers, Kathy Danielson, and Jill F. Russell*

Collaboration between a metropolitan university's college of education and urban and suburban school districts is described via an initiative to support dissemination of effective elementary practices across 7 districts. The effort focused on the creation of 4 booklets that described best practices as identified through the research-based literature. Parent involvement, literacy instruction, multiage classrooms, and brain-based learning were the areas targeted for attention. Two conferences to share the information were also a part of the plan for dissemination. Trust and camaraderie evolved as faculty members, teachers, and administrators worked together to create a product and share it with their colleagues.

SHERI ROGERS *is Associate Professor, Department of Teacher Education, University of Nebraska, Omaha.*

KATHY DANIELSON *is Professor, Department of Teacher Education, University of Nebraska, Omaha.*

JILL F. RUSSELL *is Assistant Dean of the College of Education, and Executive Director of the Metropolitan Omaha Educational Consortium, University of Nebraska at Omaha.*

Requests for reprints should be sent to Sheri Rogers, Department of Teacher Education, University of Nebraska at Omaha, Kayser Hall, 514, Omaha, NE 68182. E-mail: sheri_rogers@unomaha.edu

This is the story of one of many collaborative ventures between a metropolitan university's college of education and seven area school districts. The umbrella for the collaboration is the Metropolitan Omaha Educational Consortium (MOEC). The specific collaborative initiative to be highlighted focuses on effective elementary practices. In particular, the initiative was intended to identify what the research says about effective practices and to communicate that information in persuasive ways to those who are in a position to implement effective practices.

This article describes the context and background for this collaborative effort, the goals and strategies, and the outcomes. It also discusses the barriers that had to be overcome, the factors contributing to success, and the causes for celebration.

## Views of the Authors

The authors are Sheri, a faculty member in the University of Nebraska at Omaha's Department of Teacher Education; Kathy, also a faculty member in Teacher Education; and Jill, the executive director of MOEC, who is also assistant dean of the college. As a group we believe:

> We are strengthened by our shared community. The opportunity to listen to another's perspective strengthens and reinforces our own resolve. Colleges of Education are seen as models of working together toward a common goal: educating our community's children well. If we do not work together, what kind of message are we sending to teachers, to students, and to parents in that community? To work together, we must pull together to support our individual success stories and to offer nonjudgmental advice to those between successes.

## MOEC

MOEC was established in 1988 by the dean of the College of Education at the University of Nebraska at Omaha in cooperation with five local school district superintendents. After just a few more years two additional districts had joined, comprising essentially all of the urban/suburban public districts of the metropolitan area. The goals of MOEC are to serve as a catalyst to promote the best education for youth and educators and to provide a vehicle for communication and action across educational institutions.

Member organizations pay dues. The consortium is housed at the university out of the dean's office. Oversight is provided by the Executive

Steering Committee whose membership is the superintendents and the dean. Staff includes two full-time equivalent professionals and a part-time assistant. The primary means of accomplishing work is through task forces. There are 12 or so task forces in place that deal with such issues as assessment, middle level, technology, personnel, staff development, and so forth. These task forces include representatives from the school districts and the college. In addition, there are several ongoing projects that have been institutionalized, including a mentor training program, a graduate induction program, and a summer leadership program.

## History of the Effective Elementary Practices Initiative

Three task forces have contributed to the initiative to be described herein. The Effective Elementary Practices, Early Childhood Committee, and Reading and Literacy Task Force groups had merged several years previously when it was recognized they were discussing many of the same issues. The Combined Task Force met on a regular basis throughout the school year in various locations around the metro area.

The Effective Elementary Practices group had originally been established to help design a model elementary school in conjunction with a local group connected with the Chamber of Commerce. Kathy had been the university representative of this group. This had been a very politicized activity. One of the issues of contention was: How would governance of such a model school be handled with respect to seven different school districts? After the group had identified the characteristics of a model elementary school, the members of the MOEC Executive Steering Committee had decided they would like to see these characteristics in all the elementary buildings, not just in a single model school. The Task Force was asked to redirect their efforts toward assisting all schools in developing model school characteristics.

The Early Childhood Committee was actually the oldest of the three task forces. It had been in place for about 8 years. This group had addressed a wide range of topics and had previously produced program directories and a monograph on the need and value of early childhood education and parent involvement programs.

The Literacy Task Force was the newest group of the three. Sheri had asked that this group be created. Her story about its establishment is as follows:

One of the reasons I had accepted my position at the University of Nebraska at Omaha in the first place was because of the preexisting connection to the area schools offered by MOEC. My research is done in schools, and I was leaving connections to local schools behind with my former position. MOEC's preexisting scaffolding allowed me a foothold in the community I wished to learn with and from. During my interview with the MOEC staff while on my prehire visit to the university, I had asked about a literacy task force. There was none, but several others were suggested that I joined when I was hired: the Assessment Task Force and also the Safe Schools Task Force. Although I enjoyed my time with the committed individuals on each of these task forces, I never felt that I was making a meaningful contribution.

Later, I asked again if it would be possible to create a Literacy Task Force. One of the reasons I asked the question was because I thought I would be allowed to do so. I trusted that my suggestion would not be ridiculed or belittled. Friendly, helpful, and supportive people are easier to work with. Although this seems obvious, it is not always the case that individuals involved in collaborative situations are open to new ideas. I found that because I knew my question would, at the very least, be valued, I was willing to ask it. The immediate response was, "Okay, we'll ask the superintendents and the dean."

The willingness the staff displayed to work with me toward the positive possibilities, instead of insisting on pointing out the danger inherent in beginning anything new, made all the difference. My ideas were appreciated, not demeaned. Problems, when they developed, have been put in their appropriate perspective, not seen as the be all and end all of any of our particular goals.

I was never once told: "That isn't the way we do things here." It was mentioned that a professor had never asked for a task force previously, but there was no insistence that because it had never happened before it couldn't happen now. The removal of roadblocks was essential to the beginning of this entire project.

One of the priorities of the committee, in addition to sharing literacy research and successful practice, was to include teachers in our task force makeup. We didn't think we could accomplish the literacy changes that would be necessary if we relied only on administrators and reading specialists. Teachers had to buy into the ideas we were presenting. Teachers had to close their classroom doors and try some of the things our committee would talk about. Teachers had to lead other teachers to an integration of literacy theory and literacy practice. This priority has been a struggle, but we continue in our desire to hold meetings when teachers can attend.

As we gathered together as a task force, we were joined by other task forces with similar ideas. We began to reshape our goals based on what emerged as the number one common goal: to put quality educational research on common themes into the hands of practicing teachers and administrators. This goal consumed the time of the task force during the first year.

With that as a backdrop, the Combined Task Force chose to identify the research behind effective elementary practices and to create user-friendly booklets that shared the rationale and research behind the preferred methods and structures. It was intended the booklets would bridge the research-to-practice gap for teachers and administrators, as well as provide evidence that could be shared readily with board members, parents, or the media who may be questioning certain methods. Along the way, two conferences were planned to help with the dissemination of information.

## Activities

The Combined Task Force, together with the MOEC offices, offered the following concrete activities:

1. A sharing of professional readings, drafting of booklets, reflecting, discussing, defending, and synthesizing our own professional philosophies of quality learning and teaching.
2. Development of professional research booklets: Parent Involvement Programs, Multiage Classrooms, Principles of Brain-Based Learning, and Effective Literacy Instruction. (Note that all of the booklets are available online at the following site: http://www.unocoe.unomaha.edu/booklets.htm.) The booklets answered the questions: What does research say? How may this be manifested in the classroom? Where can I go and see this kind of practice? What Internet sites may I go to if I have additional questions?
3. A professional research conference in which practitioners, many of whom were listed in the booklets, offered their advice about the research from a first-hand perspective.
4. An additional conference with Dr. Brian Cambourne from Australia to offer follow-up to the first conference and to further integrate the collaboration across MOEC member organizations.

### Goals of Research Booklets

The primary goal of the research booklets was to address the constant challenge of integrating theory with practice. The topical areas of educational research identified by the Task Force as needing to be addressed in our metropolitan schools were the Multiaging Classroom, Parent Involvement Programs, Effective Literacy Instruction, and Principles of Brain-Based Learning. These areas were researched extensively with a great deal of support and help from the Dean's Office at the College of Education. This allowed the subcommittees to read, reflect, discuss, and eventually write a synthesis of the research, as well as identify sites of best practices involving local practitioners.

Primarily because the brain-based group insisted on providing a reader-friendly format, we offered a "less-is-more" axiom. The goal of the booklets was to have them read. To ensure that this would happen, we wanted them to present the essentials in a nonthreatening format.

*Goals of Conference*

Although the subcommittees insisted on the existence of a booklet-sharing conference, they did not necessarily have the time to plan the conference. This job fell primarily to the three of us. The subcommittees wanted these booklets read, and because the booklets themselves offered the subcommittee members as natural presenters, they and the same practitioners listed on the booklets became the conference presenters in many instances. These individuals are still the experts people turn to as they seek to follow the model established by these individuals, their schools, and their districts. The point was to encourage practitioners to be helping other practitioners.

Representatives from all of the districts and the university were included in the conference agenda. It was decided to invite undergraduate and graduate classes at the university to participate in the conference at no charge. Faculty who chose to do so allowed students to attend the conference instead of holding class that day. This allowed the natural integration of the College of Education, its faculty and administrators, the Career Advancement and Development for Recruits and Experienced Teachers (CADRE) associates (the MOEC–teacher education graduate induction program), together with the preservice and in-service teachers we serve, to illustrate the layers of learners in a concrete, formal conference. The conference further allowed us to illustrate in a less concrete fashion the power of such a collaboration. Without the prior 10 years of successful collaboration, this connection would have been less than natural. It would have been false and suspect. With the MOEC scaffolding firmly in place, we were able to build on the in-place structure and soar to new heights.

As professors, one of our goals for the conference was to allow our preservice teachers to see firsthand what in-service teachers do: Learn throughout their careers. The connections our students made with in-service teachers were priceless, but they also discerned that they were learning, in their university courses, pertinent information that was viable for real life.

One of Sheri's individual goals for the conference became the timely issue of Nebraska State Education Standards. Many of her graduate students were concerned that they would be forced outside of their own learning and teaching philosophies in order to adapt to the state's standards. Although many of Sheri's preservice students were not familiar with the standards, Sheri, who is also a member of a local school board, knew that these same future teachers would soon be evaluated on whether they were adequately addressing the standards. The conference was a natural way to address both concerns. The layers of learners at the Standards Sections were impressive to just sit back and watch.

In-service teachers attended sessions offered by preservice teachers, specifically in the area of Nebraska State Standards, as "students" presented their Standards sections of their professional portfolios. The self-confidence the presenters gained from this was career-choice affirming. One such preservice presenter offered:"They [in-service teachers and administrators] actually took notes on what I did!"

In addition, preservice teachers learned about MOEC in a way they had not before. They learned firsthand about the opportunities for collaboration, learning, and sharing of pertinent information. They wondered how they could be a part of this organization when they are practitioners. They will spread the word.

*Timeline*

The subcommittees met for over a year to develop their booklets. Connections were formed within subcommittees and allowed each member to not only learn from the process but also to be empowered to take the research they were reading directly back to their own buildings. The subcommittees were insisting on a conference to disseminate the booklets in a way that would not leave them lost on some storage room shelf. These individuals insisted that the fruit of their year-long labor would be devoured by the in-service teachers who would gain sustenance from the contents. We let the subcommittees lead us toward the conference.

*Outcomes*

Several outcomes were unplanned, but probably the most powerful were the following:

1. The opportunity to plan the conference and the booklets afforded the three of us to work together toward common goals. This has spawned many additional projects.

2. A model of collaboration. Sometimes it only takes asking, "Can I do this?" Perhaps we did not completely trust that administrators would be delighted to take on additional work for themselves. We have found that administrators are not only quite easy to work with, but if change is required, they can be very powerful allies to ensure it is not squashed by the ever-present, negative individuals always happy to offer their thoughts on why you cannot do something.

3. Our collaboration offered a valuable service-learning opportunity for our preservice and in-service students. Not only did the booklets provide this opportunity, but also the conferences, and the planning of conferences have offered opportunities for students to assist with nontraditional learning experiences. In addition, those students who were presenters at the conference have continued in their pursuit of learning.

4. The reading, writing, listening, and speaking on professional educational research topics was a priority that we have continued in our future plans. The very act of reading, writing, listening, and speaking about educational research outside of the classroom, and the opportunity to learn with and from each other in a nonthreatening atmosphere, was its own positive outcome.

5. We came together as a group who cared about continued growth, and we were afforded the opportunity to do so from an empowered stance. The choice of particular strands or themes, as well as individual research studies, was offered. The opportunity for many group members to participate in Internet searches, sometimes for the first time, was invigorating to witness. This was an empowered group that will only increase their learning through additional professional experiences.

6. The College of Education students who were lucky enough to attend the conference, or who have benefitted from the booklets, feel invited into what Frank Smith (1992) called the "literacy club." Early invitations to the expanded literacy club, the MOEC club, ensure the continued strength of this community of learners.

*Causes for Celebration*

When the booklets were finally completed and printed, the hard work of all of the subgroups was in a tangible format and thus warranted celebration. Committee members were proud of the appearance and content of the booklets.

The successful conference was also a cause for celebration. We had nearly 250 participants at our early June conference (after the school year had ended). Feedback was very positive. In fact, many said they wished it had gone on all day, or for several days.

Another cause for celebration was the networking that had taken place during the process of writing the booklets. Professors, teachers, and administrators shared information that was useful to each group of professionals. Teachers now knew some names and faces at the university, and professors knew some excellent teachers in the field that they could call on for practicum experience or for guest speakers in college classes.

*Future Plans*

The collaboration has provided the opportunity to expand our future plans to include whatever seems appropriate given the quick-changing education climate. The collaboration with administration ensures that we have the support we need to be flexible. As Sheri defends the MOEC budget at area school board meetings, she is proud to do so as she offers what our task force specifically has accomplished. We only envision further collaborations to best serve quality learning and teaching.

The Combined Task Force's current goal involves establishing a professional reading group. At our first organizational meeting this year, the committee spent time talking about what they wanted to read next. The interest and enthusiasm is infectious, and to know the members will pass this excitement for learning to others is all the more rewarding. This is all because people were willing to work together on an equal basis for a common cause.

We want to ensure that our task force practices what it preaches: Lifelong learning is essential for good teaching. We are learning through reading and reflecting, and we also continue to learn through our collaboration.

## Analysis of Pertinent Factors

The following is an attempt to step back and consider the impact of various factors on the collaborative venture. It includes an examination of faculty involvement, contributors to success, and problems to be overcome.

*Faculty Involvement*

Encouraging faculty to become involved on yet another committee can be difficult. We were successful in getting four literacy professors involved in this project by underscoring the importance of faculty input in the writing of each of the booklets. We also told participants that many classroom teachers were involved and that this was a way for professors to network with local teachers. For two relatively new professors, this was an important component of becoming involved because it gave them information about local schools and possible practicum placements for their college students.

Each of the four faculty members helped with the writing of the booklets. In several instances, the faculty member was the chair of the booklet writing committee and spearheaded the search for research and professional reading. Allowing faculty to point out important pieces to read gave some direction to a potentially unending task of reading lots of material about each subject area.

In addition, we enlisted the help of CADRE Associates. CADRE Associates are experienced classroom teachers who mentor first-year teachers in a cohort graduate induction program. These experienced teachers were then able to pass on useful information to their mentees (first-year teachers) and to their fellow mentors.

Faculty were also involved in the planning of the conference. Together, we brainstormed with other committee members about local teachers who would do wonderful presentations in the areas we had identified as important issues.

Faculty also helped with announcing the conference. Several professors required students in their summer classes to attend the conference if they did not have other class conflicts. A number of graduate and undergraduate students then benefitted from attending the conference.

*Contributors to Success*

One of the factors that contributed to the success of the booklet writing was that we shared common goals. We wanted to give teachers and administrators research-supported, up-to-date information that would be helpful. When working on the booklets, we reminded ourselves that too much information would be overkill; thus, we tried to keep our booklets precise and meaningful. By reading, discussing, and then gleaning out the most important pieces of information to share, we modeled our own lifelong learning processes.

A big factor in the success of these booklets was the help of a graduate student who located countless articles we requested from her. Every meeting would find her giving us stacks of articles to read or research pieces that we had requested. Her help in this process was very valuable.

Another factor contributing to the success of this program was the camaraderie and sense of community that had been established. Groups met fre-

*Effective Elementary Practices*

quently and got to know one another. We were comfortable sharing information, editing one another's work, and working toward a well-written product.

We were fortunate to have a variety of people on each committee, ranging from professors, administrators, and classroom teachers. All points of view were considered in the writing of the booklets and in the planning of the conference. This multiple perspective enhanced the process as well.

*Problems Encountered and How Overcome*

One of the problems always encountered when working with a large group of busy people is finding time to meet. Often only a few members of the subgroups were able to meet with the entire committee, but care was taken to make sure the subgroups met at times that were convenient to them. Special consideration was given to times that would be convenient for classroom teachers.

There was a spelling subgroup committee writing their own booklet, from which the literacy subgroup felt they needed input. Eventually, the literacy subgroup adopted what the spelling group had developed and incorporated it into the literacy booklet so that spelling was not considered separate from literacy.

The whole notion of whether to have a summer conference was a bit of a conflict, especially at the end of March when we started planning it. Instead of tabling the conference, we felt those booklets needed to get in the hands of teachers. We went ahead with the conference, despite the comments of a few members of the committee who had low attendance at summer conferences they had planned in previous years. We were glad we did—for the conference was a huge success and had great attendance.

Conclusion

As partners in this undertaking to take a long-term approach to bringing research to bear on classroom and building practices, we enjoyed the engagement in our own learning, the connections with colleagues in other organizations, and the sense that our combined efforts will impact on teaching and learning for educators as well as P–12 youth.

Collaboration is an effective means of furthering a professional's own goals, his or her organization's goals, and the broader education community's goals. It is, though, a step-by-step, day-by-day evolving phenomena rather than a tidy, preplanned process. In that sense it cannot always be directed or predicted because it allows all partners the opportunity for influence, growth, and changing opinions.

Real change and ongoing learning by organizations require team learning and shared vision (Senge, 1990). Heisenberg said that "science is rooted in conversations. The cooperation of different people may culminate in scientific results of the utmost importance" (as cited in Senge, 1990, p. 238). We would argue that educational improvement is also rooted in conversation, and conversation is the foundation for collaboration.

## References

Senge, P. (1990). *The fifth discipline: The art and practice of the learning organization.* New York: Doubleday.

Smith, F. (1992). *Joining the literacy club: Further essays in education.* Portsmouth, NH: Heinemann.

# Beyond Collaboration: Accounts of Partnership From the Institute for Educational Renewal Based at Miami University

*Bernard Badiali, Randy Flora, Iris DeLoach Johnson, and James Shiveley*

Collaboration between Miami University's School of Education and Allied Professions and multiple P–12 schools in the region has been institutionalized through the Institute for Educational Renewal (IER). The IER has provided a powerful means to address the puzzle of school reform and the need for simultaneous renewal of schools and educator-preparation programs. The IER partnership is described, an example of work at 2 schools is provided, and a

---

BERNARD BADIALI *is Associate Professor and Chair of the Department of Educational Leadership, Miami University, Oxford, Ohio.*

RANDY FLORA *is Director of Partnerships at Miami University, Oxford, Ohio.*

IRIS DELOACH JOHNSON *is Associate Professor in the Department of Teacher Education at Miami University, Oxford, Ohio.*

JAMES SHIVELEY *is Associate Professor in the Department of Teacher Education at Miami University, Oxford, Ohio.*

Requests for reprints should be sent to Bernard Badiali, 350 McGuffey Hall, Department of Educational Leadership, Miami University, Oxford, OH 45056. E-mail: Badialbj@muohio.edu

sample day in the life of a university faculty member who is highly involved in collaboration is depicted.

An ethic of collaboration and collaborative inquiry and action, more than anything else, characterizes the processes that go on in a school–university partnership (see Goodlad, 1994).

The creation of school–university partnerships has evolved as a powerful means by which to address the puzzle of school reform. Although it seems common sense to pool human (and other) resources for the benefit of children, creating and sustaining collaborative relations between and among autonomous institutions is not easy. More difficult yet may be describing the partnership enterprise in any comprehensive manner. In this article, we present glimpses of partnership nested within a network of schools that have chosen to work closely with Miami University. Several facets of collaboration are described through the eyes of four educators who have had various roles in creating and sustaining the Institute for Educational Renewal.

The first section of the article presents a brief history of the Institute for Educational Renewal (IER) to provide the reader with some context. The following sections of the work are illustrations of how collaboration occurs in an urban school partnership and a consortium of partner schools in the same district. We depict collaboration from the standpoints of the Director of the IER as well as from the perspectives of three professors who have incorporated work with partner schools into their teaching and research. We all share a common belief that the renewal of schools, and the people who work in and around them, should occur collaboratively and simultaneously.

## About the IER

We begin by providing some insight into the network of partnerships that we call the IER based at Miami University. There is nothing uncomplicated about the partnerships that we have tried to create between Miami and affiliated schools around southwest Ohio. As director, Randy's responsibilities are to promote collaboration within the university and between university faculty and professionals in schools, in human service agencies, and in community service positions. The university's self-interest is in building field-based learning opportunities for students and faculty, particularly in education and the allied professions that concern themselves with children, youth, families, and communities. There is a powerful realization that learning to work with children and families, whether in education or other fields, can be more productive if there are

*The Institute for Educational Renewal*

opportunities to practice with real children, their families, and future colleagues. There is a limit as to what can be learned on a university campus.

The IER has been built by many different people doing many different things for nearly a decade. Some of those people still work at Miami. Many have left. In fact, since the inception of the IER, we have had three university presidents, three provosts, three deans, and virtually 100% turnover in superintendents, principals, agency heads, and university department chairs. The IER has survived such massive change due to the quality work and sensible vision. Sustaining the IER have also been strong guiding principles and a thoughtful agenda for the simultaneous renewal of schools and professional preparation programs.

Miami University is a state-assisted, liberal arts university with graduate programs in selected fields. On its main campus in Oxford, Ohio, Miami serves more than 16,000 students and another 5,000 students on its two regional campuses. The School of Education and Allied Professions (EAP) is one of five colleges and schools in the university and is home to five departments that offer 26 majors and four degree programs. These include several education and health programs, family studies, social work, college student personnel, and sport studies. The School's National Council for Accreditation of Teacher Education-approved programs prepare future teachers, administrators, and pupil services personnel in most licensure areas provided by the State of Ohio. More than 500 new teachers leave Miami each year for professional careers in Ohio and across the nation.

Miami University has participated in the National Network for Educational Renewal (NNER) since 1991. By 1994, the university and its school and agency partners had formally created the IER. We have built our mission around a set of principles for the simultaneous renewal of schools, child and family-serving agencies, and university preparation programs. These principles refer in large part to the four moral dimensions of teaching and 19 postulates for teacher education that Goodlad (1994) formulated as a result of their research on schools and teacher education programs.

We made a special effort to frame our work in ways that would permit maximum participation by the education, family, health, and social work programs offered by the School of Education and Allied Professions. This meant that we would be working not only with schools, but also with the social service and community agencies. Furthermore, there were two powerful bodies of literature that spoke strongly to us to shape our work, namely (a) a belief in coordination of educational services for all children, including those with special needs (as described best by Will, 1986), and (b) a body of literature, known as Interprofessional Collaboration and Service Integration (best represented by Katharine Hooper-Briar and Hal Lawsone at Miami University; IER, 1994).

147

Our emerging vision became comprehensive:

- People renew the capacity of schools, families, health and social service agencies, and Miami University.
- People share responsibility for the learning, development, and well-being of all children, youth, and families (as measured through a variety of indicators, including school outcomes), with goals, strategies, and indicators being developed and agreed on locally through the participation of all partners.

Our prevailing assumption was that we could work together to create the conditions that would lead to improved outcomes for Miami students and the children and families in our partner communities. Our lofty aim is to strengthen all institutions impacting on children, families, education, health, and democratic communities. We bracketed our vision into a set of five goals and designated lead and shared responsibilities for all partners.

1. Improve education, health and social services for children, youth, and families (partner schools and agencies).
2. Improve the education of educators and health and human service professionals (Miami University).
3. Support the development and renewal of individuals school agency and university personnel—and families (shared among partners).
4. Support the development and renewal of organizations and organizational relations (shared among partners).
5. Promote inquiry—assessment, reflection, evaluation, research, and sharing (shared among partners).

We further agreed that the driving force for change would be inquiry. Our work should be informed by sound theoretical formulations, research-based knowledge, and practical wisdom. Although we thought that among us we had a considerable capacity for knowing and being able to carry on effective practice, we admitted that there still was much that we did not know and there were things that we were not doing to our own satisfaction. Hence, we decided to frame our most vexing, persisting questions as our most valuable allies; that is, we would pursue renewal with inquiry-driven strategies such as study teams, action research, continuous assessment and improvement practices, and "critical friend" critiques. Finally, we felt creating the conditions for collaboration and collegiality would spawn networks within networks and thus provide for mutual learning, support, and renewal.

We have been fortunate in having the generous support of the following organizations in helping to fund our collaborative ventures: The Danforth

Foundation of St. Louis, The Arthur Vining Davis Foundation, the DeWitt Wallace–Reader's Digest Fund, the W. K. Kellogg Foundation, The Martha Holden Jennings Foundation of Cleveland, the Procter and Gamble Corporation, and the Ohio Department of Education. Individual partnerships also have been able to obtain funding for specific projects, but the sponsors are too numerous to list. With their support and the hard work of the partners, we have been able to accomplish much. Some of our results include:

- Elementary school partnerships.
- A middle-school partnership with agency collaboration.
- High school partnerships, one of which has an interagency collaborative on site.
- New partnerships with preschools and child and family serving agencies to support Miami's new early childhood programs.
- Revised teacher education programs including integration of family, health-wellness concepts into the curriculum; diversity of settings for student placements.
- Four annual linking conferences for students, faculty, professionals, and community leaders from the schools, university programs, and agencies.
- Publications including newsletter, Web site, three monographs on service integration and interprofessional collaboration, parent involvement and empowerment and family support, and planned electronic monographs on specific renewal issues.

The impact of IER partnerships on teacher education includes the financial support that grants gave to planning the new curriculum and sponsoring faculty development, which had the participation of school and agency partners and faculty from EAP, arts and science, and fine arts. At least equal in impact is the work of partners in helping to build professional development partner schools that provide diverse kinds of experiences for students and faculty. Similarly, the partnerships have helped school communities with family involvement and empowerment and vexing teaching and learning issues (e.g., inclusion, gender issues, the achievement of low-wealth and urban African American and Appalachian students, and interdisciplinary curriculum).

We are fortunate in that many of the relationships, initiated both by school and university professionals, have evolved into promising partnerships—despite getting off to an awkward start and seeing some initiatives fizzle. That many have panned out is a tribute to the individuals involved. We have learned several important lessons.

There is an unnecessary risk of rejection associated with the act of issuing to schools a request for proposals to enter discussions toward a possible partnership. It is likely that, as we did, a university will have more schools proposing partnerships than there will be professors who can connect with them, thus necessitating selection of some schools and nonselection of others. Nonselection may be perceived as rejection. Rejection will almost certainly create political problems, especially if people in a school community believe that they were not selected because of perceived inadequacies, personality differences, and so forth. Let us make it clear to the reader that we took great pains to make our selections unbiased, yet we wanted to partner with school communities that represent the diversity of our state: urban, suburban, and rural populations in low-, medium-, and high-wealth communities; K–12 (now P–12) grade organization; and a variety of academic and social programs. Consequently, schools that were among the applicants—some potentially good partners—were not selected. We discovered that colleagues became very disappointed, and that some became soured on any future relation with the university. At the university, there were professors who did not agree with the selection team's choices and, therefore, found reason not to participate in partnership work. This became especially troubling when professors' refusal to participate impeded collaboration between the professors' teacher education team and the schools selected for partnership. We have learned that any perceived "slight" is likely to dissolve trust. Furthermore, any attempt to overcome the perception of being slighted (i.e., reconstituting trust) takes considerable time, energy, and skill because the individuals who felt slighted may influence the opinions of their colleagues.

During the 1992 through 1993 school year, we began to use grant funds to support university faculty as renewal liaisons. Each semester for several years, 15 to 17 professors were assigned to partnership work for approximately one fourth of their load—one professor each to a partner school and one each to a specific issue related to partnership development (e.g., faculty recognition and rewards, organizational development, etc.). Grant money was used to hire master teachers to teach the courses that these faculty members would not be teaching. We learned that this time was necessary for the professors and school, agency professionals, or both to participate in mutual learning (personal, organizational, issues faced by their respective organizations), develop a shared vision and agenda, and plan specific strategies and projects from which partnerships might be knitted. One of the first things that we discovered during regular meetings of these "liaisons" was that they needed to discuss what they were encountering. For some, working with a school was a new experience, notwithstanding their own experience as public school teachers and as teacher educators who worked with student teachers or as consultants on issues such as the teaching of reading. Few had ever worked with school personnel on whole-school issues; only one had experience working with school-agency collaboratives, and that was both limited and recent. We learned, too, that the regular meetings presented valuable opportunities for the professors to search for connections in the literature, speculate, and problem solve. A parallel to the liaisons and their regular meetings was IER's governing group, the partnership council, which met on a monthly basis to address issues across all partnerships.

Before we decided to reassign faculty part time from teaching to liaisoning, we had discussed our concern that this practice would be a soft money luxury. We worried about setting a precedent that elevated partnerships above teaching when we believed that partnerships provided a means by which faculty could strengthen teaching and learning in the teacher education program. We worried further that we were taking a risk by instituting a practice that may eventually be perceived as necessary for partnerships but nonsustainable from a budget perspective. Still, we went further, trusting that the group of liaisons and their colleagues in the school communities would develop an alternative. That alternative did emerge, although not seamlessly, after the soft money subsided. It came in the form of agreed-on roles, responsibilities, and resource commitments by the partners to a memorandum of understanding (i.e., between the partner school and the university partners).

As has been mentioned several times in this article, there has been considerable turnover in key leaders in the partner school communities and the university. Still, we persist. Clearly, having had external funding has helped. The funding has permitted us to (a) support numerous faculty as liaisons; (b) underwrite curriculum reconstruction, faculty development, and partnership initiatives; (c) support leadership development locally (study teams, leadership programs) and nationally (as of this writing, 16 people from IER have participated in NNER-related Leadership Associates Programs through the Institute for Educational Inquiry in Seattle); (d) publish monographs; and (e) offer networking functions such as the newsletter and the annual Linking Conference. Yes, the money has been important, but we already knew it would be. What we have learned is that our work persists and is becoming sustainable because we have paid attention to relationships. The two partnerships described in this article illustrate the importance of relations and the vision, hope, and energy they generate.

In this section, we have tried to provide some context for understanding the work of the IER during the last 8 years. Much has been left unsaid. The two illustrations that follow are meant to demonstrate what life in partnerships is actually like. These accounts are brief, but we would not call them "snapshots." Rather, these accounts are more like short videos that depict very different settings and a variety of activities all consistent with the goals mentioned earlier.

*Bloom Middle School: An Urban Partnership Setting*

A Miami preservice teacher assigned to 2 weeks at Bloom Middle School wrote,

> Today was my first day at Bloom. It was pretty interesting and I will definitely learn a lot. I have never had any experience in an inner city school before, so this is all new to me. I am pretty nervous because I am not sure what to expect, but so far everyone has been very helpful and friendly.

Another Miami preservice teacher wrote the following at the end of his first day:

> I had no idea what to expect for this experience. I can tell you that I went in with a negative attitude. I have just heard so many bad things about inner-city schools, that I thought I was going to have the worst experience. You always hear of violence and disrespect, but I really didn't see much of that today. Of course you have the occasional interruptions, but you get that at any school.

These are examples of the typical responses we get from elementary and secondary education majors at Miami University. The results of a survey given to all teacher education students before and after going to Bloom confirmed that less than one fourth of our preservice teachers had any experience in an inner-city school prior to their first observation of a class at Bloom. Realizing the need for good urban school placements for our preservice teachers, Miami University began conversations with Lafayette Bloom Middle School (Cincinnati, OH) and other urban schools to form partnerships between these schools and the EAP. In the fall of 1992, the partnership relationship with Bloom was formalized, and the first Miami liaison was assigned to Bloom in the spring of 1993.

Iris would like to share her story of Lafayette Bloom Middle School by highlighting the comprehensive nature of collaboration that takes place in our partnership throughout the school year. Bloom is located in the west end of Cincinnati, about 1 mile northwest of downtown. There are approximately 500 students in Grades 7 and 8. With an 80% poverty index, the school consists of approximately 80% African American students and 20% White students (mostly of Appalachian origins).

The partnership with Miami began under the leadership of the principal, Dorothy Battle (who retired in 1998 and became a doctoral student and instructor at Miami). In the first few years, several Miami professors assisted Bloom in obtaining grants to support the work of the school in its renewal process. There was specific support for the in-school social agencies program known as CORE (Community Organizations Relating Effectively) and for community support through a grant from the Dewitt Wallace Fund to the West End Philadelphia Improvement Council.

As Bloom continued to grow these efforts, Iris took students from her elementary mathematics methods classes to Bloom for single, half-day excursions that involved them in various interdisciplinary, hands-on activities. She and the Bloom teachers planned these visits (once or twice a semester) for approximately 60 Miami preservice teachers to coincide with class activities that could be accommodated best with more adults in the classroom. Sample activities included a mathematics measurement lab with various measurement stations, a cooperative group activity in French with various interdisciplinary stations for students to integrate their knowledge of French with other core subjects, and a science class in which we engaged students in team-building problem-solving exercises.

If CORE was one of the star attractions at Bloom for facilitating collaboration among school, university, parents, and community, then the Back-on-Track academic program was the star attraction for facilitating collaboration among teachers, parents, and students to achieve academic instruction. Most teachers at Bloom teach in core academic teams and loop from seventh grade to eighth grade with their students, generally in 2 years. However, beginning in 1990 there was one class of 25 to 30 students (and years later, two classes of 25 to 30 students each) who were chosen to receive a golden opportunity: a chance to get "back on track" with their education. These students had a record of having been retained in grade previously, reasonable ability to read, willingness to engage in rigorous academic work, and parental support. Successful completion meant moving from Grades 7 to 9 in 1 year.

The success of the Back-on-Track program drew the attention of the CEO of Proctor and Gamble, John Pepper, who responded favorably to a request to expand the program. Shortly after receiving a grant from Proctor and Gamble, one of the academic teams began to investigate ways to replicate some salient features of the Back-on-Track model with less cost to the school. As a result, Miami preservice teachers were scheduled to come in and tutor in reading, mathematics, or both. To our surprise, we discovered that students who were tutored in those two subjects began to improve in all subjects, in addition to the subject in which they were receiving tutorial instruction. As the Bloom students benefitted from some variations in teaching styles, they also benefitted from having more adults available to meet their needs. Bloom students thrived on the attention. Miami preservice teachers benefitted from working with a team of teachers who were dedicated to the academic success of their students and who also modeled how to team effectively.

As Bloom Middle School advanced in its capacity for self-renewal, the number of Miami preservice teachers assigned to Bloom for observations, methods, and student teaching increased dramatically. To take the partnership to yet another level, Miami wanted to employ Bloom teachers to provide supervision of student teachers on site (i.e., clinical supervision). Interested Bloom teachers began to enroll in professional development opportunities Miami provided on site: peer coaching, cognitive coaching, and orientation to the Miami teacher education program.

To better orient students to their urban experience, we surveyed them to determine their needs and concerns. As a result, we designed an orientation packet for students and any Miami faculty or staff who planned to visit Bloom. We also assisted in coordinating their visit to Bloom. For students in the methods block, we provided get-acquainted breakfasts (i.e., continental style) on site at Bloom to give the Miami students a chance to get a feel of their physical surroundings at Bloom and also to discover how willing the Bloom faculty and staff would be to help them make the most of their learning experience during their stay at Bloom. The Miami preservice teachers also received information about their teaching assignments well in advance, so they could be prepared for the return to the school during their assigned time. Thus, the partnership progressed as both institutions engaged in simultaneous renewal.

In spite of numerous personnel changes, the partnership continued smoothly because the relationship was strong. Additional professional development opportunities were designed and delivered to meet the specific needs of the Bloom faculty. Reading across the content areas and teaching talented and gifted students were two such needs. The faculty expressed a desire to become an Accelerated School following Henry Levin's Stanford University model. In addition, at least three teachers have served as clinical supervisors to Miami student teachers, and these student teachers have (for the most part) relished the experience as they compare their experiences with their peers who are assigned to other buildings.

Although all students who come to Bloom are asked to complete a pre- and postsurvey, methods students are asked to document their experiences in a small journal for the 2-week period. It is through reading these journals that we see growth in Bloom and in the Miami preservice teachers who are assigned there. One elementary methods preservice teacher shared the following:

> So far, overall, my experiences here at Bloom have been quite positive. I have learned a great deal about teaching students of this age level [more so] than about teaching in a "diverse" setting. Every person is unique and their experiences and backgrounds ought to be acknowledged, but

people are still people and kids are kids—you show them respect, they'll give you respect. My students have been nothing but polite and respectful. It has been great working with the kids. The experiences of their lives, and neighborhoods seem so unreal to me. So little shocks them. Yet, although, some of our backgrounds are vastly different I do not feel that I cannot relate to the students. We can still develop that teacher–student bond. When the focus is on the kids, the learning and the teaching, I do not even notice the other aspects of the school: the building structure, lack of supplies, condition of the surrounding neighborhood, etc. seem to fade into the background if the classroom environment itself is positive and productive.

We have spent more than 6 years in a relationship with Bloom Middle School. Iris has learned several important things about building partnerships, which she has summarized as follows:

- Building a partnership takes time. All must be receptive to hearing what the desires and concerns of the partners are, and must agree to disagree, if necessary.
- There will be changes in the operation and group dynamics in the school that will be beyond the university's and the school's control. Every one must be willing to go with the flow.
- Faculty, staff, or students from either member of the partnership may choose not to participate in partnership activities at any time, then may also change their minds and choose to participate. Allow for this; do not take things personally. Continue to keep the focus on the good of the students—both at the university and the school.

*Mason City: A Day of Collaboration in a School–University Partnership*

During the past 4 years as an assistant professor at Miami University, part of James's responsibilities have been to work with the Mason City Schools to promote the growth of our school–university partnership. Mason is a community of 17,500 residents 25 miles northeast of Cincinnati whose residents are typically upper-middle class college graduates who have professional positions. Four of its six schools boast federal Blue Ribbon awards. Mason Schools currently has three elementary schools (prekindergarten, Grades 1–2, Grades 3–4), a middle school (Grades 7–8), and Mason Intermediate School (Grades 5–6). William Mason High School (Grades 9–12) is a 4-year public high school accredited by the North Central Association.

Although the following "sample day" never happened, every incident mentioned has. Indeed, most events are representative of what types of activities occur on a regular basis—some are planned, most are not. The sample day format was created to compress events (but only a little) and to give the reader a sense of the complexity and multiple layers of partnership work that is typical when "things begin to fall into place" for a school–university partnership.

*Wednesday, midsemester, 8:00 a.m.* As I walk in from the school parking lot, a car full of Miami students currently enrolled in my methods class also pulls into the lot. I wait for them and, as we walk, we have an impromptu meeting about their experiences so far this week in the classroom. The students mention how exciting it is for them to observe their mentor teachers displaying strategies in their daily routine that are consistent with what they have been told is best practice for 2 years at the University. It is gratifying to know that our preservice teachers are placed in quality field settings with teachers who are using exemplary practices and who agree to work closely with our university. I recall thinking that not long ago, this was often not the case. Before partnerships, the university simply placed methods students and student teachers with whomever would take them in whatever schools we had contracts.

As we discuss what the students are learning, several in-service teachers doing their routine morning walk around the halls stop to talk. They have questions about the methods course they are teaching on one of our regional campuses. When their questions are answered, one mentions that Ms. Stanford, another teacher in the building, wants me to stop by her room later. I am told she has a question about a graduate course she wants to enroll in at Miami next semester.

I stop in the office and visit with Peggy and Judy, the school secretaries, who ask me how my wife is doing (she has been ill). They want to know when I am going to bring Morgan (my 3-year-old daughter) back for a school visit. Tom, the principal, comes through the office and tells me he has a list of teachers who have requested student teachers for the fall. The list includes 12 first and second grade teachers, three special support educators, and one speech pathologist teacher. We discuss the need to increase the number of music, art, and gifted student teachers in the building.

I then move throughout the building visiting student teachers and monitoring their progress. (There are 10 in this building this semester and 23 in the four buildings I work closely with.) I also check in with all of the student teacher supervisors to see if they have any questions, concerns, or suggestions for me this morning. (This building has four faculty members who have been hired by the university to supervise pairs of student teachers.) All of our students seem to be making satisfactory progress. Several are outstanding and will probably be hired by the school district next year. One student teacher seems to be struggling in the area of classroom management. The supervising teacher asks me if I would review a video of one of the student's lessons that was recorded by the cooperating teacher last week. I take the tape and arrange a time to discuss it with all involved during my next visit.

Before I leave, I check in on several teachers in the building who have signed up for a workshop on student–teacher mentoring. This graduate course will begin next week and will be taught after school in one of the Mason elementary schools. The fees for the course will be paid by Miami University. Five teachers from this building are attending, along with five teachers from the other elementary building.

On the way out (I am late for a meeting at the other building), I check in with Ms. Sanford about her graduate class question. It turns out that she and her team partner have another question as well. They are teaching a unit on "Regions" and would like my suggestions on some good children's literature that might fit well into such a unit. I give them three or four ideas, but also note that my students in methods class would be excellent resources because they have taken an entire course in children's literature. Perhaps I can have them look and see what else they can find.

*11:15 a.m.* I arrive at the Mason Middle School 15 min late for my meeting with the principal. As it turns out, he is busy doing his job and has not exactly been "sitting around waiting for me to show." Our meeting concerns planning the details of the workshop we will be offering this May and June in his building. The course is entitled "Building School–University Partnerships" and will be based on the benefits and challenges surrounding partnership work. It will be offered to teachers in the four buildings in which I work. It is our hope to have a team of four or five teachers from each building working on partnership-related inquiry projects during the course.

Following this meeting, I visit the student teachers and supervisors in this building. There are only four student teachers in this building with two University supervisors. While visiting in the building, I see a colleague from the University, Tom Romano, walking down the halls. He is here working with a group of teachers in the district about the craft of writing and the teaching of writing. The Mason City Schools have paid Miami University to release Tom from some of his other commitments so he could do this project. We visit briefly about the progress he and the teachers are making before he has to hurry off to an adjacent classroom.

*1:00 p.m.* Leaving the Middle School, I drive to the Central Office. A short meeting is scheduled between the Superintendent, the Assistant Superintendent, the district's elementary curriculum coordinators in math and science, a science educator from Miami, a biology Arts and Science faculty member from Miami, and myself. The meeting concerns combining our efforts toward the writing of an Eisenhower Grant for funding a new hands-on math and science curriculum. This introductory meeting lasts for about 1 hr, at which time we all agree to meet later to determine how to create the grant.

*2:15 p.m.* I arrive at Western Row (the other elementary school) and repeat the process of checking with methods students (6), student teachers (8), and supervisors (4). While making the rounds I encourage the methods students to stay after school to participate in the school-tutoring program. While visiting with student teachers, I remind them of the seminar next week to be conducted jointly by the supervising teachers in the building. The teachers have arranged to have the district personnel director, two district principals, and an assistant principal conduct a panel discussing hiring strategies.

Passing through the office, Will, the building principal, asks me if I would be able to attend a meeting next Wednesday morning. It seems that representatives from a grant they have been given will be visiting the school. One part of the grant focuses on our partnership work, and Will would like me to be around to help answer questions. I arrange my schedule to do so.

The school day is about to end and I have one last meeting to attend, a School Leadership Meeting held in this building. On my way out of the office, the school secretary, Sue, wants to know if I can get her some information on admissions procedures from Miami. Her son is a high school junior this year and is beginning to explore his college options. I tell her I will deliver some information on my next visit. I also pull up the Miami University Web page on her computer before I leave to show her where some of her other questions may be answered.

*4:00 p.m.* I am now attending the School Leadership Committee meeting. The committee is composed of key faculty from the building, administrators, and myself. Although the agenda is not specific to partnership, the forum allows for discussion into any issues that could benefit from school–university collaboration. Today's topics are dominated by the upcoming State proficiency tests. However, toward the end of the meeting our discussion turns to the possibility of more computer training for faculty and staff. I note that I could assist in the area of social studies and will also soon be sharing the results of my students' reports on finding Web pages and activities in the social studies. For this assignment, students used the Mason City School social studies curriculum as their guide.

The meeting ends at 5:00 p.m. I head home knowing that although a lot was accomplished today, many things were left unattended. (I missed getting to one building altogether.) However, there is always next week.

What occurred this day represents what happens when a partnership is working well. Both the School and the University collaborate on virtually every level for the benefit of K–12 students, university preservice teachers, faculty and staff in the school, and school administrators. Each interchange noted earlier involved a symbiotic collaboration that resulted in benefits for students, faculty, or both at some level. Collaborative decisions were made to help K–12 student learning, to enhance preservice teacher education, to foster school and university faculty professional development, or to support inquiry.

A partnership, and the simultaneous renewal of schools and universities, cannot occur without true collaboration. At Mason, collaboration is pervasive and ongoing to the point that those of us involved see it as part of our daily practice. They no longer ask who benefits most—trust has been developed to the point that it is assumed that efforts and decisions will benefit all involved. No one bothers to keep score.

Many who have written about their experiences working with a Professional Development School have included tips for those who may follow. These are either strategies that have worked for them as they grappled with the obstacles mentioned earlier or, more often, are lessons learned from the mistakes they made along their journey. The following represents a sampling of some of these:

- School buy-in is essential.
- Start small.
- Plan ahead.
- Be flexible and patient.
- Constantly communicate.
- Continually educate and reeducate.

## Reflections

We have been working very hard to build school–university partnerships at Miami for the past 8 years. The effort has been worth it based on the plethora of positive experiences we have had. Looking back, we could never have anticipated what we needed to know before trying this collaboration. So much was unforeseen. However, on reflection, there are some thoughts we can offer that may be useful for anyone planning this type of collaborative effort. We draw these not only from the aforementioned examples, but also from adopting a way of life that includes tending the borders between schools (with all of their complexities) and universities (with all of their intractable traditions). Successful partnerships depend on:

- Having and articulating mutual interests that transcend self interest.
- Creating and sustaining positive, trusting relationships that make it possible to pursue mutual interests.
- Maintaining a web of such relationships that allow for equal participation (opportunities for leadership) and complete reciprocity.
- Having a durable structure that can survive changes in individuals regardless of their leadership role.
- Having adequate resources, human and material.
- Having freedom to make decisions that work for each unique school setting.
- Having advocates with energy, good ideas, and creative problem-solving capabilities.
- Sharing on public demonstrations of accomplishments and on celebrations that acknowledge progress.
- Successful partnerships depend on collaboration, perhaps the single most important factor of all.

## References

Goodlad, J. (1994). *Educational renewal: Better teachers better schools.* San Francisco: Jossey-Bass.

Institute for Educational Renewal. (1994). *Proposal/plan for the formal creation of partnerships for simultaneous renewal.* Oxford, OH: Author.

Will, M. (1986). Educating children with learning problems: A shared responsibility. *Exceptional Children, 52,* 411–416.

# Growing Teacher Inquiry: Collaboration in a Partner School

*Thomas S. Poetter and Bernard Badiali*
*DJ Hammond*

Madeira Junior–Senior High School is 1 of many school partners in Miami University's Institute for Educational Renewal. This article presents first-person accounts of 3 individuals closely involved in the partnership as it evolved at this school site. In this case, the collaboration centered on the incorporation of a teacher-as-inquirer component into the student teaching experience. This type of activity holds greater promise for preservice and in-service teacher development than traditional and clinical supervision models.

The most commonly held view of public schooling in America is that it is both hierarchical and bureaucratic. The terms *hierarchy* and *bureaucracy* represent concepts that seem incompatible with a notion like collaboration. In school partnerships, collaboration has more to do with informal

---

THOMAS S. POETTER is Assistant Professor, Department of Educational Leadership, Miami University, Oxford, Ohio.

BERNARD BADIALI is Associate Professor and Chair of the Department of Educational Leadership, Miami University, Oxford, Ohio.

DJ HAMMOND is Chair of the English Department, Madeira Junior–Senior High School and Site Coordinator of the Madeira–Miami University Partnership, Cincinnati, Ohio.

Requests for reprints should be sent to Thomas S. Poetter, Educational Leadership, McGuffey Hall #350, Miami University, Oxford, OH 45056. E-mail: poettets@muohio.edu

cooperation, shared values, and personal relationships and less to do with highly structured working arrangements, rules, and mandates. How we think of schools, the metaphors and images we use, suggest something about our assumptions and beliefs regarding school improvement. Sergiovanni (1987) referred to those images and metaphors as "mindscapes." A *mindscape* is a way of seeing, a world view, imbedded with assumptions about the reality of school life. When we understand schools not as bureaucracies or hierarchies but as communities or ecologies, then we make space for collaboration in our mindscapes. The mindscapes with which we approach the dilemma of school renewal are very important. They determine what strategies and activities we employ as we try to make schools better.

Using the mindscape of schools as ecologies, we understand that genuine collaboration and genuine change occur slowly. Changes in relationships, changes in practices, changes in culture, and changes in habits occur similar to the rate that trees grow. Change takes time and an auspicious set of conditions. Some school ecologies are like deserts with arid climates and sandy soil, hostile to collaboration. Some school ecologies are like tropical jungles, seething with life and rich with a variety of opportunities for collaboration. Most school ecologies fall somewhere in between those extremes.

Madeira Junior–Senior High School (hereafter Madeira JSHS or simply Madeira) has an ecology akin to a well-tended garden. Since 1992, Madeira has engaged in a collaborative partnership with Miami University. Madeira is not Eden, but students develop well in this ecology thanks to dedicated teachers, supportive parents, and thoughtful leadership. The garden is productive mostly because those stewards who tend it care about learning and the value of education for everyone. Although there are a few swampy areas, Madeira's history is one of producing successful students year after year. This success is explained in part because steady, deliberate change is the constant at Madeira, and collaboration nourishes that change.

What follows is a brief account of the history of Madeira's partnership with Miami University and of the introduction of teacher research into the school's ecology. A new crop nested in healthy soil, teacher research now grows alongside other collaborative practices such as teaming, curriculum integration, cognitive coaching, mentoring, cohort learning, and participatory decision making. In this article, we share what we experienced during the attempt to initiate teacher research on a wide scale. We review the rationale for beginning the practice of using inquiry, the process used to put teacher research in place, the pitfalls we encountered, the potential benefits of shared inquiry, and examples of the inquiry projects that resulted.

*Growing Teacher Inquiry*

Brief History of the Partnership

In 1991 through 1992, Miami University's School of Education and Allied Professions joined with 12 schools in the southwest region of Ohio to become partners in what is now the Institute for Educational Renewal (IER). IER is Miami's interpretation of a center of pedagogy. According to Goodlad (1994), a center of pedagogy is a concept as well as a setting wherein schools and universities work together on mutual goals. Madeira was among the first partner schools to craft a plan for the mutual renewal of programs with Miami. Like Madeira, Miami has maintained an excellent reputation for providing students with exceptional educational experiences. Also like Madeira, Miami enthusiastically pursues opportunities for continuous improvement. The partnership puts students first by emphasizing the professional development of teachers, interns, and professors.

Madeira JSHS is located in the suburbs on the eastern side of Cincinnati, Ohio. The town of Madeira has a population of just over 12,000 people. The school district has one elementary school, one middle school, and one junior–senior high school. Madeira is a relatively small school with approximately 650 students in Grades 7 through 12. Each year about 93% of its graduates go on to higher education. It is an ideal partner school, not only because of its emphasis on academic achievement but also because of its hardworking staff and supportive community.

Madeira JSHS has received several impressive awards. It has twice been recognized by the U.S. Department of Education as a Blue Ribbon school. It has been identified by *Redbook* magazine as one of America's best schools. Chosen as one of Ohio's "Venture" schools in 1993, its students are consistently among the top performers on Ohio's academic proficiency tests. (In 1993 and 1996, the senior class at Madeira ranked first in the state.) In many respects, Madeira is an exemplary site in which to place aspiring teachers. The heart of the matter is that a critical group of faculty in the building is not content to stand on the laurels of the school's past performance. Madeira's 40 full-time teachers are determined to continually improve student learning by improving their own practice.

The focus of most of the partnership work has been on our work with student teaching interns (hereafter Miami interns) assigned to Madeira. Focusing on the Miami interns allowed for important, early discussions about student learning, curriculum, and the role of the teacher. Among the conditions described in the 19 postulates for educational renewal (Goodlad, 1992) is the creation of exemplary field sites where aspiring teachers can acquire the skills and knowledge necessary to become members of the profession in the 21st century. One criterion for an exemplary partnership site is developing a faculty willing and skillful with regard to preparing new teachers to enter the profession. For the past 8 years, Madeira JSHS and Miami have been striving to create a partnership that exemplifies mutual respect, mutual renewal, and coinquiry. If the marks of an exemplary site are the attitude and skill of the teaching staff and a willingness by the community to inquire and collaborate within and without, then Madeira has become an exemplary partnership site.

## A New Era: Partnership Activity, Student Teaching, and Inquiry

In 1998, the partnership entered a new era. A "Memorandum of Understanding," cowritten by Madeira and Miami, specified that a site coordinator would be chosen from among the Madeira JSHS staff to assume the responsibilities for supervising a regular cohort of Miami interns. The superintendent agreed to appoint DJ Hammond to assume that role because of her standing as a master teacher, her professional preparation, and her commitment to Madeira students. Due to the fact that DJ had been active in the partnership, she had a real sense of what progress had been made through partnership work and what still needed to be done.

DJ placed a high priority on action research by Miami interns (student teachers) and mentors (cooperating teachers) when she assumed the position as site coordinator:

> For the past several years, the staff at Madeira JSHS had experienced varying levels of satisfaction with the student teaching program, so we reconceived the program. As the new site coordinator, I had lead responsibility for the supervision of the interns. Working closely with Bernard, the liaison from Miami University, as well as the staff and administration from Madeira, we envisioned the best possible experience for the interns who came to Madeira.
>
> Our community expects a great deal from the teachers at Madeira, and the faculty enjoys a well-deserved reputation as caring and talented teachers. Parents and faculty had to be convinced that the presence of Miami interns at the school enhances student learning. Teachers at Madeira are encouraged to become professionally involved and take thoughtful and informed risks when designing curriculum and classes. We wanted to perpetuate this climate of reflective practice, and including an action research component as a requirement for the interns seemed like one of those worthwhile risks.

DJ saw that action research could strengthen the personal and professional relationships between and among interns and mentors. Action research projects may diminish the power differential between interns and mentors. Collaborative action research projects could forward the idea that teachers can generate their own knowledge, a powerful message for beginning as well as veteran teachers. Action research would also lead to deeper reflection about teaching and learning, perhaps the ultimate goal of professional development, and it would increase communication among faculty and would bring salient issues to their collective attention. It would make "public" what teachers throughout the school were interested in knowing, and it would begin a habit that had the potential to spread among the staff and enhance the school's culture.

As Madeira's faculty liaison from Miami since 1992, Bernard knew that DJ had not come to regard teacher research as such a worthwhile activity by chance. DJ, three other Madeira teachers, and Bernard had visited school sites in St. Louis to learn more about the process after it was suggested that it could be used with Miami's student teachers. There they saw wonderful examples of teacher research at Kirkwood High School where Marilyn Cohn, a professor at Washington University, had been working with classroom teachers. They also visited Parkway South High School and learned about the Action Research Consortium comprised of many schools in the St. Louis area, particularly in those schools with university partnerships. The Madeira team left encouraged by the impressive work in the St. Louis partnerships.

Bernard's introduction to the term *action research* first occurred during graduate work at Penn State University when a group studied the work of Kurt Lewin. Over the years, Bernard observed the practice of action research in a few schools he visited as a consultant. A real turning point in understanding the power of action research came as a result of work he did for the Danforth Foundation. In 1994, Danforth hired Bernard to do an appraisal of "teacher leadership" projects they had funded all over the country, and he found that the most successful programs emphasized some kind of action research.

Bernard has always thought of great teachers as researchers. Great teachers form a multitude of hypotheses as a natural part of their work. They test these hypotheses as part of the daily routines of teaching. Exceptional teachers work on hunches and intuition, but test their judgment through action and experimentation. To the unskilled or unwitting observer, great teachers simply look like "naturals" in the classroom, but to someone with classroom experience, particularly someone whose career is devoted to helping teachers enhance their performance, Bernard became interested in teacher research because of the efficacy it engendered and because of its implications for supervision.

In a bureaucracy, supervision is seen as an act of inspection or oversight. According to Sergiovanni (1992), supervision can hardly be counted among education's successes: "Most teachers consider supervision to be a nonevent—a ritual that they participate in according to well-established scripts without much consequence" (p. 203). No matter how indirect or caring the supervisor, this perception remains the same. What we have often done in the field of educational supervision is try to apply the model of supervision that worked in a bureaucratic milieu and extend it into ecological settings. As we become more aware that schools can become more like ecologies (or communities) and less like bureaucracies, traditional supervision becomes anachronistic. Even clinical supervision, created to yield more reflection and self-analysis, could not overcome the stigma of traditional bureaucratic supervision as a tool to achieve evaluation and inspection. If the purpose of supervision is to help teachers become reflective, self-critical, and metacognizant of the impact of their actions on students, then traditional supervision, for instance, has critical limitations. However, collaborative teacher research stands a much better chance of accomplishing what supervision has always tried to accomplish.

The notion that teacher research would enhance the relationship and the knowledge of teaching between interns and mentor teachers seemed sound to us. It also made sense to begin the habit early. In fact, Bernard wondered if any teacher preparation program would be complete without it. When DJ came to that same conclusion, we decided to include the expectation for teacher research into the Madeira experience. Knowing Tom's interest and expertise in the area of teacher research, we concluded this to be an auspicious time to pilot the project. In fall of 1998, we began.

## Pursuing the Practice of Inquiry

Bernard and DJ invited Tom to participate in the process of teaching interns and mentors about action research and actually how to do it. Several other Madeira teachers gained some initial training in action research by attending a seminar in St. Louis the previous spring in anticipation of utilizing action research in the fall. Tom saw this as an opportunity to use his past experience (Poetter et al., 1997) to further his interest in this area and to make a contribution to a partner setting. Both DJ and Bernard asked Tom to take the lead.

Tom entered the scene as an ally, with very little baggage. This can be comforting and helpful to the person coming in, in that the people on the inside may tend to view the outsider with knowledge as a helpful, benevolent friend. However, it can also be unsettling to the outsider, once Tom realized again that his reputation for being a nice guy, helpful, and somewhat knowledgeable about this type of work did not really matter once the process began. When entering a scene like this, trust had to be earned, available, and delivered under pressure. There is no way around this process, and there should not be. All anyone can hope for is to be treated fairly and to be allowed to make a contribution. The Madeira–Miami Partnership and the people involved opened these possibilities to Tom and made him feel like an integral, valued member of the team, but he knew that could change tomorrow.

When DJ and Tom met for the first time with Bernard, they developed a formal plan of action for how they would work together with students on their inquiry projects. Bernard and DJ had cowritten a grant that would help support the inquiry project, so they had a starting place that seemed solid and firm. However, they had not formally conceptualized programmatically, in curricular terms, how they would go about (a) introducing students and mentors to action research, (b) shepherding them through the process, and (c) coaching their final reports.

DJ, Bernard, Nancy Hoffmann (a graduate student from Miami committed to be at Madeira periodically to study the role of site coordinator and the inquiry project) and Tom conducted the first after-school seminar for the interns and their mentors a few weeks after school started. Almost every one of the mentors and all of the interns turned out for the session. A host of scheduling problems, and frankly the complications of starting up school at both Madeira and Miami, kept us from having this first meeting earlier. In retrospect, we should have had the meeting earlier and therefore would have had more time during the semester for the project. We set three more meetings with the group to take place during the semester.

Tom led the meeting by proposing several potential benefits of conducting an inquiry project during the student teaching experience (Poetter et al., 1997). At root lies the likelihood that inquiry will enhance the process and content of learning to teach. Students would learn to look deeper into important issues of teaching and learning in their own classrooms and therefore have a more reflective, dynamic student teaching experience as a result. As coinquirers with mentors, they would create new types of insights and relationships (Poetter, McKamey, Ritter, & Tisdel, 1999). The experience of conducting a systematic inquiry project adds understanding and capacity to teaching.

We introduced the notion of qualitative inquiry to the intern–mentor teams and defined *teacher action inquiry* as a sustained, systematic inquiry into an important problem or question that is always accompanied by intentional actions meant to address the situation at hand (Anderson, Herr, & Nihlen, 1994; Cochran-Smith & Lytle, 1993), urging them to think of describing phenomena and the nature and results of actions. Tom suggested an open approach to a problem or a question, in which they could search with their students and colleagues for various ways of getting at the deepest issues. Our goal was to have students of teaching inquire collaboratively with their mentor teachers about theories, practices, and issues confronting their actual experiences of teaching in their own classrooms.

Tom invited the teams to sketch some ideas on a worksheet that had four areas for focus: (a) problem, issue, and question; (b) potential actions; (c) data-collection ideas; and (d) anticipated findings (Anderson et al., 1994). After having some time to sketch ideas, several teams shared their ideas with the whole group. We attempted to guide, coach, and support the teams, hoping that they would start confidently and carry their energy almost immediately into their classrooms.

## Practical Considerations for Getting Started on Inquiry

We decided not to require each team to write and submit a project proposal. This led to some ambiguities. Due to the fact that we could not refer to project proposals, we had a very flexible timeline with very few requirements. However, the teams' hard work, focus, and energy along with adequate coaching during the semester led to quality projects in the end. Our lack of guidance contributed to several teams feeling as though they were "drifting." Without a written proposal, teams felt unsure of how to begin.

Perhaps this drifting feeling is inevitable. A new process like this presents new questions for, and challenges norms of, teacher education. We asked the teams to reconsider teaching, the role of research in teaching, and the process of becoming a teacher in light of an ever-present inquiry component, and so the teams struggled somewhat. The students expressed concern that the project seemed too loosely conceived at the beginning. They said things like, "Most projects in college are tightly controlled, but this one is loosely guided. This makes us uncomfortable." We had to balance our responses to the teams' discomforts with the pedagogical position we were advancing: Learning to teach (and learning itself for that matter) can not be a scripted, mechanical endeavor. Learning to teach requires openness, searching, valuing a certain uncertainty. Before clarity, there must be some measure of cloud cover that darkens the scene while simultaneously creating the warmth at the surface that makes germination possible.

We tried to schedule the meetings close enough together so that the teams would feel supported. Tom made an effort to be on the Madeira campus for at least 1 day between each scheduled meeting (about every 2 weeks). In the second meeting in mid-October, we asked the teams to present their progress to date; by that time the teams seemed more clear about their work together and seemed to be making progress.

## Encountering Tensions in Inquiry

By the third meeting in mid-November (originally scheduled for the beginning of December), we sensed a tension that had not existed prior, at least to our knowledge. As the semester progressed, interns began taking more lead responsibility for teaching while their deadlines loomed for data collection activities and for writing up their studies. Two weeks before the scheduled time for the third meeting, Nancy Hoffmann sensed students were feeling the pressure of finally realizing that they would have to write up their studies. We responded quickly by setting up a time the next week for an after-school meeting, and we met with the teams. The meeting was tense, exciting, and extremely illuminating.

At the same time people said things such as, "This project has made me think of things I never thought of before and I've been teaching this stuff for years" (a mentor) and "Through the changes we are making for the project we are finding that students who don't normally 'get it' are 'getting it'" (an intern), we heard the teams also saying, "We wonder where the time and energy comes to do this project well when student teaching is such a complex experience anyway" (a mentor), and "I feel like a guinea pig doing this project" (an intern). Concerns focused primarily on the anticipated time it would take to finish data collection and to write up their studies before the end of the semester. Interns and mentors worried that completing the project would take time away from the work of teaching and of learning to teach.

Tom knew we had serious issues to address and that he probably could not assuage them in one sitting. We did the best we could to hear people out and to honor their feelings and learning as they experienced this project.

Tom gave the best answers that he could to people's concerns. He said that this type of reaction happens often when people encounter the work of inquiry and the act of reporting it. It is hard, consuming, somewhat unnerving, especially for people who care about their work and want to make the most of it and do well. Writing a report, in fact, terrifies most writers and researchers. It takes so much time and energy and passion, and fear always accompanies the act. Nagging questions abound: "Do I have anything to say? Even if I have something to say, can I say it well enough and will anybody care?" However, writers know they must write because to do so completes the cycle of a project (as opposed to finishing it). Not to pull together what one learns is to leave undone a very important aspect of the learning process. Completing a project constitutes a crucial aspect of the learning process. Teachers themselves demand that their own students complete their work. They expect their students to follow through to the end despite the challenges and affronts to endurance and ability.

Tom's answers gave no comfort, and in fact he was defending the project and not really addressing their concerns about time and task, although the teams listened. In retrospect, a more in-depth reflection of the incident leads us to conclude that teacher research does not seem germane to the task of teaching to most who teach, to those who are entering teaching, or to those who prepare teachers. Teacher inquiry is not rooted in our culture of practice. Little in the students' preparation programs readied them for reflective, inquiring practices. There is no clear pattern in the school for this work. Therefore, teacher inquiry is seen as something added on, superfluous, distracting. Learning to view research as an indispensable root of our work and teaching others to do so constitutes new, untilled soil.

We worked individually with the teams over the next several weeks to help them find the time to finish up their projects. We decided together to extend the deadline of the project's due date another week to alleviate some of the felt pressure. Teams were encouraged to find a way to use the rhythms of each day and the semester to incorporate the remaining research activities into the classroom scene. Tom suggested that students could spend some time during the day when they were not teaching by observing teaching and learning activities, taking notes and writing in their journals, and writing—that building in daily reflective time would enhance the reflection of the teams and deepen their work as teachers. This is the essential hope of the process. In turn, Tom hoped mentors and interns would give the inquiry process a chance to work and not just treat it as something to get out of the way.

Exploring the Key Role of the Mentor in Inquiry

One of the issues that became clearer over the course of the semester was the role of the mentor in the inquiry process. At the start of the semester we were uncertain what the role of the mentor would be. We knew that we could not require the mentors to collaborate on the students' projects, although we suggested that they take an active role. All of the mentors in the first cohort supported the project among the interns, but they took different approaches in doing so.

Several mentors opened up their classrooms to inquiry, made sure interns had time to work on their projects during the school day, and attended several of the meetings, including the final presentations by students at the end of their internships. Others collaborated on the projects, having their writing, for instance, appear as part of the text of students' papers (Poetter et al., 1999). In every case, a collaborative approach to inquiry helped intern–mentor teams share ideas, investigate and practice methods, and interpret what was happening around them in their classrooms together, as colleagues. The relationship between mentors and interns "flattened out," from what might otherwise have remained a typically hierarchical, top-down relationship. Sometimes the mentor even took on the role of a student. This is a powerful, extremely positive move in a teaching and learning situation, for veteran teachers and for those just learning to teach. Perhaps the mentor–intern roles are closer in nature than we have imagined. Perhaps one benefit of systemic, shared inquiry is the realization that we are all students of teaching.

## Practicing Inquiry

During the summer months, DJ met with Jenn Reid, the intern who would be working with her 12th-grade English classes. Jenn spent July working in the Summers Scholars Program at Miami. Her area of study was adolescent girls' silence in the classroom. She had read several works about girls' experiences in school, but what she lacked were experiences working with actual adolescent females. The silence of adolescent girls has both fascinated and troubled DJ, as a teacher and a mother of an adolescent daughter, and their shared passion for the topic made choosing an inquiry project easy. Long before school started, they were trading titles of books and thinking of ways to seamlessly incorporate the classroom research into the fabric of their everyday instruction.

DJ had perhaps more enthusiasm for introducing teacher inquiry than details about how to do it, but with the help of Tom and Bernard, a series of seminars were created to help guide the interns and their mentors through the process of inquiry and classroom research. The fact that DJ was engaged in a project with her intern lent credibility to the assignment. Jenn was also working with another English teacher, Pam Murphy, so the three of them started the year with frequent discussions about literature and grammar and girls' voices. As an English teacher, DJ often talks with her students about the process they go through when writing papers, especially long analytical ones. They discuss the importance of reflecting on their own thought processes as they proceed to build that scaffolding needed to complete complex assignments. They often come to appreciate the inherent messiness of the process, and as they engage in a great deal of metacognition along the way, they become writers who have developed the habits of mind that will guide them throughout their academic careers and beyond. It takes a certain tolerance for ambiguity to launch into major writing projects, for they have not been given prescribed topics and formulaic writing patterns. Students squirm at times as they work to find their way.

At the beginning of the inquiry projects, ours included, the interns and mentors squirmed. At the beginning Jenn, Pam, and DJ struggled a bit with focus. Knowing that inequality exists between girls' and boys' participation was the first step, but knowing what to do about this inequality seemed far more important and complex. Rather than set aside specific times to talk about the inquiry project, it became a part of their everyday discussion. They could have spent such times collecting quantifiable data by charting participation, counting the number of times teachers called on boys versus girls, and calculating percentages. Another option would be listening to the voices of the girls and letting them help make meaning.

They decided on interviewing to pursue this latter direction. DJ typed up a list of possible questions, and the three set about talking with a cross-section of girls ranging from those who were outspoken to the ones who were virtually mute in any class discussion. These interviews were illuminating, and they caused them to both try different techniques and view the classroom through a lens focused by the experiences and insights of 17-year-olds.

The energy and excitement of working together on this project changed the relationship between Jenn and DJ. As her mentor teacher, DJ helped coach her on matters of classroom management and dealing with parents and meeting curriculum objectives, but as coresearchers on the inquiry project, they entered unfamiliar territory together. Having two teachers in the room allowed them to script conversations or freed one of them to interview. Students became eager to be involved in the conversation. Due to the fact that they would all talk about their inquiry projects during weekly seminars, the intern teachers became involved in their fellow interns' studies. They would jot down discussions, incidents, or anecdotes from their own classrooms and turn them in. Thoughtful discussions about the inquiry projects started to take place among the cohort of interns as they sat in the teacher workroom or on the long ride back to Miami at the end of the day.

### Interns Report Their Inquiry Projects to the Faculty

We kept the date for the scheduled third meeting in early December, making it our fourth actual meeting. Much of the nervous tension had dissipated in those weeks that included Thanksgiving break. The teams made progress on their work and gained more excitement than trepidation as they brought the projects to a close and prepared to present their findings to the faculty. They found that they had done something very special and had something to say as a result. This can be incredibly empowering and liberating for students of teaching. The confidence they gained through completing these projects was evident in the quality of their presentations, which surpassed our expectations.

We added a fifth meeting at the students' request. The interns called it so that they could get some final feedback about their projects and some coaching before they presented them to the faculty. Tom gave them some general guidelines about their formal presentations, which would take place over the lunch hours in the next several weeks and be open to anyone on the Madeira and Miami faculties who wished to attend.

Tom suggested to the interns that they take only 10 minutes each to present and that they leave plenty of time for questions. The interns should give the teachers and administrators in attendance a sense of why they took on the project and the question that drove the inquiry. Interns should present "snapshots" of the action they took in their classrooms and what they found happened as a result of their actions. They should give a description of what they found in their studies and how it has enhanced their classrooms, students' lives, and their understanding of teaching and learning.

Each project reflected a depth of attention and thought that informed the teams' work in classrooms and changed the learning community. The faculty in attendance at the meetings gave the students tremendous feedback and support, even inviting some interns to report at other faculty gatherings. Certainly the hard work of getting to this point paid dividends for the students and the school.

One project examined questions surrounding the composition of effective learning groups in seventh grade. Another discussed the use of Miller's (1952) *The Crucible* to examine universal human values over time. One study looked at what effects participating in extracurricular activities had on students' self-perception. Jenn's study examined the phenomenon of girls' silent voices in high school classrooms and the actions teachers can take to give them voice.

On the 2 days during which the interns presented their projects to the faculty, DJ was apprehensive. Despite the promise of free pizza, she did not know how many faculty or administrators would come. However, the response was overwhelming and gratifying. Interns, those teachers at the very threshold of their careers, stood in front of seasoned teachers and administrators and university professors and shared the knowledge that they had created during their semester at Madeira.

Maria, who student taught in English, for instance, remarked that the "inquiry project gave me the chance to stretch my mind." Despite the workload of the project, she declared it an inspirational experience as well as a great impetus to bond with colleagues and to communicate experiences, goals, and desires about teaching.

Tom, a student teacher in English and Theater, reported that the "project gave me a great opportunity to add an aspect of teaching that I never would have thought about: teacher as researcher." Tom maintained that the "stress of the project be damned; I think this semester ought to be difficult. If it doesn't feel like a lot of work during this program, then something is wrong."

Jenn shared that this inquiry project

> affected the way I will teach because I now see teaching as a learning process, not just as something concerned with helping students grasp knowledge, but also helping myself understand students and what can work best in my classroom. I think I became a better teacher because my reflection and understanding of my purpose increased due to this project. ... I have no doubt I will one day write again about the importance of girls' voices.

Some mentors voiced concern about the inquiry projects, whereas others saw them as very positive. The primary concern of everyone is student learning, and one mentor teacher reported that there is no way the inquiry project can diminish the experience kids have if it makes the relationship between the two teachers (the intern and mentor) more focused and better. When the inquiry projects are shared in some public forum, interns immediately have a different view of themselves as professionals. They begin to see themselves as providers of in-service to other teachers. The inquiry seems to have the potential to enrich a veteran teacher's experience. After listening to the interns present their studies, an excellent math teacher, one who had initially been skeptical about Jenn's project, was thoroughly convinced of its value. He admitted changing the way he structures class discussion and the way he interacts with students as a result of hearing the findings of our inquiry. The students in his class report that he now has frequent conversations about the level of participation by all members of the class, girls and boys.

Madeira Superintendent Michelle Hummel is in favor of the inquiry projects; the inquiry projects actually change teachers' beliefs and behaviors in significant ways. She also appreciates the fact that when interns collect data and present it to the faculty, it is nonthreatening and received with a far less defensive stance than if this same information was presented by an administrator. Interns seem to be blessed with a sort of political immunity. Principal Chris Mate sees that the presentations were valuable in that they sensitized faculty to important issues in teaching and enhanced the intern–mentor relationship. Chris and assistant principal Paul Imhoff were so impressed by the projects that they have promised to conduct an inquiry project of their own during the school year.

Although delighted with the response by the professional staff, we were most impressed by the interest shown by the 12th-grade students in our classroom. We told the students what we were researching, and many of them had been interviewed by Jenn or by DJ. On the last day before the winter holiday, the students in both of the Advanced Placement English 12 classes were asked if they would like to have a party or if they would like to eat cookies and listen to our findings and conclusions about girls' voices in the classroom. DJ guessed at the time that the students would probably choose the party, but they did not. Instead, just a few short periods away from 2 weeks of freedom and eggnog, these students held a lively and insightful conversation centered around Jenn's project. Moments like that are a gift indeed. They sustain our beliefs. They make the effort worthwhile. They add vitality and life to the ecology. They truly affirm the value of our collaborative, scholarly ventures together as teacher inquirers.

## References

Anderson, G., Herr, K., & Nihlen, S. (1994). *Studying your own school: An educator's guide to qualitative practitioner research*. Thousand Oaks, CA: Sage.

Cochran-Smith, M., & Lytle, S. (1993). *Inside/outside: Teacher research and knowledge*. New York: Teachers College Press.

Goodlad, J. (1992). *Teachers for our nation's schools*. San Francisco: Jossey-Bass.

Goodlad, J. (1994). *Educational renewal*. San Francisco: Jossey-Bass.

Miller, A. (1952). *The crucible*. New York: Penguin.

Poetter, T., McKamey, C., Ritter, C., & Tisdel, P. (1999). Emerging profiles of teacher-mentors as researchers: Benefits of shared inquiry. *Action in Teacher Education, 21*, 102–126.

Poetter, T., Pierson, J., Caivano, C., Stanley, S., Hughes, S., & Anderson, H. D. (1997). *Voices of inquiry in teacher education*. Mahwah, NJ: Lawrence Erlbaum Associates, Inc.

Sergiovanni, T. (1987). The theoretical basis for cultural leadership. In L. Sheive (Ed.), *Leadership: Examining the elusive* (pp. 116–129). Alexandria, VA: Association for Supervision and Curriculum Development.

Sergiovanni, T. (1992). Moral authority and the regeneration of supervision. In C. Glickman (Ed.), *Supervision in transition* (pp. 203–214). Alexandria, VA: Association for Supervision and Curriculum Development.

# The Changing Role of Schools and Higher Education Institutions With Respect to Community-Based Interagency Collaboration and Interprofessional Partnerships

*Dean Corrigan*

Growing numbers of children face conditions that severely limit their ability to learn and develop in good health. As a consequence, both P–12 schooling and higher education will need to modify their practices to help these children reach their full potential. Family-centered integrated services systems, in conjunction with interprofessional preparation, are proposed as being important steps in meeting the needs of disadvantaged children and families. Suggestions for implementation of family-centered programming are offered, and issues that need consideration at the postsecondary level in order to pursue interprofessional collaboration are discussed. Collaboration is essential to the process.

The purpose of this article is to comment on the development of partnerships across schools, colleges, community agencies, and families. It an-

DEAN CORRIGAN *is Professor, Department of Educational Administration, and is the Ruth Harrington Endowed Chair in Educational Leadership, College of Education, Texas A & M University, College Station.*

Requests for reprints should be sent to Dean Corrigan, National Commission on Leadership in Interprofessional Education Office, Texas A & M University, 574 Harrington Tower, College Station, TX 77843–4241. E-mail: dcc7542@acs.tamu.edu

alyzes the barriers to interagency collaboration and interprofessional training and research, the changes necessary in higher education to deal with these barriers, and the implications of lessons learned from collaborative ventures that are already underway.

The case descriptions in this special issue describe programs that range all the way from a tutoring program in reading involving one school and one university, to comprehensive partnerships that involve several colleges implementing interprofessional education programs that are linked to integrated service systems that embrace a wide variety of stakeholders. Partners include schools, families, community organizations (e.g., public and private health and human service agencies), businesses, and youth organizations. These case descriptions of comprehensive programs in this issue were used as references, as were other descriptions of programs in the United States and other countries (Bishop, 1999; Corrigan & Udas, 1996; Curtis, 1999; Hsi, 1999; Taba, 1999; Taylor-Dinwiddie, 1999).

Meaning of Collaboration

There is a great deal of difference between cooperation, coordination, and collaboration. Collaboration is the higher level activity. Individuals and groups can cooperate and coordinate without changing what they are doing. In collaboration, the expectation is that the new collaborative entity produces something that individuals or organizations could not produce alone—for example, 30 community agencies developing a single intake form for services that will now be used by all of the agencies instead of asking families to fill out an intake form for each agency, even though the information on the first four pages is usually the same. At even a higher level of collaboration, the 30 agencies agree to identify one of the agencies as the primary agency for working with a family, and the other agencies work through the identified partner. Collaboration is more like a marriage in which a partner can speak for you even though you are not at the meeting. That is why collaboration takes a long time; it cannot be developed overnight. It involves building trust and confidence, and that takes time.

As Ladd (1969) pointed out years ago, each new group participating in a collaborative venture means new help for achieving its objectives. It means that, in a sense, members of one group become the other's agents. For the new help each group expects to get from the other, over and above any explicit quid pro quo, it may have to pay, and it pays in several important ways. These include accepting and learning new habits, giving up old ways of doing things, and confronting problems that may cause misunderstanding or even resentment.

## Conditions of Children

As documented in *The State of America's Children Yearbook 1994: Leave No Child Behind* (Children's Defense Fund, 1994), the increases in poverty in this decade have been particularly dramatic for the youngest children. In 1992, 25% of children under 6 years of age were poor, as were 27% of all children younger than 3 years old. African American and Hispanic children are two to three times more likely to live in poverty than White children. However, poverty is not restricted to minorities. Among Whites, the poverty rate rose from 9.7% in 1973 to 15.6% in 1992, the highest rate of increase for any racial group (National Center for Health Statistics, 1993).

Schools see more and more children who are doomed to fail before they ever start. One out of three 6-year-olds is not ready for formal education (Boyer, 1991). Once in school, untold numbers cannot learn adequately because they come to school hungry, suffer neglect or abuse at home, or have birth defects and illnesses. The children of poor families are the victims of savage inequalities (Kozol, 1991, 1995).

After documenting the conditions of children in *Ready to Learn: A Mandate for the Nation,* Boyer (1991) charged that America is losing sight of its children. In decisions made every day, the needs of children are placed at the very bottom of the agenda despite the evidence that such decisions have grave consequences for the future of the nation.

> It is intolerable that millions of children are physically and emotionally disadvantaged in ways that restrict their capacity to learn, especially when we are aware of the terrible price that will be paid for such neglect, not just educationally, but in tragic terms as well. (p. 3)

In an article on the children's crusade (Gleick, 1996), Nelson, director of the Annie E. Casey Foundation, stated,

> It may well be that the nation cannot survive—as a decent place to live, as a world class power or even as a democracy—with such high rates of children growing into adulthood unprepared to parent, unprepared to be productively employed, and unprepared to share in mainstream aspirations. (p. 33)

These conditions signal the need for changes in our human service delivery systems and in professional training and practice.

Family-centered programming and integrated services delivered through an interprofessional approach may be the key to improving these conditions. The future of the education, health, and social service professions and the aforementioned conditions are inextricably interlocked.

## Integrated Services Systems

The concept of integrated education, health, and human services systems, and the development of research and development programs to support them, are ideas whose time has come—again. Although interest in integrated service systems is not new, the call for collaboration in developing integrated service systems and interprofessional education programs is now coming from our partners in other human service professions who serve the same children and families. In fact, pediatricians and social workers appear to be taking the lead in this effort (Bishop, Woll, & Arrango, 1993; Grason, Aliza, Hutchins, & Minkovitz, 1998; Sia, 1992; Zlotnik, 1998). As education, social services, and health care concerns have expanded and grown in complexity, it has become evident that the professional responsibility for specific services are often uncoordinated and dysfunctional (Hodgkinson, 1989, 1992). In addition to professional practitioners, an increasing number of federal and state policymakers and legislators now recognize that new organizational relations at the family and community level must be developed among schools, universities, health agencies, and other human service organizations, making a systemic, collaborative approach imperative.

The rationale for collaboration is rooted in the premise that children bring more than educational needs to the classroom. For a growing number of children, the conditions they face outside of the classroom have a dramatic impact on their ability to learn. If agency services were not only collocated but also coordinated according to goals developed and shared by the family and all agencies involved, fewer of a child's needs would go unmet and his or her behavior and performance in school would improve (Behrman, 1992). Collaboration in the delivery of service is the key concept. Therefore, connecting and educating the network of professional partners is essential to achieve family-centered, community-based education and health and human services.

The message is clear: No single profession or institution can assume the full responsibility for creating the conditions that children need to flourish (Melaville & Blank, 1998). To respond adequately, it will take interprofessional collaboration, public awareness, financial support, and a renewed commitment to the notion that "it takes a whole village to raise a child" (African proverb, author unknown). Moreover, integrated education, health, and human service systems cannot, by themselves, solve the problems of poverty and the quality of life; it will take jobs and a new sense of urgency. These jobs must be healthful, build self-esteem, and benefit the community. Business and industry must be full partners in this effort.

It is important to recognize that the movement to create collaborative, family-centered, community-based education and health and human service systems is value laden. At the heart of the entire effort is the notion of advocacy for the most vulnerable children and their families—it is a professional, moral imperative. It recognizes that education is an instrument for social progress and that colleges must produce the kind of professionals who are committed to implementing democracy's highest ideals.

## Interprofessional Training for Family-Centered Practice

Based on conversations with families, the National Commission on Leadership in Interprofessional Education has generated the following recommendations regarding development of family-centered programs (Corrigan & Bishop, 1997):

1. Families are needed as partners in improving the preparation programs that train service providers and in improving service delivery systems.
2. Each program is unique, must emerge from the cultural setting in which it will operate, and be planned by the people who will make it work.
3. Families must be involved in developing the plans to improve their neighborhoods in order to have a sense of ownership in these plans and sustain them over time.
4. The primary job of service providers is to create the conditions for change. Their primary goal is to enable families to act on their own behalf.
5. Perhaps the greatest barrier to change is "learned helplessness." Hopes have been dashed so many times that ordinary human beings give up. The "cultivation of optimism" must replace the "spiral toward futility."
6. A shared vision of the future is what will bring us together.

## Characteristics of Interprofessional Programs

A review of over 50 case studies of interprofessional education programs compiled by the National Commission on Leadership in

Interprofessional Education (1998) indicates that postsecondary institutions most often begin their interprofessional programs with a seminar that is held in conjunction with field experiences in a variety of human service settings serving children and families (schools, health agencies, social services, criminal justice, etc.). Instructors usually include adjunct faculty who work as practitioner mentors in field sites as well as interdisciplinary teams of professors from affiliated departments in the university. Field experience seminars that provide opportunities to reflect on practice are typically followed by the establishment of team-taught interdisciplinary courses designed to provide a common body of knowledge and skills relevant to the creation of family-centered, community-based integrated services. This content emerges out of the needs and strengths of clients to be served. Relevant courses, identified in several different departments, are cross-listed with the credit hours distributed to the home department of the instructors. New interprofessional, team-taught courses are designed in relation to the cultural setting in which the program operates. Dual appointments and centers and institutes are other strategies used to facilitate cross-departmental program implementation.

At the Office of Educational Research and Improvement conference on "School-Linked Comprehensive Services for Children and Families," the Task Force on Interprofessional Education (1995), which included representatives from 17 universities, summarized the lessons that its members had learned from their experience in developing programs:

1. Learning occurs in multiple contexts.
2. Real experience is the best teaching method; simulation is okay; the didactic is worst. Espoused theory must be translated into theory in use.
3. Professional behavior must be driven by personal vision to enable children and families to deal with problems.
4. No one model or approach to teaching collaborative behavior is desirable.
5. The learning process determines what will be learned.
6. Experiential learning with the clients develops bonding and advocacy.
7. Collaborative practice involves simultaneous renewal.
8. In trying to change the status quo, interprofessional education will confront many barriers.
9. Interprofessional collaboration must begin with individuals, requiring vision and respect for and understanding of colleagues.
10. Overall vision must begin with family, from prenatal on.
11. Service structure must be adaptive, fluctuating between centralization and decentralization for task completion.

12. Attitude and orientation are as important as skills and knowledge in promoting relationships rather than individual orientation.
13. Respect for social, ethnic, and professional differences is required of professionals who are working together.
14. Universities could be part of the answer, not part of the problem.
15. Interprofessional education must be grounded in history, culture, and local relationships.
16. Leadership requires letting go and giving over; it involves creating conditions so that others can succeed.
17. Mutual respect for all participants is essential.
18. Involvement of all players in initial planning promotes development of ownership.
19. Interprofessional education must be understood as a developmental process; therefore, programs must ensure continued support and linkage to similar-minded cohorts.
20. It takes more than education agencies to develop interprofessional collaborators.
21. Interprofessional collaboration works best when it is coequally governed.
22. Interprofessional collaboration is time consuming, difficult, complex, expensive, necessary, fun, and challenging.
23. As a field, interprofessional collaboration is already highly competitive and in danger of becoming the victim of turf battles among the professions involved.
24. Interprofessional collaborators need to be watchful of their language both among themselves and outside the professions.
25. Interprofessional collaborators need to avoid project mentality.
26. There are many experts who can work with interprofessional collaborators to develop outcome measures and evaluation schema; accountability is essential to credibility.
27. Interprofessional education is not dependent on school-linked services; it is broader. Achieving intended outcomes requires more than school-linked service.

## Implications for Schools

When one steps into a schoolhouse today, it does not take long to realize that the persistent life situations of many students and their families call for a multiple-agency, multiple-profession response (drugs, suicide, AIDS, teenage pregnancy, violence, poverty, etc.). To accomplish their primary goal of intellectual development (creating humane centers of intellectual inquiry creating communities of learning), educators must work with their professional partners in the rest of the human service delivery system (Young and Rubicam Foundation, 1991).

The fact that schools have an advocacy role for children and are the institution that all children attend does not mean that education, health, and human service professionals should provide all of their services on the school site. The extent to which the school becomes the site for access to services will depend on the community. In many communities, however, the school is already a community center serving people of all ages throughout the day, the evening, and the weekend with a wide variety of programs (Office of Educational Research and Improvement, 1999; Partnership for Family Involvement in Education, 1998).

## Implications for Professional Preparation Programs

Central to the concept of integrated services and interprofessional education as a means for reforming education, health, and human services delivery is the recognition that schools, colleges of education, and community agencies should be interrelated and interacting components of one system. Schools and teacher education must be linked with the community and vice versa. Lawson (1994), in reporting lessons learned from his journey throughout the United States studying schools, universities, and communities involved in interprofessional collaboration, pointed out that family-centered, community-based schools are not just engaged in structural changes. The changes go much deeper. Purpose and substance are changed by actually developing schools as family-friendly support environments.

Reinventing family–community schools requires a simultaneous reconceptualization of the training and development arm of the profession. When schools are designed and utilized as centers of inquiry for preservice and in-service training and research, as well as one of the hubs in the network of community-based integrated service programs, they become *interprofessional development schools.*

From the perspective of those who design professional development schools, it seems like an appropriate time to add an interprofessional dimension to the original concept developed by the Holmes Group (1990). In fact, the interprofessional development school is a natural setting in which to start interprofessional training and research because that is where the interface of professions is taking place and where it will take place in the future. Interprofessional development schools have great potential as vehicles for enhancing collaboration as well as adding vitality and meaning to preservice and in-service training and research.

Conceptualizing interprofessional development schools as centers of intellectual inquiry that will lead their communities in developing a system of integrated services and help children and families meet the intellectual, economic, demographic, and social challenges of the 21st century is a significant enough purpose, with important enough consequences, to be a powerful motivator. Due to the fact that schools are the only community institutions that see every child every day, school leaders will need to accept the responsibility to help mobilize community resources, and colleges of education must prepare their graduates for this interprofessional mission.

In addition to preparation in their particular fields of specialization, each of the aforementioned professional partners must possess a common core of knowledge that is derived from the conditions faced by their mutual clients. They must also have access to the kind of interprofessional education that prepares them to work together across agencies in collaboratively developed family-centered, community-based delivery systems.

New organizational patterns must provide the flexibility needed to build curriculum, teaching, and research around problem solution as well as around disciplines. The traditional departmental structure of the university—which is an outmoded mechanism for managing knowledge—must change.

School–university cross-disciplinary teams must have flexible work schedules that provide opportunities to meet on and off campus and funding mechanisms that support collaboration with adjunct faculty in community sites where their students will participate in interprofessional internships and seminars. Other structural changes include the cross-listing of courses, team teaching with provisions for distributing credit hours back to the home unit of the instructors, dual appointments, and the creation of interdisciplinary and interprofessional centers and institutes on and off campus.

### Barriers

Creating integrated service systems among major service providers, families, children, and communities and linking them with interprofessional programs in universities is a radical departure from the current state of the art. In effect, professional training and research programs become instruments for improving conditions in schools and communities. It should be expected that efforts to change funding, organizational structures, evaluation policies and procedures, and even the definition of who the client is, incur significant resistance.

Following is an analysis of some of the most often cited barriers that have been encountered by those involved in developing collaborative systems.

Many of the conflicts cluster around issues of governance, finance, information sharing, participant alignment, accreditation and licensing, and class conflict. These barriers apply to interprofessional development programs as well as community-based, integrated service systems (Corrigan & Udas, 1996).

*Governance and Organizational Structure*

When a particular agency is perceived as owning an interagency partnership, other agencies are likely to participate in name only (Gardner, 1992). In effect, the partnership becomes a facade. In addition, restructuring the reporting lines and relationships among personnel to best serve the collaborative will often present difficulties.

Collaboration implies shared decision making. The challenge is how to get involved everybody who should be involved and get anything done. The more comprehensive the collaborative, the more difficult it is to involve everyone equally within the time frames often laid on the collaborative venture. Many participants are very busy, especially "community voices." They often hold two minimum wage jobs and are trying to raise a family. Even though it is difficult, these constituents must be involved in order for them to feel any sense of ownership in decisions that will affect them. Furthermore, they must be involved from the beginning. They want to be at the first planning meeting to design the plan, not the second or third meeting. They do not want to be the only family representative at the meeting. They want equal representation all around the table, where a variety of positions can be expressed by different community voices. They do not want to be treated as a monolith or a symbol of community representation just to get the grant.

*Finance, Funding, and Other Resources*

If a particular agency is seen as being in charge of the collaborative, it may be difficult to attract funding from other agencies. Maintaining a flow of funds can be derailed if funding agencies are not involved in deciding on desired outcomes and evaluation tools (Gardner, 1992). If the funding agency is not included, it may not know when the program is progressing successfully, or it may not agree with the program coordinator's progress and outcomes assessment. In addition, the uncertainty associated with temporary or undependable funding streams can make planning difficult and cause instability in the program (Chase & Cahn, 1992; Schmid & Dawes, 1992). Funding streams to public agencies are normally categorical

(Bruner, 1991), which tends to reduce agency flexibility and impose artificially narrow definitions on eligibility and use of funds (Farrow & Joe, 1992). Resources and funds must be shared within a collaborative (Melaville & Blank, 1992), and categorical funding can make resource sharing difficult (Bruner, 1993). The lack of organizational and personal resources other than funding also acts as a barrier (Chase & Cahn, 1992). Three resources cited as lacking in organizations that affect the development of collaboratives are time (Gardner, 1992; Schmid & Dawes, 1992), personnel (Bruner, 1991), and facilities (Gardner, 1992).

*Projectitis*

Too often, the primary strategy for change is to set up model programs or projects, a condition that Gardner (1994) called *projectitis*. Most of the models last only as long as the government or private sector funding keeps flowing. When the "soft" money runs out, or the political advocate for a particular model project dies or moves on to other priorities, the reform fades into the night. Needless to say, this reform strategy does not work. Programs must be institutionalized, but still remain flexible. Hard money must be provided to support the work load and operating costs for interprofessional efforts for each of the partners involved.

State and federal legislation and policy guidelines must be integrated and funding mechanisms simplified and coordinated across agencies. Currently, to develop a comprehensive program grant, applications have to be written to many agencies. If one of the pieces is not funded or the grant application schedule is on a different time line, the ability to work together is impeded.

*Information Sharing*

Collaborative ventures require sharing of resources, and information is one of the most important resources needed to run a service organization or university/school/community collaborative. Although a necessity, client information confidentiality can pose a barrier to effective collaboration (Gardner, 1992). Greenberg and Levy (1992) suggested applying a "need-to-know" standard and a rigorous information delivery system to facilitate the exchange of confidential information. A second barrier to effective information sharing is poorly designed or obsolete information systems, both computerized and manual (Gardner, 1992). Another is language—not only the language of various ethnic groups, but also the language of different professions.

*Participant Alignment*

Turf battles emerge as changes in roles and role relations become necessary to achieve the goals of the new collaborative. There are many barriers to participant alignment in a collaborative. Some of the barriers are: (a) not including constituents in all phases of the process (Gardner, 1992); (b) professionals trained to specialize, not generalize (Farrow & Joe, 1992); (c) different views among the professions regarding the importance of achieving near-term and long-term goals (Chase & Cahn, 1992); (d) differences in bureaucratic structures among collaborating organizations (Chase & Cahn, 1992); (e) differences in attitudes regarding the necessity to get involved in politics; and (f) the collaborating organizations open themselves to having their structures, professional assumptions, and reward systems challenged (Bruner, 1991).

*Accreditation, Certification, and Licensing*

Requirements for licensure and certification dictate most courses in professional programs, and there is little room for electives. Interprofessional courses have to compete with or replace existing courses, or existing programs have to be extended to include interprofessional components. Accomplishing either of these changes requires extensive discussion among universities, professional associations, and accrediting agencies (Tourse & Mooney, 1999). Of specific concern is the fact that discipline-specific accreditation standards may complicate the acquisition of the competencies and experiences needed by professionals being prepared to work interprofessionally (Brandon & Meuter, 1995; Gelmon, 1996; Hogan, 1996; Lawson, 1996).

*Class Conflict*

Perhaps the most difficult challenge in developing collaborative efforts in education, health, and human services is that the most needy clients of community-based collaboratives are often the poorest and most vulnerable children and families with the least amount of power. It is a monumental task to cut across wealthy suburbs and inner cities, to get wealthy suburbanites to take seriously the problems of the community they may have fled or to get a small rural community to admit that it has hungry and homeless children and families who are in need of services. As Hodgkinson (1992) pointed out, it is difficult to get together economic classes to change the status quo. In the United States today, an increasing number of places exist where Whites, African Americans, Hispanics, Asians, and Native Americans live and work together in peace and harmony, but places where rich and poor people live and work together in peace and harmony are rare. Much of what appears to be a problem between races in America is actually a problem between classes (Fredericks, 1993).

Although the problems of reluctance to change the status quo, turfism, organizational restructuring, blending of funds, and lack of interprofessionally prepared personnel are formidable barriers, probably the greatest challenge for leaders in education, health, and human services is to convince this generation of Americans to accept responsibility for ensuring the human rights of others as well as their own rights—to achieve a sense of human connectedness. In the future, all of the children of all of the people (rich and poor) must have access to the opportunity to become all they are capable of becoming. Collaboration, like everything else that is important, is a question of values.

The degree to which the aforementioned factors are understood, anticipated, and planned for by leaders of new collaborative ventures will determine, in large measure, success or failure.

## Special Concerns Regarding the Role of Universities

Analysis of case descriptions of community-based collaborative systems indicates great concern regarding the particular role of universities. Needless to say, universities will have to change dramatically if they intend to participate in this new movement.

### Different Views of Research

The quality of research associated with the establishment, operation, and evaluation of community-based collaborative systems is likely to have an impact on the support of programs and influence on future public policy. Due to the fact that so much is at stake, there is a great deal of debate about appropriate research designs and tools for data collection and dissemination. Perhaps most important is the debate about the purpose of research itself.

The concept of participatory research is being considered as an alternative to, or used in addition to, agency-centered research (Center for Study of Social Policy, 1993; Levin & Greene, 1994). The Center for Study of Social Policy has suggested that evaluation designs focus on the sum total of the collaborative system's efforts. In participatory research, individual units track their own performance as a subsystem to maintain accountability on that level. This arrangement requires the collaborative to identify goals, needs, and strengths as well as design a systematic process to conduct research and self-evaluation.

Levin and Greene (1994) developed a cogent argument for the use of participatory program evaluation for integrated service and interprofessional education programs. Participatory evaluation compliments collaborative service development and delivery in both structure and philosophy. Participatory program evaluation, like interprofessional collaboration, involves a multitude of diverse program stakeholders. Participatory design allows all stakeholders to contribute to the system in a constructive, meaningful way. The information generated from research is fed back into the system for reflection and analysis. As feedback, the information is used for program improvement, not just for publication and presentation. Beyond the benefits of fostering group ownership, consensus, and responsibility regarding the system, a diverse group of stakeholders helps provide contextually rich information from multiple perspectives that will likely improve the capacity of the system and quality of decisions. In addition, participatory research is consistent with democratic ideals associated with empowerment (Levin & Greene, 1994).

Even though several of the programs described in this issue focus on inquiry and action research as the engines that drive the programs, this approach is in sharp contrast to the way most university research is designed today. Historically, university research has been defined rather narrowly, with the participant acting primarily as a passive participant. Practitioners, families, and children are often the participants of research on program development and evaluation, but are not usually involved beyond that. Ironically, practitioners and clients are likely to have the most direct access to data and are often most qualified to interpret the data. Who knows more about why some kids miss school than a child that has lived in several homeless shelters? Who can better estimate the effects that alcohol and substance abuse have on employability, school attendance, and child abuse than those who live with those conditions? Who really knows why an unwanted or unexpected pregnancy occurred? Members of the service population know. It also would not be entirely unexpected to find that data contained in eviction records, medical records, and police records would provide some insights into why some children miss school. School workers such as custodians, grounds keepers, cafeteria employees, and secretaries can amass an incredible amount of knowledge regarding how things really work in the school and community and where potential health and safety hazards exist.

An important revelation regarding the activities of clients, peers, and other practitioners is that the data to which they have access is useful to other people in the system. Unfortunately, so long as individuals performing formal research isolate investigators engaged in living research, this potential for meaningful inquiry is lost. It is only when living research is considered legitimate and clients and practitioners are allowed to participate in research design, execution, and analysis that this resource can be realized.

In this scenario, research is viewed as a means, not an end. The expected end of participatory research is to create effective collaborative education, health, and human service delivery systems that produce healthy learners who possess the knowledge, skills, and values needed to get and keep a job, create healthy families, and know how to work together to create healthy human communities. Research, as well as training, are means to achieve this end. This view of research, as a means not an end, will require far reaching changes in the prevailing attitudes and reward systems of universities, as well as in the perceptions of the public (clients) regarding the role and value of university-based research.

*Track Record*

Feedback from community-based clients and staff involved in integrated service programs indicates that they do not trust or have confidence in the university's long-term commitment to collaborative action. Community residents, especially those from lower socioeconomic sections, and practitioners in community agencies who serve these constituents see the university faculty as a separate, elite culture that wants to change others while it remains the same. When professors come into the community to help, they come as experts, or worse, they come with their predetermined frameworks that immediately put the client's problems into categories. The problem of setting up interprofessional development programs that respond to the needs of homeless children and families who live under a bridge does not fit nicely into the current infatuation with national standards and testing. Research professors sometimes cannot think outside of their own paradigms. They suffer from a hardening of the categories. They are unable to put themselves inside the skin of the people they are studying or preparing students to serve. Most of the current research paradigms and modes of inquiry do not look at the needs of the whole child, the whole family, or the whole community.

Successful involvement with universities seems to occur in situations where the university is a partner in a community-based entity that takes the lead. Instead of the university faculty making a frontal attack, as experts they share their talents in the areas where they are asked to assist. They respond to needs identified by clients. They focus on community strengths and asset inventories, not just deficits. They exert leadership by honestly participating with others in solving mutual problems facing their communities.

To create the conditions for full university involvement, it is essential that the collaboratively developed, community-based entity define its own policies, roles, rewards systems, and expectations from a child- and family-centered service perspective and assist participants in getting their home institutions and departments to accept these conditions as part of the contract for their institutions' participation. Memorandums of agreement must formalize the process and clearly state commitments of each of the partners.

*Reward Systems*

The clarification and sanctioning of roles to accomplish identified collaborative missions is essential. Often when faculty members are involved in responsibilities away from their home setting, colleagues do not see that activity as being important to their department. The only way to protect and be fair to participants engaged in collaborative efforts is to make sure that from the beginning there is communication and commitment to the collaborative mission by everyone who will have input into a participant's performance evaluation. This includes faculty members on promotion and tenure committees as well as department heads, deans, and provosts. Due to the fact that peer review is part of the process, it is not enough to get formal agreements just from administrators. Within this environment, university participants are evaluated for promotion, tenure, and merit pay on the quality of their performance in the role as defined in terms of the collaborative venture's mission, not some unrelated criteria pulled out of the back pocket of a university committee member. Multiple definitions of the term *professor* must exist to accomplish multiple missions. A variety of faculty profiles related to teaching, research, and service must be sanctioned, from the research end of the knowledge continuum to the informed practice end.

In the development of collaborative community-based systems research grows out of practice and returns to practice to improve it. In this context, research and evaluation become instruments for improving services to clients. If someone gets an article or two out of the experience or a book, that is fine, but the quality of the research undertaken is judged by how much it helps to solve the problems of clients, not how much it adds to the research professor's resume or how good a paper presentation at the American Educational Research Association conference or article in a refereed journal it will make.

In this approach, university researchers do not submit their research and evaluation reports of the program and run away. They stick around and work on implementing the findings that come out of their research, and they build their next research effort on the problems discovered in implementing the recommendations they have made in their reports. Their relationship is reciprocal. The quality of their work is judged on the same criteria as other service providers involved in the collaborative venture: Does their work contribute to improvement in the conditions of the clients served by the program?

This research rationale is based on the notion that some of the most important knowledge that needs to be discovered today is knowledge of how to use knowledge to improve the quality of life. As Boyer (1990) pointed out in *Scholarship Reconsidered: Priorities for the Professoriate*, in addition to the scholarship of discovery, the university must begin to enhance and reward the scholarship of integration, application, and teaching. Communities need scholars who can act on thinking—scholars whose espoused theory matches their theory in use. Such scholars must be valued by the academy.

In addition, involvement in community-building activities carries some risks for university administrators that other missions do not. Being an equal partner in shared community governance and collaborative decision making presents special problems for the university. The most successful programs operate from three of the most fundamental principles of change: (a) people who are going to implement a plan must be involved in developing the plan, (b) never do for others what they can do for themselves—people must be empowered to act on their own behalf, and (c) programs cannot be transplanted from one setting to another—they must emerge from the cultural setting in which they will operate. When community leaders and their clients jointly develop strategies based on these principles, education problems, health problems, and human service problems often become political problems that require political action. Universities have difficulty getting involved with political problems: They find it hard to be advocates for anything political or controversial that may get in the way of their own self-interest with the neighboring community or legislature.

This must change, if the university is to play its essential role. Higher education—indeed society in general—needs a new generation of visionary university leaders who can restore a sense of social purpose to the university. These new leaders will have to convince the public and policy makers that knowledge (research) is as critical to the moral and social development of a nation as it is to scientific and economic development. These leaders will have to do what they say; they will have to be personally involved in community building. Only then will they develop the trust and confidence necessary to be a full partner in collaborative community-based ventures.

## Conclusion

The most important question that those of us who work in universities must ask ourselves is: Are we obsolete? If we are not to become obsolete, we must connect professional preparation programs to the solution of society's problems. We have important work to do with our partners in the other helping professions. Our society and the professions charged with education, health, and human services delivery have to get beyond the "I'll take care of mine, you take care of yours" syndrome. We have a common stake that we must accept and profess to others.

In order for leaders from the various professions to interact effectively, an understanding of the professional cultures of each must be acknowledged. This can only occur as dialogue among groups is fostered through interprofessional training and research programs. Only as a new generation of interprofessionally oriented leaders view today's education, health, and social problems from each other's perspective, and learn to walk in each other's shoes, can barriers be replaced with bridges of understanding.

United, the education, health, and human service professions constitute the largest work force in the world. Undergirded by a new interprofessional ethic and driven by a common mission—child advocacy—such a force could accomplish whatever it set out to do. The potential of such a coalition to influence the various forces that develop policies and programs designed to serve children is unequaled. As we work with our professional partners to place children at the top of the agenda where they belong, we may rediscover the primary purpose of colleges of education.

Collaboration in education, health, and human services today is not an option: It is a necessity and an obligation of professional leadership.

## References

Berhman, R. E. (1992). *The future of children.* Los Altos, CA: David and Lucile Packard Foundation.

Bishop, K. (1999). [Partnerships for change: A family-centered interprofessional project]. Unpublished raw data.

Bishop, K. K., Woll, J., & Arrango, P. (1993). *Family/professional collaboration for children with special health needs and their families.* Burlington: University of Vermont, Department of Social Work.

Boyer, E. (1990). *Scholarship reconsidered: Priorities for the professoriate.* Princeton, NJ: Carnegie Foundation for the Advancement of Teaching.

Boyer, E. (1991). *Ready to learn: A mandate for the nation.* Princeton, NJ: Carnegie Foundation for the Advancement of Teaching.

Brandon, R., & Meuter, L. (1995). *Proceedings of the National Conference on Interprofessional Education and Training.* Seattle: University of Washington, Human Services Policy Center.

Bruner, C. (1991). *Thinking collaboratively: Ten questions and answers to help policy makers improve children's services.* Washington, DC: Education and Human Services Consortium.

Bruner, C. (1993). *Examining the costs of failure.* Unpublished manuscript, Center for the Study of Social Policy, Washington, DC.

Center for the Study of Social Policy. (1993). *Community services and supports to improve the outcomes for children.* Washington, DC: Author.

Chase, Y., & Cahn, K. (1992). Schools of social work and child welfare agencies: Barriers and bridges to better collaboration. In K. Hooper Briar, V. Hooker Hansen, & N. Harris (Eds.), *New partnerships: Proceedings from the National Public Child Welfare Training Symposium* (pp. 113–125). Miami: Florida International University.

Children's Defense Fund. (1994). *The state of America's children yearbook 1994: Leave no child behind.* Washington, DC: Author.

Corrigan, D., & Bishop, K. (1997). Creating family-centered integrated service systems and interprofessional education programs to implement them. *Social Work in Education, 19,* 149–163.

Corrigan, D., & Udas, K. (1996). Creating collaborative, child and family-centered education and health and human service systems. In J. Sikula (Ed.), *Handbook of research on teacher education* (2nd ed., pp. 901–910, 914–917). New York: MacMillan.

Curtis, K. (1999). [Interprofessional collaboration program]. Unpublished raw data.

Farrow, F., & Joe, T. (1992). Financing school-linked, integrated services. In R. B. Behrman (Ed.), *The future of children: School linked services* (pp. 56–67). Los Altos, CA: Center for the Future of Children.

Fredericks, B. (1993). *Integrated service systems for troubled youth.* Unpublished manuscript, Western Oregon State University, Teaching Research Division.

Gardner, S. L. (1992). Key issues in developing school-linked, integrated services. In R. B. Behrman (Ed.), *The future of children: School linked services* (pp. 85–94). Los Altos, CA: Center for the Future of Children.

Gardner, S. (1994). Afterword. In L. Adler & S. Gardner (Eds.), *The politics of linking schools and social services* (pp. 189–192). Washington, DC: The Farmer Press.

Gelmon, S. B. (1996). Can educational education drive interdisciplinary learning in the health professions? *Journal on Quality Improvement, 22,* 213–222.

Gleik, E. (1996). The children's crusade. *Time, 147*(23), 31–35.

Grason, H., Aliza, B., Hutchins, V., & Minkovitz, C. (1998). *Twelve stories: Pediatrician-led community child health initiatives.* Baltimore, MD: John Hopkins University Press.

Greenberg, M., & Levy, J. (1992). *Confidentiality and collaboration: Information sharing in interagency efforts.* Denver, CO: Author.

Hodgkinson, H. L. (1989). *The same client: The demographics of education and service delivery systems.* Washington, DC: Institute for Educational Leadership.

Hodgkinson, H. L. (1992). *A demographic look at tomorrow.* Washington, DC: Institute for Educational Leadership. (ERIC Document Reproduction Service No. ED 359 087)

Hogan, P. (1996). Transforming professional education. In K. Hooper-Briar & H. Lawson (Eds.), *Expanding partnerships for vulnerable children, youth, and families* (pp. 222–230). Alexandria, VA: Council on Social Work Education.

Holmes Group. (1990). *Tomorrow's schools: Principles for the design of professional development schools*. East Lansing, MI: Author.
Hsi, A. (1999). [Project UNITE]. Unpublished raw data.
Kozol, J. (1991). *Savage inequalities*. New York: Crown.
Kozol, J. (1995). *Amazing grace: The lives of children and the conscience of a nation*. New York: Crown.
Ladd, E. (1969). *Sources of tension in school-university collaboration*. Atlanta, GA: Emory University, Urban Laboratory in Education.
Lawson, H. (1994). *Serving children and youth and families through interprofessional collaboration and service integration: A framework for action*. Oxford, OH: Miami University, The Danforth Foundation and the Institute for Educational Renewal.
Lawson, H. (1996). Credentialing issues for interprofessional education and practice. In K. Hooper-Briar & H. Lawson (Eds.), *Expanding partnerships for vulnerable children youth and families* (pp. 203–221). Alexandria, VA: Council on Social Work Education.
Levin, R., & Greene, J. (1994). Evaluation of coordinated children's services: A collaborative participatory approach. In R. Levin (Ed.), *Greater than the sum: Professionals and a comprehensive services model* (pp. 174–183). Washington, DC: American Association of Colleges for Teacher Education.
Melaville, A. I., & Blank, M. J. (1992). *What it takes: Structuring interagency partnerships to connect children and families with comprehensive services*. Washington, DC: Education and Human Services Consortium.
Melaville, A. I., & Blank, M. J. (1998). *Learning together: The developing field of school–community initiatives*. Flint, MI: Mott Foundation.
National Center for Health Statistics. (1993). *Children's health*. Unpublished report, Office of Public Affairs, Washington, DC.
National Commission on Leadership in Interprofessional Education. (1998). [Survey of interprofessional preparation programs]. Unpublished raw data.
Office of Educational Research and Improvement. (1999). *21st century community learning centers program*. Washington, DC: U.S. Department of Education.
Partnership for Family Involvement in Education. (1998). *Keeping schools open as community learning centers*. Washington, DC: U.S. Department of Education.
Schmid, D. L., & Dawes, K. J. (1992). North Dakota model of collaboration. In K. Hooper Briar, V. Hooker Hansen, & N. Harris (Eds.), *New partnerships: Proceedings from the National Public Child Welfare Training Symposium* (pp. 101–111). Miami: Florida International University.
Sia, C. J. (1992). The medical home: Pediatric practice and child advocacy in the 1990's. *Pediatrics, 90*, 419–423.
Taba, S. (1999). [Health and education collaborative project]. Unpublished raw data.
Task Force on Interprofessional Education. (1995). *School-linked comprehensive services for children and families*. Unpublished report.
Taylor-Dinwiddie, S. (1999). [Interprofessional initiative]. Unpublished raw data.
Tourse, R. W. C., & Mooney, J. F. (Eds.). (1999). *Collaborative practice: School and human service partnerships*. Westport, CT: Praeger.
Young and Rubicam Foundation. (1991). *The one place: A new role for American schools*. New York: St. Martin's Press.
Zlotnik, J. L. (1998). *Preparing the work force for family-centered practice: Social work education and public human services partnerships*. Alexandria, VA: Council on Social Work Education.

# Commonalities Across Effective Collaboratives

*Jill F. Russell*
*Richard B. Flynn*

This article looks across effective collaborations involving schools and colleges of education and other organizations to identify most commonly voiced reasons for collaboration and factors perceived as being most important to collaboration. Partnerships are often founded as means for a school or college of education to better fulfill its own mission through working with other departments on campus, community organizations, and schools. Those involved with effective collaboration report that willingness to listen, mutual respect, long-term commitment, frequent communication, flexibility, and careful selection of partners were key factors in the success of their collaboratives.

This theme issue is intended to expand on the idea and practice of collaboration involving colleges, schools, or departments of education. This article in particular serves to provide commentary and reflection on the previous case descriptions of collaborative efforts. The issues of why to collaborate and factors contributing to effective collaboration are highlighted.

JILL F. RUSSELL *is Assistant Dean of the College of Education, and Executive Director of the Metropolitan Omaha Educational Consortium, University of Nebraska at Omaha.*

RICHARD B. FLYNN *is the President of Springfield College, Springfield, Massachusetts.*

Requests for reprints should be sent to Jill F. Russell, Assistant Dean, College of Education, Kayser Hall 208, University of Nebraska at Omaha, Omaha, NE 68182. E-mail: jill_russell@unomaha.edu

Four primary sources of information are used for this commentary: (a) the broader literature on collaboration, (b) the case descriptions that comprise this issue, (c) responses by the theme issue authors to a survey about factors affecting collaboration, and (d) input from a long-time group of collaborators with whom the co-guest editors have worked for a number of years.

## Why Collaborate?

The reasons to collaborate can be as many and as varied as there are potential collaborations. One compelling reason is that collaboration helps fulfill the institutional mission. Boyer (1994) proposed a "New American College," which would be a "connected institution, committed to improving, in a very intentional way, the human condition" (p. A48). Use of the term *connected* connotes collaboration and partnership. Boyer (1990) also spoke of how the institutional mission of scholarship includes applied scholarship. Again, use of the term *applied* implies collaboration with community partners.

Being responsive to external pressures is a second reason to pursue collaboration. Mulhollan (1998) pointed out that the "business as usual" model of the traditional college or university is less acceptable in a period when the problems of cities, for example, are so pressing. Hackney (1994) went so far as to say: "For universities to stand aloof from the task of revitalizing our nation's schools and communities, when society has clearly decided that it is an urgent priority, simply will not be tolerated" (p. 9). Harkavy (1996) agreed, suggesting

> The financial, public relations, and political costs of institutional aloofness are becoming too steep to bear. It is untenable to be perceived as a distant island of affluence in a rising sea of poverty and despair. It is particularly untenable given the major role universities play in shaping modern society. (p. 9)

A third reason to collaborate is to be able to put in place practices and programs that are of benefit to the college, school, or department's students and constituents. These would include many new or, shall we say, rediscovered concepts receiving much attention in higher education circles today. Among them are outreach, service learning, interprofessional preparation, and strategic alliances.

*Outreach* has been defined by Fear and Sandmann (1995) as "a form of scholarship that cuts across teaching, research and service. It involves generating, transmitting, applying, and preserving knowledge for the direct benefit of external audiences in ways that are consistent with university and unit missions" (p. 113). Although land grant institutions have their tradition of working with the agricultural community, this heightened focus on external audiences is a new one for many colleges and universities.

*Service learning* is the incorporation of hands-on, community-based activities within the course work structure of the college or university. It would include some long-standing traditions such as student teaching, as well as newer applications such as having students in English composition courses help write and edit newsletters for community agencies.

*Interprofessional preparation* supports opportunities for the joint preparation of professionals from multiple fields (e.g., educators and social workers). It presumes that professions that deal with different aspects of children's or families' lives could benefit by working together and training together. Hence, it encourages learning about the perspectives and practices in other disciplines, how to work in teams, and holistic approaches to service delivery.

*Strategic alliances* involve a college or university determining through a long-range planning process that certain goals are best accomplished through partnerships with certain types of organizations. Hence, it is a targeted approach to collaboration, rather than a random encouragement of any and all collaboration (Gaines, Kelley, & Spencer, 1997).

*Theme Issue Authors' Views on the "Why" of Collaboration*

The theme issue authors have presented a range of reasons for their collaborative efforts. The Boston College project came out of recognition of the institution's "responsibility to address the issues and problems confronting society" (Walsh et al., 2000/this issue, p. 7). In addition, there was a desire to link action and inquiry. The University of Kentucky project was initiated because of a felt need to interact with and provide support to a long-ignored population or community. The youth apprenticeship program affiliated with the University of Wisconsin–Whitewater was created to provide a common solution to multiple problems. The school district wanted to achieve a higher rate of success for at-risk youth, a local employer needed access to trained labor, and the University's College of Education wanted opportunities for placing preservice and in-service teachers in nontraditional educational settings. The University of Missouri–St. Louis' 21st century College of Education model was established to assure readiness by teachers for the demands of the coming century and to assist with future work readiness of the teachers' K–12 students. The Florida Early Literacy and Learning Program was instituted to address the need for improved reading skills among pre-school children in

*Commonalities Across Effective Collaboratives*

the region. At Springfield College, the goal of collaboration was fulfillment of the college's Humanics mission. The Ohio State University's efforts were based on the idea that interprofessional preparation would be a more effective approach to professional preparation. The original vision was that professions such as medicine, law, theology, social work, nursing, allied medicine, and education could work together to study societal issues too complicated for one profession alone to be able to successfully address. The University of Nebraska at Omaha's consortium with the schools was founded to provide a vehicle for communication and action with the intent of improving education for youth and preparation of educators. The Institute for Educational Renewal at Miami University (of Ohio) is a part of the National Network for Educational Renewal, which advocates simultaneous renewal of K–12 education and colleges of education.

When looking across the case descriptions, several themes emerge: service learning, applied research, interprofessional preparation, preparation of new professionals in collaboration with practitioners, new ways of interacting with the community, and an orientation toward family and community perspectives. Collaboration becomes the vehicle to implement these concepts.

*Views of Long-Time Collaborators*

Seven school district superintendents and the College of Education dean at the University of Nebraska at Omaha who comprise the Executive Steering Committee of the Metropolitan Omaha Educational Consortium (MOEC) were asked their opinions on the issue of collaboration (Group Meeting, 1998). MOEC has been a successfully operating partnership for educators in the metropolitan Omaha area for over 10 years, so this group has had the opportunity to see the benefits of collaboration. They named 18 reasons why they felt collaboration was important. These reasons are listed in Table 1.

Basically, the leadership of the MOEC partner organizations believes that the consortium supports achievement of each organization's own goals, as well as those goals common across the organizations. The superintendents and dean feel collaboration leads to improved problem solving, greater efficiencies, enhanced communications, and the opportunity for a united front.

Factors Contributing to Effective Collaboration

For the purposes of this discussion, an effective collaboration is one that

199

Table 1
*Perspectives on the Importance of Collaboration*

---

Supports the provision of the best education for youth
Leads to improved problem solving through an interdisciplinary approach
Reorganizes power to get things done
Builds consensus leading to easier implementation
Leads to efficiencies
Enables sharing of personnel
Provides a source of new allies
Allows strength in numbers
Responds to public expectations
Builds on strengths of all participants
Permits learning about multiple perspectives on various issues
Allows participants to set better goals
Encourages understanding of other sectors' goals
Helps communication both internally and externally
Furthers each partner's own agenda and the potential for influencing other partners' agendas
Supports capacity building to address issues
Allows opportunity to "wake the town and tell the people" about the high quality of education provided by the partner organizations
Encourages budget support from constituents' arrangement

---

- Is sustainable (i.e., partners wish to continue working together, sufficient resources can be generated to continue operations).
- Is viewed positively by all partners, which may be due to a variety of reasons, but would generally include the perception that the collaboration was useful and productive.
- Generates positive outcomes in accordance with the goals and purposes of the collaborative entity.
- Creates a means of open and equal communication and decision making.
- Provides an improved mechanism to achieve common purposes more readily (e.g., more efficiently, at reduced cost, with better quality) through partnership than alone.

As a part of the process of identifying those projects to be described within this issue (see the "Setting the Stage for Collaboration" article by Russell and Flynn for more information on how projects were chosen for inclusion), and then working with those who agreed to provide case descriptions, a research opportunity seemed to present itself to the co-guest editors. Based on a previous qualitative research effort (Russell & Flynn, 1997), 26 factors had been identified as contributing to the effectiveness of collaborative ventures involving postsecondary institutions and organizations from other sectors, such as business and industry, government, and schools. As a follow-up to that earlier research, Russell and Flynn (2000/this issue) were surveyed regarding the extent to which they felt those same 26 variables were a factor in the success of their own collaborative effort.

*Methodology*

The methodology, therefore, involved conducting a survey of the authors of the other 11 articles within this issue (one survey was completed per project). The survey responses represent projects from across the nation, from public and private colleges and universities, and are inclusive of partnerships with P–12 schools, other departments and units on campus, business, government, and community groups—all with the intent of improving the skills and knowledge of postsecondary students, P–12 students, parents, citizens, professionals in various disciplines, and individuals in leadership positions. However, these projects do not constitute a randomly selected group. In fact, they are likely not to be representative in the sense that selection for inclusion was intentionally designed to push the envelope, depict a wide variety, showcase excellence, and demonstrate partnerships in nontraditional areas.

In addition to requesting information about the respondents' perceptions on factors affecting success, open-ended questions were asked regarding any other important factors not included in the list of 26, including advice for administrators about to embark on collaborative ventures and identification of those things to be avoided when trying to establish a collaborative.

*Findings*

The 26 factors with their corresponding mean rating are presented in rank order in Table 2.

The six factors receiving the most support for having greatly contributed to the effectiveness of the collaboration were: (a) willingness to listen to other partners, (b) mutual respect, (c) long-term commitment, (d) frequent communication, (e) flexibility in ways of working together (regarding types of goals and strategies), and (f) careful initial selection of partners.

In response to the question, "Are there any additional factors which you feel were critical, but which were not listed previously?," the following were suggested: (a) trust building; (b) creating a broader collaborative vision; (c) demonstrating opportunities and rewards to university faculty

Table 2

*Mean Ratings of Factors Contributing to Successful Collaboration*[a]

| Rank Order | Factor | M Rating |
|---|---|---|
| 1 | Willingness to listen to other partners | 3.00 |
| 2 | Mutual respect | 2.82 |
| 3 | Long-term commitment | 2.73 |
| 4–5–6 | Careful initial selection of partners | 2.64 |
| 4–5–6 | Flexibility in ways of working together and types of goals and strategies | 2.64 |
| 4–5–6 | Frequent communication | 2.64 |
| 7–8–9 | Involvement of all necessary partners from the beginning | 2.55 |
| 7–8–9 | Open decision making in group settings with all partners present | 2.55 |
| 7–8–9 | Top administrative support from each partner's organization | 2.55 |
| 10–11–12 | Early establishment of a common agenda and expectations | 2.45 |
| 10–11–12 | Assignment of responsibilities for follow through | 2.45 |
| 10–11–12 | Time | 2.45 |
| 13–14–15 | Some form of operational structure in place | 2.36 |
| 13–14–15 | Equity for all | 2.36 |
| 13–14–15 | Acknowledgement of differences in operating styles, norms, and so forth | 2.36 |
| 16–17–18 | Explicit clarification of benefits to involvement for all involved | 2.27 |
| 16–17–18 | Selection of projects with tangible outcomes | 2.27 |
| 16–17–18 | Built-in system to support networking and sharing | 2.27 |
| 19 | Political awareness and savvy | 2.18 |
| 20–21–22 | Willingness to engage in creative and flexible financing | 2.09 |
| 20–21–22 | Recognition of funds, staff, and energy requirements for success | 2.09 |
| 20–21–22 | Use of the partnership for multiple, ongoing purposes | 2.09 |
| 23–24 | Multiple short-term projects, especially at the beginning | 1.91 |
| 23–24 | Incorporating all three college and university mission foci—teaching, research, service | 1.91 |
| 25–26 | Clear rewards for participation | 1.82 |
| 25–26 | Previous successful history of working with partners | 1.82 |

*Note.* Rated on a 4-point scale ranging from 0 (*contributed negatively*) to 3 (*contributed greatly*).

[a] $N = 11$.

and student in the areas of teaching, research, and service; and (d) sustaining the project after initial funds are depleted.

When asked, "What one piece of advice would you share with a dean, director, [or] chair about to embark on a collaborative venture?," the following were offered: (a) strive for simultaneous reform, (b) clarify goals with the partners, (c) recognize the value of relationship building and the time it will take, (d) empower key internal and external participants, and (e) provide adequate administrative support and resources.

When queried as to what should be avoided above all else, respondents indicated: (a) power struggles, (b) allowing any one individual or partner to control the agenda, (c) early failures, (d) being overly time driven, (e) trying to accomplish too much too fast, and (f) involving people who are not respectful of different opinions.

Miscellaneous comments included the points that decision making is different in private industry from that in public postsecondary institutions, and that some of the strongest work with students and strongest scholarship can come through collaboration.

*Discussion*

Successful organizational collaboration is a complex relationship or process. Its prerequisites are the same as that for a successful individual relationship—careful selection of partners, mutual respect, willingness to listen, commitment, an equal power base, frequent communication, and flexibility. It should not be entered into lightly. Building trust and creating a shared vision take time and resources. Working with others in different sectors automatically places one in a position of having to deal with different norms, values, and operating styles—all of which are the breeding ground of potential conflict as well as potential growth and enlightenment.

On the basis of the research one may conclude effective collaboration is an illusory ideal too complex or time consuming for achievement by mere mortals. However, the authors of the descriptions suggest otherwise. Effective collaborations can be created and prosper, with the recognition of the necessary factors.

## Conclusions and Recommendations

There are multiple reasons for and means of collaboration involving departments, schools, and colleges of education, but there are also some approaches that may be more effective than others. Participants in collaboration often come to realize the journey is at least equally important as the destination. The act of building relationships, creating trust, and working together toward mutually held goals almost becomes an end in and of itself. In *The Tao of Physics: An Exploration of the Parallels Between Modern Physics and Eastern Mysticism*, Capra (1991) suggested that life is about patterns of interactions. Using that premise, quality of life would be determined by the extent to which patterns of interaction are perceived to be positive and productive. In that sense, practicing the art of collaboration becomes an effort to improve quality of life through enhanced interactions. Although that description may seem somewhat esoteric, it appears to describe the sentiments of the authors whose works comprise this theme issue.

## References

Boyer, E. (1990). *Scholarship reconsidered: Priorities of the professoriate.* Princeton, NJ: Carnegie Foundation for the Advancement of Teaching.
Boyer, E. (1994). Creating the new American college. *The Chronicle of Higher Education, 40*(27), A48.
Capra, F. (1991). *The Tao of physics: An exploration of the parallels between modern physics and Eastern mysticism* (3rd ed.). Boston: Shambhala.
Fear, F., & Sandmann, L. (1995). Unpacking the service category: Reconceptualizing university outreach for the 21st century. *Continuing Higher Education Review, 59,* 110–122.
Gaines, S., Kelley, S., & Spencer, L. (1997). Creating health-focused academic–community partnerships. *Metropolitan Universities: An International Forum, 8,* 27–39.
Group Meeting. (1998, June 19). *Executive Steering Committee of the Metropolitan Omaha Educational Consortium.*
Hackney, S. (1994). Reinventing the American university: Toward a university system for the 21st century. *Universities and Community Schools, 4*(1–2), 9–11.
Harkavy, I. (1996). Urban university–community partnerships: Why now and what could (should) be next? *Journal of Public Service and Outreach, 1,* 8–14.
Mulhollan, P. (1998). The importance of changing universities through COPC projects. *Metropolitan Universities: An International Forum, 8,* 83–87.
Russell, J., & Flynn, R. (1997). Overview. *Metropolitan Universities: An International Forum, 8,* 7–12.
Russell, J. F., & Flynn, R. B. (2000/this issue). Setting the stage for collaboration. *Peabody Journal of Education, 75*(3), 1–5.
Walsh, M. E., Brabeck, M. M., Howard, K. A., Sherman, F. T., Montes, C., & Garvin, T. J. (2000/this issue). The Boston College–Allston/Brighton Partnership: Description and challenges. *Peabody Journal of Education, 75*(3), 6–32.

For Product Safety Concerns and Information please contact our EU representative  GPSR@taylorandfrancis.com
Taylor & Francis Verlag GmbH, Kaufingerstraße 24, 80331 München, Germany

www.ingramcontent.com/pod-product-compliance
Lightning Source LLC
Chambersburg PA
CBHW050635300426
44112CB00012B/1802